MASTERING

ECONOMICS

J. HARVEY

M

First edition 1982
Reprinted 1982 (twice), 1983 (twice)

Published by
THE MACMILLAN PRESS LTD
London and Basingstoke
Companies and representatives throughout the world

Typeset by
Reproduction Drawings Ltd, Sutton, Surrey

Printed in Hong Kong

This book is also available under the title
Basic Economics, published by
Macmillan Education.

ISBN 0-333-31287-2 (hard cover)
    0-333-30477-2 (paper cover – home edition)
    0-333-31063-2 (paper cover – export edition)

CONTENTS

CONTENTS

CONTENTS

CONTENTS

TABLES

PREFACE

Mastering Economics is written for those who are embarking on a study of economics. While its main aim is to cover basic examinations in schools and colleges, it will also meet the requirements of most professional syllabuses and will provide preliminary reading for university students.

For the general reader seeking guidance in understanding economic problems and policies, the book sets out the essential background and introduces in simple form the techniques used by economists.

Particular attention has been paid to current views regarding the defects of the 'laissez-faire' system in solving the economic problem, the role the government can play in a 'mixed' economy, and the increase in the importance of the public sector over the past thirty-five years — subjects which are inclined to be glossed over in elementary texts.

I would like to thank Andrew Leake, senior economics master at Latymer Upper School, and David Whitehead, lecturer in education at the University of London, who read the original typescript and made many helpful suggestions.

Harvey

ACKNOWLEDGEMENTS

The author and publishers wish to thank the Controller of Her Majesty's Stationery Office for permission to reproduce extracts from official publications.

ACKNOWLEDGEMENTS

PART I

INTRODUCTION

ISBN 0-333-30477-2

SOLVING THE PROBLEM
OF SCARCITY

1.1 THE ECONOMIC PROBLEM

(a) Wants and limited resources

Have you been window-shopping lately, gazing longingly at the various goods on display? If only you had the means to buy them! This is the *economic problem* – unlimited wants, very limited means. You just can't get a quart out of a pint pot.

While we can never completely overcome the difficulty, we can, by 'economising', make the most of what we have. Thus the housewife buys that assortment of goods which will give a maximum satisfaction from her limited housekeeping allowance. Similarly, the student strives to make his grant go as far as possible. And the businessman takes decisions which will achieve the maximum return on capital. The government, too, has to plan its spending in order to make the most of the funds at its disposal.

(b) Opportunity cost

Thus economics is concerned with the problem of choice – the decisions forced upon us by the smallness of our resources compared with our wants. But choice involves sacrifice. If the newspaper boy spends his earnings on a football, he will have to postpone buying the table-tennis bat he also wants. The schoolgirl who works in a store on a Saturday has to forgo the game of tennis she would otherwise have played. When the farmer sows a field with wheat, he accepts that he will have to go without the barley it could have grown.

Because resources are limited, having 'this' means going without 'that'; or, as the Yorkshireman says, 'There's no owt for nowt in this world'. We speak, therefore, of *opportunity cost* – the cost of something in terms of the best alternative gone without.

Usually economising does not mean a complete rejection of one good in favour of another, but rather deciding to have a little bit more of one and a little less of the other. In short, as we shall see it involves choice at the *margin*.

Fig 1.1 *the economic problem*

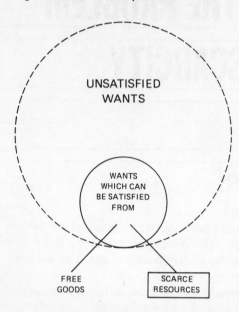

(c) 'Free' and 'scarce' goods

Few goods are so plentiful that nobody will give anything for them. Air is one of the few exceptions. In some years, too, there is such an abundant apple harvest that a farmer says, 'Help yourself.' Such goods are termed 'free' goods. But most goods are 'scarce' – they can be obtained only by going without something else. With these goods we have to economise, so they are referred to as 'economic goods'. They are the subject-matter of economics – the study of how people allocate their limited resources to provide for their wants. It is against this backcloth of limited resources that all decisions by consumers and firms have to be made.

1.2 ECONOMIC SYSTEMS

(a) The role of the economic system

In primitive economies, the individual uses his resources directly to provide what he wants. Thus Robinson Crusoe had to decide how much time to spend hunting, fishing, growing corn and relaxing in the sun according to the strength of his preferences for meat, fish, bread and leisure. Similarly, in a subsistence economy the farmer's output is mainly for his own family's needs.

Today, however, decisions as to what shall be produced are linked only indirectly with the actual consumer. Man now specialises in production, obtaining the variety of goods he wants by exchange. Thus, on the one hand, we have what we will call 'households', the units which both consume goods and services and supply the resources, such as labour, to produce them. On the other hand, we have 'firms', the organisations which decide what goods and services to produce, and use accordingly the resources supplied by households (fig. 1.2).

Fig 1.2 *the flow of goods and resources in an economic system*

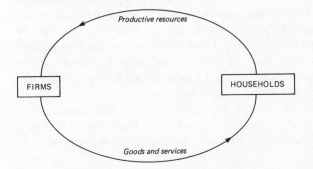

But if the greatest possible satisfaction is to be obtained from limited resources there must be a link between households and firms. Put briefly, the following questions have to be answered:

(i)   *What* goods and services shall firms produce?
(ii)   *How much* of each good and service shall be produced?
(iii) *How* shall the goods and services be produced?
(iv)   How shall products be *divided* between households?

To solve these problems we need some form of economic system; in short, the economic system provides the link between households and firms.

(b) Different forms of economic system

Man's first exchanges were quite simple: there was a direct swap of one good for another – a 'market' was established (see p. 45). Eventually a 'go-between' – money – was developed, allowing goods to be 'priced' and sold more easily. The subsistence economy had now evolved into the *market economy*, where answers to the above questions follow from people's decisions in the market.

In contrast to the market economy, there is the *command* or *centrally directed economy*, where the state decides what to produce and directs the factors of production accordingly. Furthermore, what is produced is distributed according to the decisions of the central body, the emphasis being 'to each according to his need' rather than on financial ability to pay.

Our task now is to examine in turn the respective strengths of these two systems.

1.3 THE MARKET ECONOMY

(a) Outline of the market mechanism

In the market economy, emphasis is laid on the freedom of the individual, both as a consumer and as the owner of resources.

As a consumer he expresses his choice of goods through the price he is willing to pay for them. As the owner of resources used in production (usually his own labour) he seeks to obtain as large a reward as possible. If consumers want more of the good than is being supplied at the current price, this is indicated by their 'bidding-up' the price. This increases the profits of firms and the earnings of factors producing that good. As a result, resources are attracted into the industry, and supply expands. On the other hand, if consumers do not want a particular good, its price falls, producers make a loss, and resources leave the industry.

The *price system* therefore indicates the wishes of consumers and allocates the community's productive resources accordingly (fig 1.3). There is no direction of labour; people are free to work wherever they choose.

Fig 1.3   *the allocation of products and resources through the market economy*

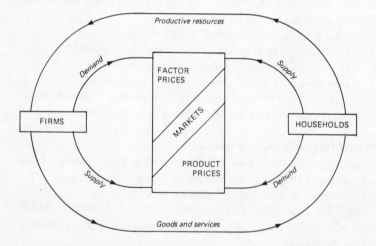

Efficiency is achieved through the profit motive: owners of factors of production sell them at the highest possible price, while firms keep production costs as low as they can in order to obtain the highest profit margin.

Factor earnings decide who is to receive the goods produced. If firms produce better goods or improve efficiency, or if workers make a greater effort, they receive a higher reward, giving them more spending power to obtain goods in the market.

In this way the price system acts, as it were, like a marvellous computer, registering people's preferences for different goods, transmitting those preferences to firms, moving resources to produce the goods, and deciding who shall obtain the final products. Thus, through the motivation of private enterprise, the four problems inherent in economising are solved automatically.

(b) Defects of the market economy

Unfortunately, in practice the market economy does not work quite so smoothly as this. Nor are its results entirely satisfactory.

First, some vital *community goods*, such as defence, police, justice and national parks, cannot be adequately provided through the market. This is mainly because it would be impossible to charge a price since 'free-riders' cannot be excluded. Indeed, in most advanced countries, the state usually goes further. Thus it may take responsibility for *public goods*, such as TV programmes and parks, where there is no reduction in the quantity available for others when one person has more, and the cost can be covered by taxation. Moreover, it usually provides a safety-net when people are unemployed, sick or old, and gives assistance towards *merit goods*, such as education, housing, museums and libraries, on which people might underspend through either ignorance or miscalculation of future benefits.

Second, the consumers with the most money have the greatest pull in the market. As a result, resources may be devoted to producing luxuries for the rich to the exclusion of necessities for the poor. While this is really brought about by the unequal distribution of wealth and income rather than by the market system, the fact is that the latter tends to produce, and even to increase, such inequality.

Third, the *competition* upon which the efficiency of the market economy depends *may break down*. An employer may be the only buyer of a certain type of labour in a locality. If so, he is in a strong position when negotiating rates of pay with individual workers. The state may therefore have to intervene, e.g. with minimum-wage agreements, as in the 'sweated' industries (see p. 150). Similarly, on the selling side, one seller may be able to exclude competitors. This puts the consumer in a weak position because he cannot take his custom elsewhere.

Fourth, *competition itself may sometimes lead to inefficiency*. Small units may not be able to secure the advantages of large-scale production. Duplication of research and competitive advertising may waste resources. Uncertainty as to rivals' plans may hold back investment.

Fifth, *consumers' sovereignty may be distorted* by large firms which use extensive advertising simply to convince consumers that the goods they have produced are just what people want.

Sixth, in practice the price mechanism may function sluggishly, through *imperfect knowledge* or *immobility of factors of production* (see p. 147). As a result supply is slow to respond to changes in demand.

Seventh, the private-profit motive does not always ensure that *public* well-being (as distinct from the sum total of *private* wealth) will be maximised. There may be *social benefits* (often referred to as *spillovers* or *externalities*). Thus, in providing a car park, a supermarket attracts customers; but there is an additional social benefit in that it reduces congestion for all road users. On the other hand there may be *social costs*. A manufacturer does not consider the soot which falls from his factory chimney onto nearby washing-lines; but, although not a cost to him, it is one to the surrounding community.

Lastly, and most important, in a market economy where individuals decide what to produce, resources may remain *unemployed* because firms as a whole consider that profit prospects are poor.

1.4 THE COMMAND ECONOMY

(a) Central decision-making
With the command economy, the decisions regarding what? how much? how? and for whom? are taken by an all-powerful planning authority. It estimates the assortment of goods which it considers people want and directs resources into producing them. It also decides how the goods produced shall be distributed among the community. Thus economic efficiency largely depends upon how accurately wants are estimated and resources allocated.

Fig 1.4   *the allocation of resources and products through a command economy*

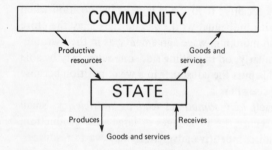

(b) Merits of the command economy
The merits of the command economy correspond closely to the defects of the market economy. The central planning authority can: (i) allow for the uneven distribution of wealth when planning what to produce and in

rewarding the producers; (ii) ensure that adequate resources are devoted to community, public and merit goods; (iii) eliminate the inefficiencies resulting from competition; (iv) use its monopoly powers in the interests of the community, e.g. by securing the advantages of large-scale production, rather than make maximum profits by restricting output; (v) use advertising to inform rather than simply to persuade or 'brainwash'; (vi) allow for external costs and benefits when deciding what and how much to produce; and (vii) employ workers in order to keep them occupied although to do so may be unprofitable in the narrow sense.

(c) Defects of the command economy

Nevertheless the command economy has inherent defects which lay it open to criticism on both economic and political grounds.

First, estimating the satisfaction derived by individuals from consuming different goods is impossible – although some help can be obtained by introducing a pricing system through markets, changes in prices signalling changes in wants.

Second, many officials are required to estimate wants and to direct factors of production. Inasmuch as such officials are not needed in a market economy they represent wasted factors of production. Moreover, the use of officials may lead to bureaucracy – excessive form-filling, 'red tape', slowness in coming to decisions and an impersonal approach to consumers. At times, too, officialdom has been accompanied by corruption.

Third, even when wants have been decided upon, difficulties of co-ordination arise. On the one hand, wants have to be dovetailed and awarded priorities. On the other, factors have to be combined in the best proportions. Usually plans are co-ordinated through numerous committees, directed at the top by a central planning committee. Yet members of this committee tend to be primarily politicians with little experience of administration, especially in coping with the difficulties of managing a large organisation (see p. 200).

Fourth, it is argued that state ownership of resources, by reducing personal incentives, diminishes effort and initiative. Direction of labour may mean that people are dissatisfied with their jobs; officials may play for safety in their policies (see p. 196). Thus production may be less than under private enterprise.

Fifth, and probably most important, there is the political danger. Once individuals have given power to the state to decide what is good for them, to own all factors of production and to direct labour, it may eventually seize absolute political power. Individuals would then exist for the state, and not the state for the individual. Thus the ultimate choice between a market economy and a command economy (in their extreme forms) really hinges on whether people prefer to run the risk of dictatorship or to accept the defects of the market economy which allows them to choose their own jobs.

1.5 BRITAIN'S MIXED ECONOMY

(a) The 'middle way'

Fortunately a community does not have to make a complete choice between these two extremes. Instead it can compromise, allowing the state, to act, not as a dictator, but more like a wise parent who gives children much personal freedom but plans ahead to avoid many of the pitfalls into which they may stumble.

Thus, in an attempt to get the best of both worlds, the UK has a 'mixed economy' in which four-fifths of production is carried out by the private sector through the market (though subject to varying degress of government control), while for the other fifth the government is directly responsible through the public sector. Moreover, chiefly by income re-distribution and subsidies, the government influences the allocation of the goods and services produced.

(b) Summary of the objectives of government economic policy

The objectives of government economic policy in the UK fall into three broad categories: allocation of resources, stabilisation of the economy and re-distribution of income.

The government may influence the allocation of resources by producing goods and services itself. This occurs when they would not be provided adequately by the private sector, as with community goods, or when they can be produced more efficiently by the state, as with the nationalised industries and certain activities of local authorities, e.g. the provision of roads and libraries.

But other defects of the market mechanism are often dealt with by influencing the operation of the price system in order to: (i) protect individuals from the operations of powerful interests, such as monopolies; (ii) overcome frictions, e.g. in the movement of labour; (iii) relieve short-ages when these would entail hardship, as with housing; and (iv) allow for the external costs and benefits of a firm's own plans, e.g. with planning controls.

In general the government modifies the operation of the price system either by physical controls or by market intervention. The most rigid form of physical control is legislation. For example, pornographic literature (and certain drugs) must not be sold freely, and certain forms of cigarette advertising are forbidden. Controls can be flexible, however, when they are administered by the authorities under general powers conferred by Act of Parliament. Thus under the Town and Country Planning Acts local authorities exercise planning functions which take into consideration the external costs and benefits of various uses of land and of the erection of buildings. As we shall see, other direct controls operate over certain prices, proposed mergers of firms and foreign trade.

Alternatively the government can avoid the rigidity of physical controls by intervening in the market itself. Thus it can adjust its own demand and supply to affect price, as with agriculture (p. 63), government bonds (p. 237) and foreign exchange rates (p. 226). It may also influence demand, supply and price by indirect taxes and subsidies.

While such intervention is best discussed in terms of the specific topics concerned, other government policy is more widespread in its effects and is therefore considered separately. Thus chapters 18–21 cover international trading relationships, full employment, regional development, price stability, economic growth and the re-distribution of income through government expenditure and taxation.

(c) Private and public sectors
In examining how a mixed economy works, it is convenient to distinguish between the 'private sector' and the 'public sector'. The former includes those firms which are privately owned and where decisions are taken in response to market signals. The latter includes government departments, local authorities, the nationalised industries, and public bodies such as the University Grants Committee. All are distinguished by the fact that their capital is publicly owned and their policies can be influenced through the ultimate supply of funds by the government. Thus the existence of the public sector enables the government to exercise an important measure of control over the economy. Moreover, decisions on what to produce can be based on need rather than demand (see p. 178).

1.6 THE NATURE OF ECONOMICS

(a) Welfare and wealth
The economist who is concerned with human welfare must recognise that in the last resort people do not want goods as such, but simply the satisfaction they obtain when consuming those goods. Yet it is quite impossible to measure satisfaction. It is probable, for instance, that a schoolgirl derives more enjoyment from £15 spent on a new tennis racket than a millionaire does from £15 spent on a dinner. Yet we can never be sure – satisfaction, like love or pain, is a personal feeling which cannot be measured objectively.

So the economist, working on the principle that two loaves are better than one, measures the output of goods and services and declares that any increase over a given period of time indicates an increase in welfare.

Nevertheless, as we see in chapter 13, this is only an approximation, and its limitations have to be constantly borne in mind.

(b) The role of economics

It will be appreciated that in practice many economic decisions involve subjective judgments; that is, they cannot be made solely by an objective appraisal of the facts but depend to some extent on personal views in interpreting facts. Thus the relative size of the public sector and the extent to which the government interferes with the operations of firms in the private sector are determined largely by the political philosophy of the elected government.

The economist tries to be as objective as possible, establishing principles which, given certain conditions, show how the economy works and can be used to predict the likely results of policies.

Decision-makers may brush these principles to one side, either because facts necessary for a complete answer are not available or because different weight is given to assumptions. But at least economics provides a reminder of where objectivity ends and subjectivity begins.

THE POPULATION
AS CONSUMERS
AND PRODUCERS

2.1 GROWTH OF POPULATION

(a) Changes in population size

The people of a country are its consumers. They also provide the labour force for production. A study of the population of the UK, therefore, will give us a bird's-eye view of the community for which the economic system must provide, and also of the size and nature of the available labour force.

At any one time the structure of the population is largely the result of demographic factors prevailing some fifty years earlier. It is necessary, therefore, to consider such factors in order to explain the UK's present pattern of population and how it is likely to change in the future. Owing to the difficulty of obtaining consistent figures for Northern Ireland, the

Fig 2.1   *population, 1801-1971, Great Britain*

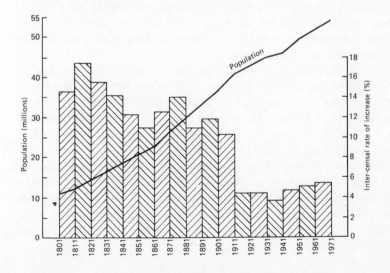

discussion concentrates on Great Britain. The basic conclusions, however, apply equally to the UK as a whole.

Table 2.1 and fig 2.1 reveal that, while the UK's population increased quite rapidly during the nineteenth century, there was a marked falling-off in the rate of increase in the twentieth century. This poses three main questions. (i) Why was there such a rapid growth during the nineteenth century? (ii) Why did that rate fall so markedly during the twentieth century? (iii) What is likely to happen during the rest of the twentieth century?

(b) Causes of changes in the rate of growth

The factors affecting population changes are shown in fig 2.2. On the one hand we have the natural increase – the excess of births over deaths; on

Fig 2.2 *factors affecting population*

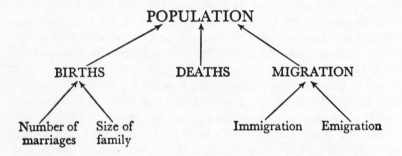

the other, migration – the balance between immigration (inwards) and emigration (outwards). In fact, apart from the years 1931–41 and 1951–61, Great Britain has lost by migration about half a million people each decade. Changes in the rate of growth, therefore, have resulted chiefly from changes in the natural increase.

For our purposes crude rates are adequate for examining changes in the rate of births and deaths. The *crude birth rate* (CBR) is the number of births per year per thousand of the population. For example, if the total population is 50 million and the number of births in the year is 1 million, the CBR is 20. Similarly the *crude death rate* (CDR) is the number of deaths per year per thousand of the population.

The reason for the high rate of increase during the nineteenth century was that, while the birth rate remained high, the death rate fell considerably (probably from about 33 in the mid-eighteenth century). This fall was the result of improved medical knowledge, better sanitation and water supplies, and the higher standard of living following the agricultural and industrial revolutions.

Table 2.1 *Population (in 000s) 1801-1978*

Date	Great Britain (England, Wales and Scotland)	Northern Ireland
1801	10,500	1,442
1851	20,817	1,237
1901	37,000	1,371
1951	48,854	1,536
1971	53,979	1,539
1978 mid-year est.	54,296	(not avail.)

Source: Annual Abstract of Statistics

Table 2.2 *Crude birth rate (CBR) and crude death rate (CDR) for England and Wales, 1851-1977*

Date	CBR	CDR
1851	35.5	22.7
1900-2	28.7	17.3
1950-2	16.0	11.9
1961	17.9	12.0
1971	16.2	11.6
1977	11.8	11.7

Source: Annual Abstract of Statistics

But the situation changed in the twentieth century. The death rate did not fall so rapidly. More important, the birth rate fell considerably. The reason was a decrease in the average size of family – from between five and six children to just over two. A variety of factors contributed to this: improved methods and social acceptance of birth control; the increased economic burden of parenthood – due, for instance, to the gradual raising of the school-leaving age; the higher standards which parents generally set themselves for their children's welfare; the growth of competing alternatives to children, such as holidays, foreign travel, the cinema and the motor-car; the emancipation of women, politically, economically and socially, with the consequent desire to be free from home ties; and the momentum which social example, smaller houses and advertisements provided once the movement towards smaller families had started. In 1949 there was a real possibility that Britain's population would have declined in number by the end of the century!

Today, however, it seems that such a decline is unlikely to occur, for people appear to be having slightly larger families. Various reasons can be suggested for this: younger marriages, greater economic prosperity, increased government help for the family, and more facilities for young mothers to resume work. Even so, over the past thirty years population projections have been continually revised downwards; for, after the 'baby booms' immediately following the war and in the early 1960s, the birth rate fell, and it continues to do so. The size of the family appears to be settling only slightly above the 1930 level. Although couples are marrying younger, they postpone having children so that wives can continue working full-time, while smaller families enable them to resume work sooner. In this they are aided by improved methods of contraception.

While any projections of population depend upon the reliability of assumptions, especially as regards birth and migration, it now seems likely that the population of the UK will be about 57 million at the end of the century. Whether such an increase is desirable or not will now be examined.

2.2 THE IMPLICATIONS OF CHANGES IN THE SIZE OF THE POPULATION

(a) The Malthusian theory of overpopulation

Until the middle of the eighteenth century, the population of Britain grew slowly. But, from then on, growth became more rapid, and in 1798 Thomas Malthus's first essay on *The Principle of Population as it affects the future improvement of Society* made it a major subject of discussion.

Malthus began from two postulates: (i) that the passion between the sexes is necessary and will remain nearly in 'its present state'; and (ii) that food is necessary to the existence of man. Given these two postulates, his arguments forced him to conclude that: (i) the population will, if unchecked, double itself every twenty-five years; and (ii) the means of subsistence can, at a maximum, increase by only the same amount every twenty-five years. In other words, while population multiplies in a geometric progression, food supplies increase in an arithmetic progression.

The first conclusion was based on information collected by Malthus on the populations of various countries. But the second was supported by no evidence whatsoever. In order to substantiate it, Malthus appealed to the 'known properties of land'. Here he was virtually relying on the *law of diminishing returns* (see p. 106), although that was not precisely stated until some fifty years later.

From these two conclusions the important result followed that the power of population to increase was 'infinitely greater than the power of the earth to produce subsistence for man'. In short, the population would always tend to outgrow its food supply.

Since man cannot live without food, what, Malthus asked, kept population within its means of subsistence? The answer he found in certain 'checks'. First, there were 'positive checks', involving misery – famine, war, disease. Second, there were 'preventive checks' – which, with one exception, all involved 'vice', including contraception. The exception was 'moral restraint', by which was meant deliberately refraining from marrying at an early age. Since this was a remote possibility, the outlook for civilisation was gloomy: in the long run mankind could only expect a subsistence level of existence. Moreover, social policies to alleviate poverty would be self-defeating.

(b) Malthus's 'blind spots'

Although at the beginning of the nineteenth century Malthus's views were widely accepted, the final tragedy of starvation, the logical outcome of his two conclusions, has not occurred. Where, therefore, did Malthus go wrong?

First, we must note that to some extent his argument was illogical, for he did not deal with the fact, well known at the time, that, in spite of the rapid increase in the population over the previous fifty years, people on the average were no worse off. This showed that the means of subsistence must at least have increased in proportion. Had Malthus possessed a precisely formulated law of diminishing returns, he could have based his argument on a fixed total supply of land which would sooner or later make itself felt as the population increased.

Second, Malthus was preoccupied with people as consumers. He failed to see that, by and large, a consumer is also a producer, for 'with every mouth God sends a pair of hands'. Here again a fixed supply of land with consequent diminishing returns could have overcome this objection.

Third, Malthus did not foresee change. On the one hand the geometric increase in Britain's population did not come about, because of emigration and above all because of the reduction in the size of the family. On the other hand, improved agricultural techniques and the vast increase in imports meant that Britain's food supplies were not limited to increasing in an arithmetic progression.

Thus Malthus's arguments have validity only when there are fixed resources, such as land or energy reserves. It is, for instance, the limited supply of land which brings about a Malthusian situation in the Far East today – and, as we shall see, increases Britain's difficulties as she tries to produce a larger proportion of her foodstuffs at home.

(c) The concept of an 'optimum population'

To Malthus, increasing numbers were a bad thing, as they pressed on the means of subsistence and lowered the standard of living. But his views lost ground towards the middle of the nineteenth century, for, as the capital investment of the industrial revolution began to yield benefits, the standard of living was seen to be keeping pace with the increase in population.

Indeed, at the turn of the century, Professor Edwin Cannan showed that population could be too small to take full advantage of available technical knowledge. For example, a larger population might justify large-scale production, with more use being made of division of labour, specialised machines and technical discoveries. In short, a doubling of the population could lead to more than doubling production.

Since, therefore, population can either be too large or too small, there must be an intermediate point where it is just right: the optimum population at which, given existing technical knowledge, capital equipment and possibilities of exchange with other countries, average output per head is at a maximum. Thus, with reference to table 6.1 on p. 107, the optimum population for the example given would be four labourers. It follows that any country is over- or underpopulated if its population is respectively more or less than the optimum.

But the concept of an optimum population is not without difficulties. In the first place it is unjustifiable to specify 'given existing technical knowledge, capital equipment and possibilities of exchange' and then to speculate as to what production would be if the population were larger or smaller. Had the population increased differently, these variables them-selves would have been different. The same mistake is apparent in J.S. Mill's argument in the middle of the nineteenth century that the world would have been better off if, with the improvements that had taken place, population growth had been less. The truth is that such improvements would not have taken place, for a large and rapidly growing population accumulates knowledge and equipment differently from a smaller or slowly growing one. Even more important is that, from the practical point of view, the concept is of little help. Any optimum population at which a country was aiming would only remain the optimum so long as technical knowledge, etc., did not change. Thus, before an optimum was achieved, some new figure would have taken its place. All that can be done, there-fore, is to consider the present composition of the population, forecast the population which will result from it, and then relate this population to likely changes in capital accumulation and technical discoveries.

We now apply this procedure to a study of Britain's population.

(d) The advantage to Great Britain of an increasing population
An increasing population has certain advantages which stimulate growth:

(i) *It increases the size of the home market*
The additional output needed for a larger population should benefit industries working under conditions of decreasing costs, e.g. those produc-

ing aircraft, computers, nuclear reactors. It should be noted, however, that this applies only if the extra output is provided by existing firms and not by additional firms entering the industry. Moreover, it is possible to obtain large-scale economies by specialising on a narrow range of goods and exporting, as in Switzerland.

(ii) *It facilitates labour mobility*
With an increasing population, unemployment resulting from the immobility of labour presents fewer problems. This is because the decline of older industries is slower and can be covered by natural wastage with fewer redundancies, while expanding industries can obtain most of their additional workers from new entrants to the labour force.

(iii) *It encourages investment*
An increasing population makes it easier to maintain the level of replacement investment. More than that, the extra consumer demand necessitates additional investment in machinery, factories, schools, houses, transport, etc. Consequently it stimulates improved techniques, thereby accelerating the replacement of existing equipment.

(iv) *It promotes vitality*
By weighting the age distribution in favour of youth, an increasing population ensures more workers per retired persons and makes for energy, mobility, inventiveness and willingness to accept new ideas.

It should be noted that the disadvantages of a decreasing population could be stated as the opposite of these.

(e) The disadvantages of an increasing population
Against the advantages given above it is necessary to set certain disadvantages which may make it difficult for an increasing population to raise present living standards. Resources have to be used in adding to capital equipment instead of in producing consumer goods or improving existing buildings. The growing population in Britain since the war, for example, has delayed slum-clearance and re-housing schemes since new houses have had to be built for the extra people.

Above all, an increasing population adds to the pressure on the fixed supply of land available in Britain. The saying that 'with every mouth God sends a pair of hands' ignores two important facts. The first is that not every person is a producer – for a time the additional mouths have to be provided with food, education, etc., by the working group. The second is more important: the increase in the number of labourers on a fixed amount of land may well bring the law of diminishing returns into operation, with a consequent fall in living standards.

It is the law of diminishing returns which pinpoints the problem of increasing numbers. In the Far Eastern countries there is simply a lower output per head, as extra people have to obtain their subsistence from a fixed amount of land. But for Britain the problem is presented in a slightly different form. Some of her additional food supplies can be produced at home by improving techniques. But, in the main, Britain produces her food in her workshops, by exporting machinery, oil, electrical equipment, etc., for the meat, cereals, fruit, etc., that she requires. What Britain has to ask, therefore, is: can exports be increased sufficiently to pay for the extra imports required by the larger population? In short, can she maintain a healthy balance-of-payments position so that she suffers no reduction in her standard of living if population grows?

Throughout the nineteenth century Britain proved that this was possible. Indeed, a balance-of-payments surplus allowed her to invest heavily abroad. But since then the problem of finding and holding foreign markets has become more difficult – one of the causes of her frequent balance-of-payments difficulties.

Moreover, it must be remembered that any increase in the population necessitates a much larger proportional increase in exports if the standard of living is to be maintained. Any expansion of present food production in Britain could encounter rapidly diminishing returns. Most of the extra foodstuffs, therefore, would have to come from abroad (not just one half, which is the present proportion). In addition the extra population would require imported goods, such as cameras and cars. Finally, to increase exports, a large proportion of the raw materials from which they are made would have to be imported.

Nor does this take into consideration any possible deterioration in Britain's terms of trade, the rate at which exports exchange for imports (see p. 280). Will the prices of Britain's imports rise as under-developed countries' demand for their own raw materials and foodstuffs increases as they industrialise and improve their incomes? Or will the latter lead to a vastly increased demand for British exports? At present the rising price of North Sea oil is moving the terms of trade in Britain's favour.

Finally, with population growth, environmental problems intensify. As city congestion increases and more open space is required for housing, roads and industry, arguments for conservation and control of pollution gain momentum.

(f) Conclusion

At present Britain is managing to support increasing numbers while improving living standards. But the overall level of the future population must be watched by the government and, if necessary, influenced by immigration policy and the level of child benefits. Social as well as economic considerations have to be taken into account.

In the Far East a Malthusian situation exists. While the death rate is falling through better medical services, the birth rate remains high. By the end of the century an almost doubled population could be seeking to live with little increase in land. Possible solutions are birth control, improved agricultural techniques, the development of export industries, and economic aid from developed countries.

2.3 AGE DISTRIBUTION

Any change in the birth or death rates will affect the age distribution over time. Thus the boom in births after the war and in the early 1960s produced a bulge in new young workers some sixteen years later.

The present overall pattern is of an ageing population brought about by the fall in the rate of increase during the twentieth century (fig 2.3).

Fig 2.3 *changes in the age distribution of the population of Great Britain, 1851-1971*

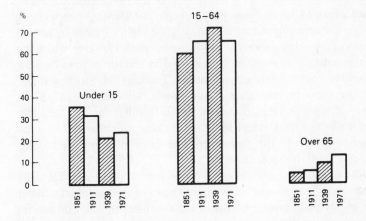

Until the end of the century, the working age-group should form a slightly higher proportion (65%) of the total population, but those under 15 years will fall to 20% and those over 65 rise to 15%.

(a) The effects of an ageing population
It should be noted that in part this trend is due to a normal development, the fall in mortality. This means that we have to adjust to the change: trying to prevent it by raising the birth rate will also increase the size of the population – which, as we have seen, presents problems.

It is essential, therefore, to anticipate the possible economic, social and political difficulties resulting from changes in the age structure so that the necessary adjustments can, with planning, occur smoothly.

(i) *Economic*

First, there is an increased dependence of retired persons on the working population. Current wants can only be provided for by current production. An ageing population means that the proportion of workers to consumers is falling. Whereas in 1851 there were over 12 people of working age for every person over 65, in 1978 there were only 4½. One particular result will be the increased burden of retirement pensions, more pensioners having to be supported by proportionately fewer contributors.

Second, a changing pattern of consumption will result. An ageing population means, to take extreme examples, that bath-chairs will be wanted in place of prams, walking-sticks in place of hockey-sticks, tea in place of milk. For many of these new wants, consideration has to be given well in advance. We must, for instance, make more provision for aged couples when planning the housing programme. (On the other hand, the later 1940s and early 1960s bulges have to be provided with housing and jobs, and further education, respectively.)

Third, an older labour force is less mobile. In the past, expanding industries have obtained labour from young people just starting their working lives, while the decaying industries have declined fairly quietly by natural wastage – not replacing workers as they leave or retire. However, where the working population is static in size, expanding industries have to draw older workers from the declining industries. 'Teaching old dogs new tricks' and moving them to new areas is not always easy (see pp. 147-8). A high level of unemployment increases the difficulties, for it is the older workers in the declining industries who are likely to remain out of a job the longest. Thus both the government and firms must provide training schemes and re-location incentives.

Fourth, an older population tends to be less progressive. While older people are more patient and experienced than younger people, the latter excel in energy, enterprise, enthusiasm and the ability to adapt themselves and to learn new skills.

(ii) *Social*

Where old people are more numerous and live longer, their children find greater difficulty in caring for them. Thus there is an increasing need for the state to provide home-care services (such as 'meals-on-wheels' and home helps), old people's homes and geriatric wards in hospitals.

Similarly, there is a greater demand for advice from Citizen's Advice Bureaux, since older people need more help in sorting out difficulties relating to housing, gas and electricity bills, social-security benefits and so on.

(iii) *Political*

Political decisions have to be made as a result of the disadvantages of an ageing population. To what extent should younger generations be augmented by a liberal immigration policy, bearing in mind the social stresses which could arise? Can adequate defence be provided by the use of more sophisticated weapons, or will the falling proportion of young people necessitate conscription? Should TV and radio programmes give greater weight to the type of entertainment preferred by old people? And, since older people own the larger share of the nation's capital but are adverse to taking risks, should the state assume responsibility for providing funds for the riskier types of enterprise, such as North-Sea-oil prospecting and development, the building of nuclear power stations and the exploration of outer space?

Indeed, the ageing population may even influence the election of governments, for older people tend to be more conservative.

2.4 SEX DISTRIBUTION

In 1978 the population of the UK was 55,835,000 of whom 27,170,000 were males and 28,666,000 females. Thus females outnumbered males by 496,000. This fact influences the pattern of consumption and the nature of the labour force, and may affect the number of births. We shall examine the latter question.

Since nine-tenths of children are born to married mothers, the number of births depends to a great extent on the number of marriages. But where the numbers of the sexes are unequal, especially at the usual age of marriage – that is, between 16 and 49 – the proportion of people likely to get married will be smaller.

Table 2.3 *Proportion of females to males, 15–49 age-group, Great Britain*

Date	Percentage
1911	108
1921	113
1931	110
1939	106
1951	104
1961	100.4
1971	97.9
1978	97.7

Source: Royal Commission on Population Report, 1949, and Annual Abstract of Statistics

The balance of the sexes in the 15–49 age-group has changed remarkably over the last 60 years. Until 1961, females outnumbered males. Since then males have outnumbered females (table 2.3). We can explain the change as follows.

The proportion of male to female births has hardly varied from 106:100. But until 1961 the number of males in the 15–49 age-group was decreased by: (i) the wars of 1914–18 and 1939–45; (ii) emigration; and (iii) the higher male mortality rate in general.

After 1961 these factors became less significant. First, the generations of men affected by World Wars I and II have passed out of the age-group. Second, there is an increased proportion of women emigrants. Third, males in this age-group have benefited more than females from the fall in mortality rates.

In 1978 the normal ratio of females to males in the age-group was 97.6%, and it should stay at this. If mortality declined further, the ratio could fall to 96.6, since males would probably benefit the most.

Present numbers in the age-group are 12,737,000 males and 12,439,300 females. Thus, even if every female marries, at least 300,000 males are likely to remain bachelors.

Above 50 years of age the mortality of males compared with females increases considerably, so that females outnumber males. Indeed, in the 85+ group there are three times as many women.

2.5 THE INDUSTRIAL DISTRIBUTION OF THE WORKING POPULATION

(a) The working population

Great Britain's population in 1978 was estimated to be 54,296,000 persons. Of these, 25,745,000 persons are described by the Department of Employment as 'the working population'.

The working population is defined as persons over school-leaving age 'who work for pay or gain or register themselves as available for such work'. It therefore includes all persons who are: (i) in civil employment, even if they are over retirement age or working only part-time; (ii) in the armed forces; or (iii) registered as unemployed. Excluded by the definition are: (i) children under 16 and students over 16 who are receiving full-time education; (ii) persons, such as housewives, who do not work for pay or gain; (iii) persons who, having private means, do not need to work; and (iv) retired persons.

The size of the working population depends upon:

(i) The numbers within the 16–65 age-group.
(ii) The activity rates within this group, especially as regards young people and female workers. The tendency over the last twenty years has been for a higher proportion of young people to remain

in further education, thus reducing their activity rate. On the other hand, a higher proportion of women are now entering the working population. The expansion of the service and light-manufacturing industries has provided increased job opportunities for women, while the changed attitude to women workers is reflected in the Equal Pay Act 1970 and the Sex Discrimination Act 1975. Above all, the smaller family, the availability of crêches and school dinners, and new labour-saving domestic appliances have allowed married women to work.

(iii) The extent to which people over retiring age continue to work, something which is largely influenced by the level of pensions.

(iv) The employment opportunities available – the tendency being for the working population to contract in a depression (mainly through withdrawal of married women).

Table 2.4 *Industrial distribution of the working population, 1901–1978*

	Distribution (%) Great Britain		Numbers (000s) G.B.
	(1) 1901	*(2)* 1978	*(3)* 1978
Agriculture, forestry and fishing	9.0	1.5	377
Mining and quarrying	5.8	1.3	341
Manufacture (including gas, electricity and water supply)	32.6	29.2	7,504
Construction	8.1	4.8	1,233
Transport and communication	9.3	5.5	1,426
Distributive trades		10.4	2,683
Financial, professional and scientific services	15.4	18.3	4,709
Public administration	1.4	6.2	1,586
Catering and domestic services	15.3	3.4	884
Miscellaneous services	2.0	5.7	1,480
Armed Forces	1.1	1.2	318
Registered unemployed	–	5.4	1,381
Employers and self-employed	–	7.1	1,825
TOTALS	100.0	100.0	25,745

Sources: Col (1) compiled from Colin Clark, *Conditions of Economic Progress* (quoting Booth, *Journal of Royal Statistic Society*, 1856). Cols (2) and (3) compiled from *Annual Abstract of Statistics*

(b) Changes in the industrial distribution of the working population

Table 2.4 shows that the chief changes in the distribution of the working population between 1901 and 1978 were:

(i)   A large decrease in the percentage of the population employed in the primary (extractive) industries – agriculture, mining and fishing.

(ii) A relatively small decrease in the secondary – manufacturing and construction – industries.

(iii) A relatively large increase in the tertiary industries – the distributive trades, public administration and services – with the notable exception of domestic servants.

The basic explanation of these broad changes can be found in the increase in real income (which more than doubled) over the period. In this respect the changes are merely a continuation of the trend of the previous century. As income increases, people tend to spend a smaller proportion on food, and more on comforts and luxuries. In 1901, for example, the average labourer spent 60% of his income on food; by 1978 only 23%. Now the distribution of labour between industries is largely a reflection of the way in which people spend their incomes.

Thus, as agriculture declined in relative importance, workers moved into the new luxury industries, particularly those providing services.

But there have been other influences at work, especially important in explaining changes within these broad groups. Briefly, these influences are:

(i)   Changes in exports (e.g. mining) and in imports (e.g. agriculture).

(ii) Improved techniques and increased use of machines (e.g. in agriculture, construction, transport, mining).

(iii) The increase in exchange (e.g. insurance, banking and other services).

(iv) The increase in state activities (public administration).

(v)   The acceptance of women workers in industry and commerce, where high wages attracted them from domestic service.

2.6 THE GEOGRAPHICAL DISTRIBUTION OF THE POPULATION

Geographically, the population of the UK is dominated by two features: it is *concentrated*, and it is *urban*. Both are the result of moving from an agricultural to an industrial economy.

(a) The concentrated nature of the population

As a result of the industrial revolution industry migrated to the coalfields in the Midlands and north of England. And today, even though electricity frees industry from being located on the coalfields and the basic industries of these areas have declined, they still remain important centres of industry and population (Fig 2.4).

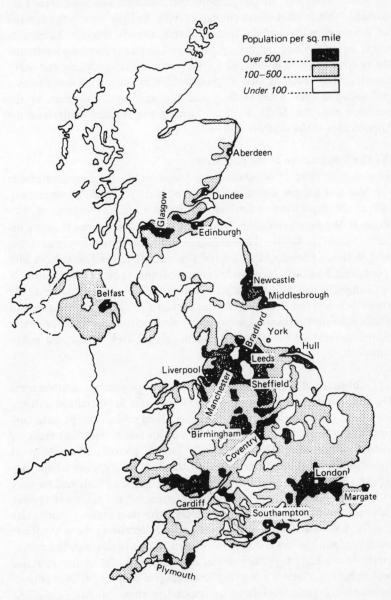

Fig 2.4 *geographical distribution of the population of the UK*

Population per sq. mile

Over 500 ....

100–500 ....

Under 100 ....

There are two main reasons for this. First, many industries remain because of acquired advantages, particularly the availability of labour (see p. 96). Second, new industries have been attracted by the government's Development Area policy (see p. 314).

Nevertheless, since World War II the main areas of natural expansion have been the Midlands and south-east England (particularly London and the home counties). In comparison, the coalfields and rural areas have declined. This is what one might expect with the expansion in the demand for light-engineering and electrical products, aircraft, motor vehicles, consumer durable goods and luxury goods and services of various kinds, and the relative decrease in demand for the products of agriculture and heavy industry. The result is that at present 55% of the population live in a coffin-shaped area with south Lancashire and west Yorkshire at the northern end, the Midland region forming the broader centre and the London area at the southern end.

(b) The urban nature of the population
This concentration of population is in towns (unlike the concentrations in the Nile and Ganges deltas, which consist mainly of rural communities). 80% of the population of England and Wales is urban. Furthermore, 30% of Great Britain's population lives in the seven conurbations (continuous built-up areas) of Greater London, south-east Lancashire (Manchester), the west Midlands (Birmingham), central Clydeside (Glasgow), west Yorkshire (Leeds and Bradford), Merseyside (Liverpool) and Tyneside (Newcastle).

Changes in population take place within the main centres, however. As towns become too crowded, as the standard of living improves and as offices take over residential areas, so people tend to move from the centre to the suburbs or even further, commuting to work by car and public transport.

(c) Problems resulting from the concentration of population in urban areas
The concentration of population in large urban areas has certain advantages. Such areas can offer better and more specialised schools, shops, entertainment and other services. Fast road, rail and air communications facilitate travel between cities. They can usually provide a variety of employment opportunities, enabling firms to recruit the different types of labour they require. But conurbations often involve travelling long distances to work within the urban area, putting a heavy stress on the transport system. There are also problems of inner-city decay, with poor housing, inadequate schools, pollution and lack of open spaces. Moreover, there are fewer social ties, and the lower community spirit results in vandalism and petty crime. Above all, where these areas are faced with the decline of major local industries, there is a 'regional' problem (see chapter 19). Not only do government organisations have to respond to these conditions, but the development of urban areas may itself lead to the re-organisation of local and regional government.

PART II
PRIVATE-SECTOR
PRODUCTION

THE OPERATION OF
THE FREE MARKET

3.1 MARKETS

(a) Value and price

In the market economy a want is significant only when a person is prepared to give up something in order to satisfy it. As the strength of the different wants varies, so will the amounts which people are willing to give up. In other words, different goods have different *values*, value being the *rate* at which a particular good or service will exchange for others. In modern economic systems the values of goods are expressed in terms of money, as *prices*.

Changes in *relative* prices, if supply conditions have not changed, indicate a relative shift in the importance of the goods concerned. Thus price changes signal changes in what people want. We must therefore examine the mechanism by which these signals are flashed up. We begin by looking at the *market*.

(b) What is a market?

'I am offered £350 for this heifer. No more offers? For the last time of asking, any advance on £350? Going at £350, going, gone.' Down comes the hammer. 'Sold at £350 to Mr Giles on my right.'

This is the local cattle-market. On his stand above the cattle-ring is the auctioneer. Inside the ring, a black-and-white heifer is appraised by local farmers and dealers. Some are buyers, some sellers. The market fixes the price at which those who want something can obtain it from those who have it to sell.

Note that it is only exchange value which is significant here. The farmer selling the heifer may have felt that it ought to have made more than £350. Or, as it was the first calf reared by his son, it may have had great 'sentimental value' to him. Such considerations, however, mean little in the market economy.

Of course, prices are not always fixed by auction. This is the method usually employed where there are many buyers but the seller only comes to the market infrequently, or wishes to dispose of his goods quickly. If there are few buyers and sellers, e.g. in the purchase of a house or a second-hand car, the final price may be arrived at by 'haggling' – the seller's meeting the prospective buyer personally and bargaining with him.

But where goods are in constant demand the above methods take too long. Thus most goods, such as foodstuffs, clothing and household utensils are given a definite price by the shopkeeper. But buyers will still influence this price. If it is too high, the market will not be cleared; if it is too low, the shopkeeper's stocks will run out.

A market need not be formal or held in a particular place. Secondhand cars are often bought and sold through newspaper advertisements. Secondhand furniture may be disposed of by a card in a local shop window. Foreign currency, gold, base metals, raw cotton and other goods which can be accurately described are dealt in over the telephone.

However, in studying the market economy it is essential to understand how price is determined. Since this is done in the market, we can define the market simply as *all those buyers and sellers of a good who influence its price*. Within the market there is a tendency for the same price, allowing for costs of transport, to be established for the same commodity.

(c) World markets

Today modern transport allows many commodities to have a world market – a price change in one part of the world affects the price in the rest of the world. Examples of such commodities are wheat, vegetable oils, basic raw materials (such as cotton and rubber), gold, silver and base metals. What conditions must a commodity fulfil to obtain a world market?

First, there must be a wide demand. The basic necessities of life (e.g. wheat, frozen meat, wool, cotton) answer this requirement. In contrast, such goods as national costumes, books translated into little-used languages and postcards of local views have only a local demand.

Second, commodities must be capable of being transported. Land and buildings are almost impossible to transport. Personal services are limited by the distance the consumer can travel. Labour, too, is particularly immobile, especially when it comes to moving to a different country (see chapter 8). Furthermore, governments may, by import taxes and quotas, effectively prevent the entry of certain commodities into the country.

Third, the costs of transport must be small in relation to the value of the commodity. Thus the market for diamonds is worldwide, whereas that for bricks is local. Similarly wheat and oil are cheap to transport compared with coal because they are more easily handled – although, as sea transport is relatively cheap, coal mined near the coast can be sent long distances.

Last, the commodity must be durable. Goods which perish quickly, such as milk, bread, fresh cream and strawberries, cannot be sent long distances. Nevertheless modern developments, such as refrigeration, canning and air freight transport, are extending the market even for these goods.

(d) Perfect and imperfect markets

In any market the price of the commodity in one part affects its price in another part. Hence the same price tends to be established. Where price differences are eliminated quickly, we say the market is a 'perfect' market. (Note that this is not quite the same as 'perfect competition' – see chapter 6).

For a market to be perfect certain conditions have to be fulfilled. First, buyers and sellers must have exact knowledge of the prices being paid elsewhere in the market. The development of communications, particularly the telephone, has facilitated this. Second, both buyers and sellers must base their actions solely on price, and not favour one particular person out of loyalty or mere inertia. Thus, if one seller puts up the price of his good, his customers immediately go to another who is cheaper. Alternatively, if he lowers his price, customers will so flock to him that he would sell out quickly unless he raises his price to that asked elsewhere.

Examples of perfect markets are the precious-stones market of Hatton Garden in London, and above all the organised produce markets and the stock exchange (see below). In these markets the two essential conditions are fulfilled, for prices are watched closely by professional dealers. As a result of their operations, variations in price are quickly eliminated.

But such conditions are rarely satisfied in other markets. Buyers and sellers neither have perfect knowledge nor act solely on the basis of price. The ordinary housewife, for instance, cannot afford the time to go from one shop to another in order to compare the prices of her everyday purchases, though she is usually much more careful when spending on the more expensive goods bought at infrequent intervals. Similarly, shopkeepers do not always know what competing shopkeepers are charging for their goods. Moreover, purchasers may be influenced by considerations other than price. Thus they may continue to deal with one particular trader, even though he is charging a slightly higher price, because he has given them good service in the past. Finally, although two goods may be virtually the same physically, by 'product differentiation' and advertising the merits of his own brand a producer may convince the consumer of its superiority. Such 'persuasive' advertising, which accounts for over a half of present advertising expenditure, makes the market less perfect, and must be contrasted with 'informative' advertising, which increases knowledge and thus helps to make the market more perfect.

Where price differences persist, markets are said to be 'imperfect'. As we have already hinted, such markets are often found in retailing.

(e) Organised produce markets

As explained above, the market for certain commodities is worldwide. Moreover, many of these commodities are in constant demand, either as basic raw materials or as main foods or beverages for a large section of the world's people. They therefore figure prominently in international trade, and are the subject of the following discussion.

England's foreign trade began with the export of raw wool in the thirteenth century, and it was extended by the subsequent development of the chartered companies. These were based in London, and it was there that merchants gathered to buy and sell the produce which the companies' ships brought from abroad.

The big change, however, came about with the expansion of international trade following the industrial revolution. The UK became the greatest importing and exporting nation in the world. London, her chief port and commercial city, not only imported the goods which were required for the people of her own country but, assisted by the fact that British ships were the carriers of world trade, built up an important entrepôt business, acting as a go-between in the distribution of such commodities as tea, sugar, hides, skins and wool to many other countries, particularly those of western Europe.

Hence formal 'organised markets' developed. These markets are distinctive in that buying and selling takes place in a recognised building, business is governed by agreed rules and conventions, and often only certain persons are allowed to engage in transactions. They are thus a highly developed form of market. Today London has exchanges or auction centres for such commodities as rubber, wool, tea, coffee, furs, metals (tin, copper, lead and zinc), grain, and shipping freights (the Baltic Exchange). It must not be thought, however, that such organised produce markets exist only in London. Liverpool has exchanges for cotton and grain, and most of the other large trading countries have exchanges too. Although today many of the goods go directly to other countries, the earnings of London dealers are part of the UK's income from 'invisible exports' (see p. 285).

Broadly speaking, organised markets fulfil three main functions. First, they enable manufacturers and wholesalers to obtain supplies of commodities easily, quickly and at the competitive market price. Because they are composed of specialist buyers and sellers, prices are sensitive to any change in demand and supply. Thus they are perfect markets.

Second, 'futures' dealings on these markets enable people to protect themselves from heavy losses through price changes. Thus a cotton grower prefers to know what price he will receive before his output is actually delivered to the market. On the other hand a cotton spinner has to protect himself from a rise in the price of raw cotton between the time he quotes a price for his yarn and the time of its actual manufacture. Where a good is bought today for delivery today, the deal is known as a 'spot' transaction and the price is the 'spot price'. With many goods, however, it is possible to buy today for delivery in the future. The good may not even be in stock, but the seller contracts to obtain and deliver it at the agreed time. The price agreed upon is the 'future' or 'forward' price. For a commodity to be dealt in on a futures market certain conditions must be fulfilled: (i) the commodity must be durable, thereby enabling stocks to be carried; (ii) the commodity must be described in terms of grades which are internationally uniform; (iii) dealings must be frequent enough to occupy professional dealers; and (iv) the commodity must be subject to price fluctuations.

Where futures dealings take place, the market is usually divided between brokers and dealers. The broker merely carries out the wishes of his client, whereas the dealer uses his expert knowledge to make a profit on what he considers will be the future price of the commodity. At any time a dealer will quote a price (according to the view he takes of the future movement of prices) at which he is prepared to buy or sell at some future date. Thus a cotton grower can cover himself against a possible fall in price by selling his produce forward, while a cotton spinner can quote a weaver a price for yarn and guard himself against loss by buying the raw cotton forward.

Such dealing usually performs the third function of organised markets – evening out price fluctuations. At a time when an increase in supply would cause the price to fall considerably, the dealer adds his demand to the normal demand in order to build up his stocks, and thereby keeps the price up. On the other hand, when the good is in short supply he releases stocks and so prevents a violent rise in price. The difficulty is that speculation on the future price may dominate the real forces which influence it, prices fluctuating violently in response to changes in optimism and pessimism.

3.2 FORCES DETERMINING PRICE

(a) Demand and supply

'That animal was cheap, remarks Dan Archer as the auctioneer's hammer falls. 'And no wonder,' replies Fred Barrett. 'This has been a long winter. We're now in the middle of April, and the grass is hardly growing. Hay's running short, and breeders are being forced to sell sooner than expected. Old Giles is about the only farmer who'll take the risk of buying extra cattle.'

What can we learn from Fred Barrett's observations? Simply that the £350 at which the heifer was sold was not really determined by the final bid. The real factors producing the relatively low price were the reluctance of farmers to buy and the number of young animals being offered for sale. In short, the price was determined by the interaction of the forces of demand and supply. We shall look at each in turn.

(b) Preliminary assumptions
First, we examine how these forces work in an imaginary market – for eggs. To simplify, we shall assume that:

(i) All eggs are exactly the same in size and quality.

(ii) There are no transport costs within the market.

(iii) The market consists of so many small buyers and sellers that there is keen competition.

(iv) That it is a perfect market: price differences are quickly eliminated because buyers and sellers (1) have complete knowledge of prices and conditions in other parts of the market, and (2) act solely on the basis of price.

(v) There is no interference by the government in the operation of market forces, e.g. by price control, regulating supply, etc.

(c) Demand
Demand in economics is the desire for something *plus* the willingness and ability to pay a certain price in order to possess it. More specifically, it is how much of a good people in the market will buy at a given price over a certain period of time.

It is helpful if we separate the factors affecting demand into (i) price, and (ii) the conditions of demand.

(i) *Price (the conditions of demand remaining unchanged)*
Normally a person will demand more of a good the lower its price. This is because, once you have some units of a good, you have partly satisfied your want and so will only buy more at a lower price. This conforms to our everyday observations. 'Winter sale, prices slashed' announce the shops when they wish to clear their stocks of clothing.

We can draw up a table showing how many eggs a person would be willing to buy at different prices. If they are very expensive, other foodstuffs will, as far as possible, be substituted; if they are cheap, people may even buy them to pickle. By adding up the demand from all buyers of eggs in the market at different prices over a given period of time, it is possible to obtain a *market demand schedule* (table 3.1).

Note that this schedule does not tell us anything about the actual market price or how much is in fact sold. It is an 'if' schedule. All it says is: 'If the

Table 3.1 *Demand schedule for No-Such Market for the week ending 26 January 1980*

Price (pence per egg)	Eggs demanded (thousands)*
12	3
10	9
8	15
6	20
4	25
2	35

*what buyers would take at each price

price is so much, then this quantity will be demanded.' Plotting this schedule on a graph, and assuming that demand can be obtained for intermediary prices, gives the demand curve D in fig 3.1.

Fig 3.1 *quantity demanded and price*

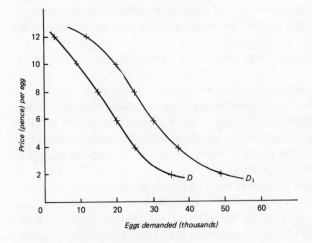

(ii) *The conditions of demand*

Something may occur to cause housewives to demand more eggs at a given price. In other words, the demand schedule alters. Suppose, for instance, farmers unite in an advertising campaign describing tasty egg dishes. As a result more eggs are demanded at all prices (table 3.2).

Plotting this revised demand schedule gives curve D₁ to the right of D. Had conditions so changed that demand decreased, the new demand curve would have been to the left.

The influence of both (i) price, and (ii) the conditions of demand, on

Table 3.2 *An increase in demand*

Price (pence per egg)	Eggs demanded (thousands)
12	12
10	20
8	25
6	30
4	37
2	49

the quantity demanded is thus shown on the graph. The former determines the shape of the demand curve – its slope downwards from left to right. The latter determines the position between the axes – an increase in demand shifting the curve to the right, a decrease to the left. For clarity's sake, a change in demand resulting from a change in price will in future be referred to as an *extension* or *contraction* of demand; a change in demand due to new conditions of demand will be described as an *increase* or *decrease* in demand.

Conditions of demand may change in a *short* period of time through:

(1) A CHANGE IN THE PRICE OF OTHER GOODS

Goods compete for our limited income and are thus, to some extent, substitutes for each other. When the prices of other goods fall, the particular good under discussion becomes relatively dearer and therefore less of it is demanded. When the prices of other goods rise, it becomes relatively cheaper, and so more of it is demanded.

But the effect on the demand for a particular good is more pronounced when the price of a close substitute changes. Suppose that fried tomatoes are an alternative to eggs for breakfast. If the price of tomatoes falls, housewives will tend to buy them rather than eggs. Thus, although there has been no initial increase in the price of eggs, demand for them has decreased. Similarly, where goods are complementary, a change in the price of one good has a pronounced effect on the demand for the other. For example, a fall in the price of cars results in more cars being purchased, leading eventually to an increase in the demand for petrol and tyres.

(2) A CHANGE IN TASTES AND FASHION

A campaign advertising eggs would increase demand; a scare that eggs were the source of infection would decrease it

(3) EXPECTATIONS OF FUTURE PRICE CHANGES OR SHORTAGES
The fear that the price of eggs may rise considerably next week will induce people to increase their demand now in order to have eggs in stock.

(4) GOVERNMENT POLICY
A tax on eggs paid by the consumer would raise the price and lead to a decrease in demand; a rebate paid to the consumer would have the opposite effect (see chapter 21).

Over a *longer* period the conditions of demand may change through:

(5) A CHANGE IN REAL INCOME
If there were an all-round increase in income, people could afford more eggs, and demand would probably increase. On the other hand it might now be possible to afford mushrooms for breakfast, and these would take the place of eggs.

(6) GREATER EQUALITY IN THE DISTRIBUTION OF WEALTH
The wealth of a country may be so distributed that there are a few exceptionally rich people whereas the remainder are exceedingly poor. If many poor people felt they could not afford eggs, greater equality of wealth would be likely to increase the demand for eggs.

(7) A CHANGE IN THE SIZE AND COMPOSITION OF THE POPULATION
Additional people coming into the market will, with their extra income, increase demand, especially if eggs figure prominently in their diets.

(d) Supply
Supply in economics refers to how much of a good will be offered for sale at a given price over a given period of time. As with demand, this quantity depends on (i) the price of the good, and (ii) the conditions of supply.

(i) *Price (the conditions of supply remaining unchanged)*
Normally more of a good will be supplied the higher its price. The real reason for this is explained in chapter 6. But even a brief consideration of how the individual farmer reacts to a change in price will show that it is likely to be true. If the price of eggs is high, he will probably consume fewer himself in order to send as many as possible to market. Moreover, the higher price allows him to give his chickens more food so that they can lay a few extra eggs. When we extend our analysis to the market supply it is obvious that a higher price for eggs enables farmers - including the less efficient - to produce more.

Hence we are able to draw up a *market supply schedule* - the total

54

Table 3.3 *Supply schedule for No-Such Market for the week
ending 26 January 1980*

Price (pence per egg)	Eggs supplied (thousands)*
12	40
10	32
5	25
6	20
4	13
2	7

*what sellers would offer at each price

number of eggs supplied at different prices by all the sellers in the market
over a given period of time (table 3.3).

Once again it must be noted that this is an 'if' schedule, for all it says
is: 'If the price is so much, then this quantity will be offered for sale.'

We can plot this schedule (figure 3.2); assuming supply for all intermediate prices, a supply curve S is obtained.

Fig 3.2 *quantity supplied and price*

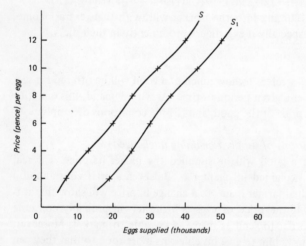

However there is a fundamental difference between demand and supply.
Whereas demand can respond almost immediately to a change in price, a
period of time must usually elapse before supply can be fully adjusted. For
the first day or two the only way in which the farmer can send more eggs
to market is by eating fewer himself. By the end of the week he may have

increased output by giving the hens more food or by leaving the light on in the hen-house all night; the higher price covers the extra cost. But to obtain any sizeable increase the farmer must add to his hens; if all farmers are following the same policy, this will take about five months, the period required to rear laying hens from chicks.

These different periods of time are dealt with more fully in chapter 6.

(ii) *The conditions of supply*
The number of eggs supplied may change even though there has been no alteration in the price. In the spring, for instance, chickens lay more eggs than in winter. Thus more eggs will be supplied at all prices in the spring, and fewer in winter, as shown in table 3.4.

Table 3.4   *An increase in supply*

Price (pence per egg)	Eggs supplied (thousands)
12	50
10	43
8	36
6	30
4	25
2	19

Table 3.4 shows that, whereas in winter only 25,000 eggs were supplied at 8p each, during the spring 36,000 were supplied. Or, looked at in another way, 25,000 eggs can be supplied in the spring at 4p each compared with 8p in the winter. When plotted, the revised supply schedule gives a curve S_1 to the right of the old one. Had supply decreased, the new supply curve would have been to the left.

Like demand, therefore, supply is influenced by both (i) price, and (ii) the conditions of supply. The former determines the shape of the curve – its upward slope from left to right. The latter determines its position between the axes – an increase in supply shifts the curve to the right, a decrease to the left. To distinguish between the two we shall refer to a change in supply resulting from a change in the price of a commodity as an *extension* or *contraction* of supply; a change in supply due to new conditions of supply will be described as an *increase* or *decrease* in supply.

In general, conditions of supply may change fairly quickly through:

(1) A CHANGE IN THE PRICES OF OTHER GOODS, ESPECIALLY WHEN IT IS EASY TO SHIFT RESOURCES AND THE GOOD IN QUESTION IS IN 'JOINT SUPPLY'

Suppose, for instance, that there is a considerable increase in the price of chicken meat, including boiling fowls. It may pay the farmer to kill some of his laying pullets. Thus fewer eggs are supplied at the old price.

(2) A CHANGE IN THE PRICES OF FACTORS OF PRODUCTION
A fall in the cost of pullets or of their food would reduce the cost of producing eggs. As a result more eggs could be supplied at the old price, or - looked at in another way – the original quantity could be produced at a lower price per egg. A rise in the wages of workers on chicken farms would have the opposite effect.

(3) CHANGES RESULTING FROM NATURE
(e.g. the weather, floods, drought, pest) and from *abnormal circumstances* (e.g. war, fire, political events).

(4) GOVERNMENT POLICY
A tax on the output of eggs or an increase in employers' national insurance contributions would result in fewer eggs being offered for sale at the old price. That is, the supply curve moves to the left. On the other hand a subsidy, by decreasing costs, would move the supply curve to the right (see p. 64).

Other changes in supply take longer, occurring through:

(5) IMPROVED TECHNIQUES
Technical improvements reduce costs of production, shifting the supply curve to the right. Thus automatic feeding devices might be developed, or selective breeding produce hens which lay more eggs over a given period.

(6) THE DISCOVERY OF NEW SOURCES OF RAW MATERIALS, OR THE EXHAUSTION OF EXISTING SOURCES

(7) THE ENTRY OF NEW FIRMS INTO THE INDUSTRY

3.3 THE DETERMINATION OF PRICE: MARKET CLEARING

The demand and supply curves can be combined in a single diagram (fig 3.3).

Let us see how this analysis helps as a first approach to understanding how the market is cleared. The assumptions we have made so far are:
(i) Many buyers and sellers.
(ii) Keen competition between buyers, between sellers, and between buyers and sellers.
(iii) More will be demanded at a lower price than at a higher price.

Fig 3.3 *the determination of equilibrium price*

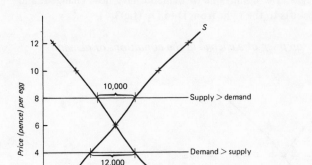

(iv)   Less will be supplied at a lower price than at a higher.

Given assumptions (iii) and (iv), the two curves slope in opposite directions. Thus they cut at a single point – in our example, where the price is 6p. It can be predicted that in No-Such Market, where these conditions of demand and supply exist, the price of eggs will move towards and eventually settle at 6p. This is the *market* or *equilibrium price*.

This proposition can be proved as follows. Suppose that initially the price of eggs is fixed at 8p. Here 15,000 will be demanded but 25,000 supplied. There is thus an excess supply of 10,000. But some sellers will want to get rid of their surplus supplies, and therefore reduce the price being asked. As this happens some supplies are withdrawn from the market, and there is an extension of demand. This continues until a price of 6p is reached, when 20,000 eggs are both demanded and offered for sale. Thus 6p is the only price at which there is harmony between buyers and sellers: given existing demand and supply, the market is 'cleared'.

Similarly, if the initial price is 4p, 25,000 will be demanded, but only 13,000 offered for sale. Housewives queue to buy eggs, and sellers see that their supplies will quickly run out. Competition among buyers will force up the price. As this happens, more eggs are supplied to the market, and there is a contraction of demand. This continues until a price of 6p is reached, when demand equals supply at 20,000 eggs.

3.4 CHANGES IN THE CONDITIONS OF DEMAND AND SUPPLY

The equilibrium price will persist until there is a change in the conditions of either demand or supply.

Let us begin with our market price of 6p. Suppose tastes alter, and people eat more eggs. The conditions of demand have now changed, and the demand curve shifts to the right from D to D_1 (fig 3.4).

Fig 3.4 *the effect on price of a change in the conditions of demand*

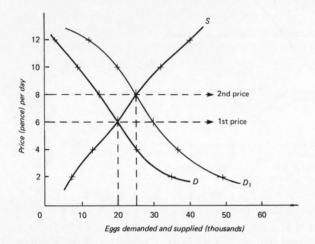

At the original price of 6p we now have an excess of demand over supply – 30,000 eggs are demanded, but only 20,000 are supplied. As explained in the previous section, competition between buyers will now force up the price to 8p, where 25,000 eggs are both demanded and supplied.

Fig 3.5 *the effect on price of a change in the conditions of supply*

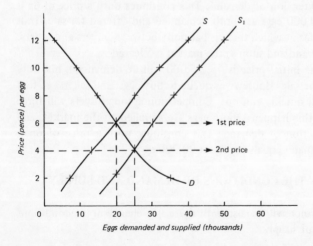

Similarly a decrease in demand – resulting, for instance, from a significant fall in the price of tomatoes – would cause the curve to shift to the left and the price of eggs to fall.

Alternatively a change may occur in the conditions of supply. At any given price more eggs can be produced during the spring, when the supply curve shifts to the right from S to S_1 (fig 3.5).

At the original price of 6p we now have an excess of supply over demand – 30,000 eggs are supplied, but only 20,000 are demanded. Here competition amongst sellers will mean that the price falls to 4p, where 25,000 eggs are both demanded and supplied.

3.5 FUNCTIONS OF PRICE IN THE FREE MARKET

Our analysis can be applied to practical problems, especially those relating to government policy. First, however, we use it to examine the role of price in the market economy.

In a free market, price both indicates and motivates.

(a) Price 'rations out' scarce goods
At any one time the supply of a good is relatively fixed. It therefore has to be apportioned among the many people wanting it. This is done by adjusting price. As price rises, demand contracts; as it falls, demand expands. At the equilibrium price demand just equals the supply. Should supply increase, the total quantity can still be disposed of by lowering the price; should supply decrease, the price would have to be raised.

We can illustrate how price works by considering, with much simplification, two current problems:

(i) *Who shall be allowed to park his car in a congested area?*
Car parking is causing traffic congestion in the centre of Barthem City. This is because it costs motorists nothing to park their cars at the kerbside. The council decides to limit parking to one side of the road and to 800 places, each with a parking meter. The demand schedule for two-hour parking is estimated to be as follows:

Price (pence)	Demand
30	450
20	800
10	1,200
0	1,800

The council therefore fixes a charge of 20p. The 1,000 motorists who will not pay this price do not, therefore, bring their cars into the city centre.

(ii) *Why do ticket touts obtain such high prices for Cup Final tickets?*

To ensure that the regular football supporter can afford a Cup Final ticket, prices are fixed by the Football Association. Let us simplify by assuming that the FA has one price, £1, for the 100,000 tickets, but that a free-market price would be £3. In fig 3.6, when the price is £3 demand equals the available supply, but at the controlled price of £1 demand exceeds supply by 150,000.

Fig 3.6 *excess demand for Cup Final tickets*

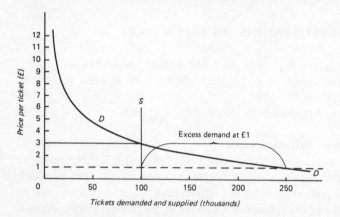

But some tickets are obtained by touts, who re-sell at a profit in a free market where demand and supply determine price. Keen club supporters, not lucky enough to have been allocated a ticket, are willing to pay more than £1. As the price rises, some people possessing tickets may be induced

Fig 3.7 *the black-market price of Cup Final tickets*

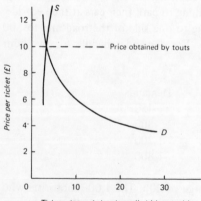

to sell them to the touts. Thus the demand and supply curves are roughly as shown in fig 3.7, giving a 'black-market' price of £10.

An important conclusion can be drawn from this example: where price is controlled below the market price, only some form of rationing can ensure that everybody gets a share of the limited supply. Normally this is achieved by the FA, which, after allocating a certain number of tickets to each finalist, limits each affiliated club to approximately two. One alternative would simply be a 'first come, first served' method of distribution, penalising those who could not queue and increasing the scope for tout activity.

(b) Price indicates changes in wants

Prices are the signals by which households indicate the extent to which different goods are wanted, and any changes in those wants.

Consider how the demand for owner-occupied houses in south-east England has increased over the last ten years through the pressure of population, higher real incomes, tax concessions, etc. As a result, prices have risen from OP to OP_1 (fig 3.8).

(c) Price induces supply to respond to changes in demand

When demand increases, price rises and supply extends; when demand decreases, price falls and supply contracts. Thus in fig 3.8 the increase in price has made it profitable for extra houses MM_1 to be supplied by new building, by transferring houses from the rented sector, etc.

Fig 3.8   *the effect on house prices of an increase in demand by owner-occupiers*

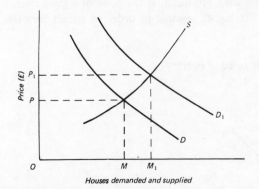

Houses demanded and supplied

(d) Price indicates changes in the conditions upon which goods can be supplied

If the cost of producing a given commodity rises, this should be signalled to consumers, who can then decide to what extent they are prepared to pay these higher costs by going without other goods. Again this is achieved through price. Assume in fig 3.9 that costs have risen·in producing good X because raw materials have risen in price. Where demand is depicted by D, most consumers pay the higher costs (price rises by PP_1) rather than do without the good. Where demand is depicted by D_1, consumers tend to go without the good as its price rises (demand falls by MM_1), substituting other goods for it.

Fig 3.9   *the effect of a change in the conditions of supply on price and quantity traded*

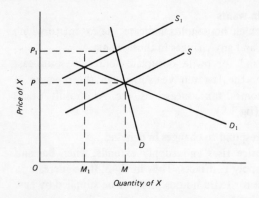

(e) Price rewards the factors of production

Payments for factors of production give their owners spending power. The relative size of this spending power determines the division (usually termed 'distribution') of the cake produced. If the price of a good rises, producers can afford to offer higher rewards in order to·attract factors from other uses.

Fig 3.10   *stabilisation of the price of butter*

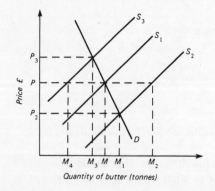

3.6 FURTHER APPLICATIONS

(a) How can the government stabilise commodity prices?
The government can use a stockpile in order to stabilise the price of basic commodities where demand or supply fluctuates.

In fig 3.10, it is assumed that the demand for butter remains constant, but that the conditions of supply change from one period to another. S_1 is the supply curve for period 1, S_2 for period 2 and S_3 for period 3. The government has a stockpile by means of which it stabilises the price of butter at OP a tonne. This it does by adding MM_2 to the stockpile in period 2 and withdrawing M_4M in period 3.

(b) How would an increase in the demand for cars affect the price of tyres?
Cars and tyres are 'jointly demanded'. With such goods prices move in the same direction. This can be seen in fig 3.11. The increased demand for cars leads to an increased demand for tyres, and the prices of both rise.

Fig 3.11 *joint demand*

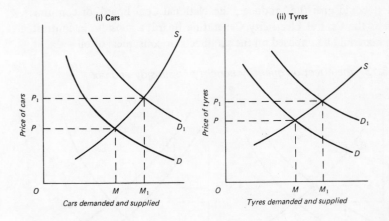

(c) How would an increase in the price of petrol affect the price of paraffin?
Petrol and paraffin are 'jointly supplied': increased production of one automatically increases production of the other. Suppose that demand for petrol increases but that there is no change in the demand for paraffin. The price of petrol rises from OP to OP_1, and supply expands from OM to OM_1 (fig 3.12). But this means that the supply of paraffin increases, although there has been no change in price. Thus the supply curve for paraffin moves from S to S_1, and the price of paraffin falls from OR to OR_1.

Fig 3.12 *joint supply*

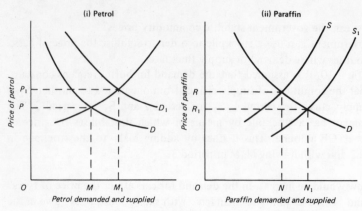

(i) Petrol — Price of petrol, Petrol demanded and supplied

(ii) Paraffin — Price of paraffin, Paraffin demanded and supplied

(d) How could the government secure greater use of coal in order to conserve the stock of North Sea oil?

Here the government must operate to alter the relative prices of coal and oil, reducing the former and increasing the latter. To reduce the price of coal it could give the producer, the National Coal Board, or consumers, such as the Central Electricity Generating Board, a subsidy. In contrast, a high tax could be imposed on the producers or consumers of oil.

Fig 3.13 *the effect on quantity bought of a subsidy and tax*

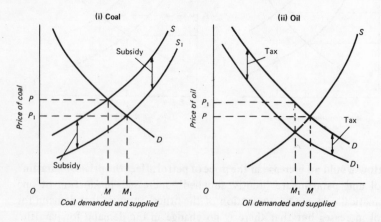

(i) Coal — Price of coal, Coal demanded and supplied

(ii) Oil — Price of oil, Oil demanded and supplied

The effect is shown in fig 3.13. Assume the NCB is given a subsidy. This allows more coal to be supplied at all prices, the supply curve moving to S_1. Price falls to OP_1 and demand expands by MM_1. On the other hand, suppose a tax is levied on consumers of oil. Their demand is reduced to allow for the tax, the curve falling to D_1. Price, including the tax, rises to OP_1, and the amount sold contracts by MM_1.

DEMAND

4.1 THE MARGINAL-UTILITY THEORY

Our assumption in chapter 3 that more of a good will be demanded the lower its price was based solely on our everyday observations. However, by examining a little more closely how the individual consumer 'economises', we can explain why this is normally so. We shall use the marginal-utility theory.

(a) Preliminary assumptions
  (i)   Our consumer is a housewife.
  (ii) She has a limited housekeeping allowance per week.
  (iii) She acts so as to obtain the maximum satisfaction from her limited income.
  (iv) During the period of time under consideration, income, tastes and the other conditions of demand do not change.
  (v)   She knows how much satisfaction each unit of a good will give.
  (vi) She is one of a large number of buyers and her demand does not directly affect the price of the good.

(b) Questions to be answered
Three basic questions have to be answered. First, what conditions will hold when the consumer has obtained the maximum satisfaction from her limited resources? In other words, what are the equilibrium conditions? Second, how does she achieve this equilibrium? Third, what happens when the equilibrium is disturbed by a price change? We deal with each in turn.

(i) The equilibrium condition
Our housewife will be in equilibrium when she would not switch a single penny of her expenditure on one good to another.

We can be more explicit by introducing the term 'utility'. In economics this simply means that a good has the power to satisfy a want, irrespective of whether it is useful. Note, too, that we cannot measure utility; like fear, it is purely subjective to the individual.

However, our housewife knows in her own mind how much satisfaction each good affords her. She is in equilibrium, therefore, when she has obtained the greatest possible utility from her income: that is, she maximises total utility.

She achieves this by careful allocation of her spending – say between cheese and margarine. All the time she is asking: 'If I spend a penny more on cheese, will I obtain more or less utility than if I spent the penny on margarine?' Only when the satisfaction she obtains from the last penny spent on cheese (in the sense of the penny she only just decided to spend) is equal to that from the last penny spent on margarine will she be in equilibrium. That is, her spending adjustments take place at the margin.

Note that we did *not* say that she obtained the same utility from the last pound of cheese as she obtained from the last pound of margarine. If, for instance, a pound of cheese were four times as expensive as a pound of margarine, that would obviously be unreasonable; we would expect four times the amount of utility.

Sometimes, however, we cannot buy goods in 'pennyworths' – the good is 'lumpy' and we have to take a whole 'lump' of it or nothing at all. Can we re-state our equilibrium condition to allow for this? Yes, but first we must define more carefully the concept of the margin and what we mean by 'marginal utility'.

Each small addition to a given supply of a good is called the *marginal increment*, and the utility derived from this increment is known as the *marginal utility*. Our original condition of equilibrium can therefore be stated in general terms:

$$\text{The marginal utility of 1p spent on good } A = \text{The marginal utility of 1p spent on good } B$$

But the marginal utility of 1p spent on good A depends on how much of a unit of good A you get for 1p. Thus:

$$\text{The marginal utility of 1p spent on good } A = \frac{\text{The marginal utility of one unit of good } A}{\text{The number of pence it costs to buy a unit of good } A}$$

Similarly with good B. Thus our original equilibrium condition can be re-written as:

$$\frac{\text{The marginal utility of one unit of good } A}{\text{Price of a unit of } A \text{ in pence}} = \frac{\text{The marginal utility of one unit of good } B}{\text{Price of a unit of } B \text{ in pence}}$$

That is:

$$\frac{\text{Marginal utility of good } A}{\text{Price of } A} = \frac{\text{Marginal utility of good } B}{\text{Price of } B}$$

The argument can be extended to cover more than two goods.

Fig 4.1 *factors affecting the equilibrium of the housewife*

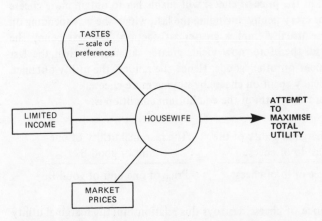

(ii) *How does the consumer achieve this equilibrium?*

The question must now be asked: How can our housewife arrange that the utility of the last penny spent on different goods is the same? The answer is to be found in the so-called *law of diminishing marginal utility*. Although wants vary considerably in their nature, they all possess the underlying characteristic that in a given period they can be satisfied fairly quickly. Thus, if a boy drinks lemonade to quench his thirst, the first glass will yield him a great amount of satisfaction. Indeed, the second glass may be equally satisfying. But it is doubtful whether he will relish the third glass to the same extent, since his thirst has now been partially quenched. If he continues to drink the lemonade, there will come a time when a glass gives him no additional satisfaction whatsoever and, in fact, it might be that he would be better off without it – there is a 'disutility'. We can therefore state a general rule that the utility derived from any given addition to a consumer's stock of a good will eventually decline as the supply increases, provided tastes and the consumption of all other goods remains unchanged.

This means that our housewife can arrange that equal utility is derived from the last penny spent on each good by varying the quantity she buys. If she buys more of a good, the stock of other goods remaining fixed, its marginal utility relative to other goods falls. Similarly, if she reduces the quantity she buys, the marginal utility of the good relative to other goods rises. She goes on making these marginal adjustments until she is in equilibrium.

(iii) *What happens when the equilibrium is disturbed by a price change?*
Suppose the price of cheese falls from 80p to 70p per pound while the prices of other goods remain unchanged. How will this affect her demand for cheese, assuming that she could still do with some more? We can proceed in either of two ways:

(1) The fall in the price of cheese will enable her to obtain more cheese than before for every penny, including the last, which she was spending on it. More cheese usually implies greater satisfaction. The last penny she spent on cheese, therefore, now yields greater satisfaction than the last penny being spent on other goods. Hence she reduces the utility obtained from the last penny spent on cheese by buying more cheese.

(2) The alternative form of the equilibrium condition is:

$$\frac{\text{The marginal utility of the last lb of cheese}}{\text{Price of lb of cheese}} = \frac{\text{The marginal utility of one unit of good B}}{\text{Price of one unit of good B}}$$

A fall in the price of cheese destroys this relationship; the marginal utility of cheese to its price is now higher than with goods B, C, etc. To restore the equilibrium relationship, the marginal utility of cheese must be decreased. Hence our housewife buys more cheese.

The reasons for this expansion in the demand for cheese can be analysed more closely. A reduction in the price of cheese means that our housewife is now able to purchase all the cheese she had before and still have money left over. This is an *income* effect of a price fall – she can now buy more of all goods, not only cheese. But, in addition to this income effect, more cheese will tend to be bought because of a 'substitution effect'. At the margin this means that a penny spent on cheese will now yield more satisfaction than a penny spent on other foods. Thus cheese is substituted for other foods. If cheese is a good substitute, marginal utility will diminish comparatively slowly as the consumption of cheese increases. A given price fall, therefore, will lead to a considerable increase in the quantity of cheese demanded.

4.2 PRICE-ELASTICITY OF DEMAND

(a) Measurement of elasticity of demand

Consider fig 4.2. At price OP, demand for both commodities A and B is OM. But when the price of both falls by PP_1, demand for A expands by only MM_1, whereas that for B expands by MM_2. Responsiveness of demand to a change in price is of obvious importance to a firm which has some

Fig 4.2 *elasticity of demand*

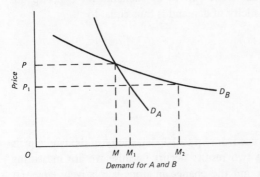

control over the price it charges. In economic terms it is interested in its 'price-elasticity of demand'.

Elasticity of demand always refers to the elasticity at a particular price, and in what follows when we talk about 'elasticity', it will be assumed that there is some price in mind.

Elasticity of demand is defined by comparing the *rate* at which demand expands to the rate at which price falls. If the former is greater than the latter, we say that demand is *elastic*; if it is smaller, we say that demand is *inelastic*. When they are equal, elasticity of demand is said to be equal to *unity*. Using this definition, elasticity of demand can be measured in two ways. One is direct, showing the degree of elasticity; the other is indirect, merely indicating whether the demand for the good is elastic or inelastic.

(i) Elasticity of demand is the proportionate change in the amount demanded in response to a small change in price divided by the proportionate change in price. That is:

$$\text{Elasticity of demand} = \frac{\text{Proportionate change in demand}}{\text{Proportionate change in price}}$$

$$= \frac{\dfrac{\text{Change in quantity demanded}}{\text{Original quantity demanded}}}{\dfrac{\text{Change in price}}{\text{Original price}}}$$

$$= \frac{\dfrac{\text{New quantity} - \text{Old quantity}}{\text{Old quantity}}}{\dfrac{\text{New price} - \text{Old price}}{\text{Old price}}}$$

We can illustrate by an example from the demand schedule, table 3.1 (see p. 51). When price falls from 10p to 8p, demand for eggs expands from 9,000 to 15,000. Elasticity of demand is thus equal to

$$\frac{\dfrac{6,000}{9,000}}{\dfrac{2}{10}} = \frac{\dfrac{2}{3}}{\dfrac{1}{5}} = 3\tfrac{1}{3}$$

Similarly, for a rise in price from 8p to 10p, elasticity of demand equals $1\tfrac{3}{8}$. The difference in the two results occurs because we are measuring from two different points and the change in price is relatively large. (It should also be noted that it is conventional to ignore the minus sign which results from the fact that the typical demand curve has a negative slope.)

(ii) If the proportionate expansion in demand is greater than the proportionate fall in price, the total amount spent on the good will increase. In other words demand is elastic when, in response to a fall in price, total outlay increases; or, in response to a rise in price, total outlay decreases. Similarly demand is inelastic when, in response to a fall in price, total outlay decreases; or, in response to a rise in price, total outlay increases. Elasticity of demand is equal to unity when, as price changes, total outlay remains the same. Thus, using the same demand schedule, we have:

Table 4.1

Price of eggs (pence)	Demand (thousands)	Total outlay (pence)	
10	9	90,000 ⎞	Elastic demand
8	15	120,000 ⎠	
6	20	120,000 ⎞	Inelastic demand
4	25	100,000 ⎠	

Between 8p and 6p, elasticity of demand equals unity.

(b) Factors determining elasticity of demand

(i) *The availability of substitutes at the ruling market price*
As a good falls in price, it becomes cheaper relative to other goods. People are induced to buy more of it to replace goods which are now relatively dearer. How far they can carry out this replacement will depend upon the extent to which the good in question is, in their own minds, a substitute for the other goods. Goods within a particular class are easily substituted for one another. Beef is a substitute for mutton. Thus, if the price of beef falls, people will buy more beef and less mutton. Between one class and another, however, substitution is more difficult. If the price of meat in general falls, there will be a slight tendency to buy more meat and less fish, but this tendency will be very limited because meat is not nearly so perfect a substitute for fish as beef is for mutton.

The success of supermarkets has been based on the high elasticity of demand for their products; people switch to them when prices of processed goods are reduced, for they can recognise the packages and tins as being almost perfect substitutes for those being sold for higher prices in other shops.

(ii) *The proportion of income spent on a good*
When only a very small proportion of a person's income is spent on a good, as for example with pepper, salt, shoe-polish, newspapers and toothpaste, no great effort is made to look for substitutes when its price rises. Demand for such goods, therefore, is relatively inelastic.

On the other hand, when the expenditure on a good is fairly large – as, for example, with meat – a rise in price would provide considerable incentive to find substitutes.

(iii) *The period of time*
Since it takes time to find substitutes or to change spending habits, elasticity may be greater the longer the period of time under review. In practice many firms try to overcome the ignorance or conservatism of consumers by advertising, giving free samples or making special offers.

(iv) *The possibility of new purchasers*
In discussing the possibility of substitution above, we have looked at elasticity of demand solely from the point of view of the individual consumer. But when we are considering market demand we must allow for the fact that, as price falls, new consumers will be induced to buy the good. In fact, with goods such as cars, TV sets, washing-machines, etc., of which most people require only one, it is the fall in price bringing the good with-

in reach of new consumers which leads to the increase in demand. Hence a fall in price which induces people in a numerous income group to buy will produce a big elasticity of demand, whereas a fall in price which affects only the higher and less-numerous income group will not produce many new customers; and hence the market demand schedule here tends to be inelastic.

(c) Uses of the concept of elasticity of demand
The concept of the elasticity of demand figures prominently in the economist's analysis and in the practical decisions of the businessman and government.

Thus a trade union will find it more difficult to obtain a wage increase for its members without creating unemployment where the elasticity of demand for the product made is high (see p. 155).

British Rail, too, have to consider elasticity of demand when fixing fares. Should they, for example, raise fares in order to reduce losses? If, at existing fares, the demand is relatively elastic, then a fare increase would mean that total revenue would fall. Losses would only be reduced if operating costs (through carrying fewer passengers) fell more than revenue. Indeed, consideration could be given to reducing fares, since the extra revenue might cover any additional cost of running more trains.

Finally, the Chancellor of the Exchequer must take account of elasticity of demand when imposing a selective tax on a particular good. The demand may be so elastic that the increase in price might cause such a falling-off in sales that the total tax received is less than it originally was.

4.3 INCOME ELASTICITY OF DEMAND

An increase in real income usually increases the demand for goods, but to a varying degree. Thus it is possible to speak of *income-elasticity of demand* – the proportionate change in demand divided by the proportionate change in real income which has brought it about. If demand increases 20%, for instance, as a result of a 10% increase in real income, income-elasticity of demand equals 2. Which goods have a high income-elasticity of demand depends upon current living-standards. In Western Europe today it is demand for such goods as cars, dishwashers, central-heating appliances and personal services which expands most as income increases. In contrast, necessities, such as salt and soap, have a low income-elasticity of demand.

SUPPLY: (i)

THE STRUCTURE

OF INDUSTRY

5.1 THE ROLE OF THE FIRM

(a) The meaning of 'production'

Early economists considered that only work in the extractive industries
(agriculture, mining and fishing) was productive. In his *Wealth of Nations*
in 1776 Adam Smith added manufacturing, but he was specific in excluding workers who merely rendered services.

This was illogical. People work, and production takes place, in order to
satisfy wants. Consequently people who render services must be regarded
as being productive. The soldier, actor and footballer are all satisfying
wants. Similarly, in a factory, the clerk who calculates the wages is just as
productive as the man who makes the nuts and bolts. All are helping to
produce the final product, a good satisfying wants.

Wants can take different forms. Most people like a newspaper to read
at the breakfast-table; thus the boy who takes it from the shop to the
customer's letterbox is productive. Most people, too, prefer to buy their
potatoes weekly; thus the farmer or merchant who stores them through
the winter is satisfying the wants of consumers, and is similarly productive.
Utility is created by changing not only the *form* of our scarce resources,
but also their *place* and *time*.

For certain purposes it may still be useful to classify industries broadly.
Primary industries cover the first steps in the productive process – agriculture, fishing, mining and oil-prospecting. *Secondary industries* use the raw
materials of the extractive industries to manufacture their own products –
flour, clothing, tinned salmon, steel girders, petrol and so on. *Tertiary
industries* are concerned with the provision of services – transport, communications, distribution, commerce, government, and professional and
other services.

(b) The legal form of the firm

In the private sector a firm can trade as a sole proprietor, partnership,
private company, public company or co-operative society. For a new firm

the choice is really between the first three, the actual decision largely resting on whether freedom from control by the Registrar of Companies compensates for unlimited liability. The legal form hardly affects its ability to raise capital for, unless it is an offshoot of a large parent company, it has to be fairly successful before outsiders can be induced to subscribe capital for large-scale development.

(i) *The sole proprietor*

The sole-proprietor or 'one-man' firm is the oldest form of business organisation. Even today, from the point of view of numbers, small firms predominate, but in their total productive capacity they are far less important than companies (see table 5.1). Such one-man firms range from the window-cleaner working on his own account to the farmer, shopkeeper and builder who employ other workers and may even own many separate units. Nevertheless these businesses all share the characteristic of being owned and controlled by a single person. This person decides the policy of the firm, and it is he alone who takes the profits or bears losses. This makes for energy, efficiency and careful attention to detail. In addition, the only accounts he has to submit are to the Board of Inland Revenue for income-tax assessment and to the Customs and Excise Department if he is registered for VAT. He does not have to pay corporation tax.

As a form of business organisation, however, the sole proprietor suffers from five main disadvantages. First, such a firm can only develop slowly, because sources of capital are limited. The success of the venture, especially in its early stages, depends mainly on the person in charge, and nobody is likely to provide capital unless he has that confidence in the proprietor which comes from personal contact. Hence the main source of capital is the owner's savings, plus any money he can borrow from relatives or close friends. In time, development may be financed by ploughing back profits, but this will probably be a slow process and sole traders generally remain comparatively small.

Second, in the event of failure, not only the assets of the business, but also the private assets and property of the proprietor can be claimed by creditors. In short, there is no limited liability.

Third, where profits are high, income tax paid on annual profits may be larger than a company's corporation tax. This is because income may be taxed at a high marginal rate of tax, whereas corporation tax is only 42% if a company's profits are less than £70,000 (with marginal relief up to £130,000, when tax is 40%). Less tax leaves more funds for investing in the business.

Fourth, it is more difficult to transfer part of a business than to transfer shares in a company.

Fifth, there is a lack of continuity; on the retirement or death of the owner, a one-man firm may cease to function.

Because of these disadvantages, sole proprietors are mainly confined either to businesses which are just setting up and to certain industries, such as agriculture and retailing, where requirements of management make the small technical unit desirable.

(ii) *The partnership*

More capital is available when persons join together in a 'partnership', though not more than twenty (except in certain professions, such as those of solicitor and accountant) may do so. Each partner provides a part of the capital and shares the profits on an agreed basis. Yet the amount of capital which can be raised in this way is still inadequate for modern large-scale business. Thus partnerships remain relatively small, predominating in retailing, insurance broking and underwriting, and among professional people (doctors, surveyors, consulting engineers and lawyers), where the capital provided is not so much in the form of money as in experience and skill, each partner often specialising in a particular branch.

Nor is the partnership without its snags. The risk inherent in unlimited liability is increased because all partners are liable for the firm's debts, irrespective of the amount of capital which each has individually invested. Only if a partner takes no share in the management of the firm, and there is at least one ordinary partner, can he enjoy limited liability. Second, since any action taken by one partner is legally binding on the others, not only must each partner have complete confidence in his fellows, but the risk inherent in unlimited liability increases with the number of partners. Finally, at any time one partner may give notice to end the partnership, and it is automatically dissolved upon the death or bankruptcy of a partner. To preserve the business, surviving partners may be put to great expense and trouble in buying the partner's share or finding a purchaser acceptable to everyone.

(iii) *The joint-stock company*

The joint-stock company dates from Tudor times, when England's foreign trade began to expand. Instead of a trading ship's being owned by one person, it was financed by a number of people who bought 'shares' in a company formed for the purpose. However, since they enjoyed no limited liability, people were reluctant to join such companies: by purchasing only one share a person risked not only the money he had invested, but all his private assets, should the company be forced into liquidation. Moreover, this made it impossible to adopt the technique of spreading risks by investing in a number of companies.

The industrial revolution, with the introduction of machines and factory organisation, made it essential that more capital should be available to industry. So, in order to induce small savers to invest, parliament granted limited liability in 1855.

Today the joint-stock company is the most important form of business organisation. The advantages it enjoys over the partnership are limited liability, continuity, the availability of capital (since investors can spread their risks and sell their shares easily) and, should the need arise, ease of expansion. Indeed, some kinds of businesses, e.g. computer production, could not be operated on a small scale. Here firms have to start as joint-stock companies, being either sponsored by important interests or developed as subsidiaries of existing large firms.

Against these advantages, however, the small joint-stock company in particular has to consider certain snags. Additional cost is incurred in submitting the annual accounts, etc., to the Registrar of Companies, while the company's corporation tax could exceed the income tax which would have been paid had the business been carried on as a sole trader or partnership. Furthermore, any assets of the company which have been built up over the years will increase the value of the original shares (usually owned by a family), so that when the time comes to wind up the company, e.g. because of retirement, this increase will be subject to capital gains tax. Finally, if the company is expanded by the issue of more shares, the original owners may lose control or even be subject to a takeover bid.

Joint-stock companies are of two main kinds, private and public.

(1) THE PRIVATE COMPANY

A private company, while conferring the advantage of limited liability, allows a business to be privately owned and managed. The formalities involved in its formation are few, but the Companies Act 1948 imposes conditions restricting its size and the sale of shares to the public.

Thus the private company is particularly suitable for either a medium-sized commercial or industrial organisation not requiring finance from the public, or for a speculative venture where a small group of people wish to try out an idea and are prepared to back it financially to a definite limit before floating a public company. While private companies are considerably more numerous than public companies, their average capital is much smaller.

(2) THE PUBLIC COMPANY

To obtain a large amount of capital it is necessary to form a public company (having a minimum of seven shareholders) and then apply for a stock-exchange quotation. The affairs of the company have to be advertised in at least two leading London newspapers while, if no new issue is being made, a supply of shares has to be made available sufficient to make dealing, and the price fixed, realistic.

Once the introduction has been completed, the capital can be raised by offer to the public, as described later.

It should be noted that a new Companies Bill is currently proceeding through parliament to implement the EEC's second directive on company law. It covers a new definition of a public company, the share capital of companies and the distribution of profits to shareholders.

(iv) *Co-operative societies*

Although there were many co-operative societies in operation before the Rochdale Pioneers of 1844, it was these twenty-eight workers who started the modern co-operative movement. By subscribing a few pence per week they accumulated an initial capital of £28, with which they rented a store and started trading with small stocks of flour, oatmeal, sugar, butter and candles. Profits were distributed to members in proportion to their purchases. Today there are over 200 retail co-operative societies in the UK, and their trade accounts for 7% of Britain's retail trade. In addition, these retail societies largely provide the capital and control the operations of the Co-operative Wholesale Society.

The minimum shareholding in a retail co-operative society is usually £1. Only if a full share is held does a member enjoy voting rights, but each member has only one vote irrespective of the number of shares held. Until fairly recently, societies distributed profits as a dividend in proportion to the value of the member's purchases. Today, however, most societies make use of the National Dividend Stamp scheme run by the Co-operative Wholesale Society. Stamps are given to customers in proportion to their purchases, and a book of stamps can be redeemed for 40p in cash, 50p in goods or a 50p deposit in a share account. Not only has this system allowed co-operative shops to compete in price with the supermarkets, but it is much cheaper to operate than the old 'divi' method. Nor does the member have to wait at least six months before receiving the dividend; and the national stamp can be given by other traders, e.g. petrol stations.

The co-operative societies described above are organised directly by consumers and are therefore called 'consumer co-operative societies'. Producers have also formed 'producer co-operative societies' to market their members' produce. They are chiefly important in agriculture, particularly where production is carried on by small farmers, as in Denmark, New Zealand and Spain. Nevertheless they have been slow to develop in the UK. Instead, marketing difficulties have been dealt with by the government's setting up marketing boards.

Co-operatives have also been established in manufacturing, e.g. the Meriden motorcycle workers' co-operative, which was established with government aid when its firm was threatened with closure. A highly successful retail co-operative is the John Lewis Partnership; and building societies can be regarded as 'co-operative' ventures.

(c) The objectives of the firm

In a market economy a firm has to cover its costs if it is to stay in business. Thus regard must be paid to 'profitability'.

But in practice are firms always single-minded in seeking to *maximise money* profits? The answer is no; there is a range of possible objectives.

Personal motives may be important, especially where the manager is also the owner of the firm. Thus emphasis may be placed on good labour relations, the welfare of the workers, the desire for power, political influence, public esteem or simply 'a quiet life'. To cover such objectives profit would have to be interpreted in a wider sense than 'money profit'.

With major companies there is in practice a gap between the ownership and its administration. The business is run by professional managers, and is too complex for shareholders to be able to exert effective control. This applies even to the institutional shareholders, who avoid being directly involved in the running of the business. Thus the motives of the full-time executive managers tend to override the shareholders' desire for maximum return on capital invested. Managers may be anxious for the security of their own jobs and, instead of taking the calculated risks necessary to earn maximum profits, tend to play for safety. More likely, they will be motivated by personal desires for status. Provided they achieve a level of profit which is satisfactory in the sense that it keeps shareholders content, their positions and salaries can be enhanced by expanding the firm to where it *maximises sales* rather than profits.

Even when there is an emphasis on money profit, a firm may stress its long-term position rather than immediate maximum profit. Security of future profits may be the dominating motive for mergers and takeovers as an alternative to developing new products and techniques. Moreover, where there is an element of monopoly, a firm can follow its own pricing policy rather than have it determined by competitive market conditions (see chapter 6). In such circumstances it may not adjust prices to short-term changes in demand and supply conditions. For one thing, there are the administrative costs of printing and distributing new price lists. For another, frequent changes in price tend to offend retailers and customers.

Again, a firm enjoying a degree of monopoly has always to assess what effect the pursuit of maximum profit may have on its overall position in the long term. Will a high price attract new entrants or encourage the development of a rival product? Will it lead to adverse publicity and eventually to government intervention, by a reference to the Office of Fair Trading or possibly by nationalisation?

Finally, a firm has often to modify its objectives in deference to government policy. Thus it may be expected to follow government guidelines regarding wage increases, to have regard to the environment in the disposal of its waste products and even to retain surplus workers for a time rather than add to an already high level of unemployment.

Yet, while we must take account of these other objectives, our analysis cannot proceed far if any are seen as the main motive force of the firm. In any case they merely supplement the profit objective, for profits have to be made if the firm is to survive. Thus it is useful to start with the broad assumption that firms seek to maximise profits. We can then establish principles concerning how resources should be combined and what output should be produced.

(d) The decisions of the firm

The firm has to decide on policies to secure its profit objective. In broad terms, these cover assessing the demand of potential customers and organising production accordingly. If it is seeking to maximise its profits, a firm will have to produce that output which secures the largest possible difference between total receipts and total costs. It will therefore always have an incentive to keep the cost of producing a given output to a minimum. This means that it must answer the following questions:

(i) What shall it produce?
(ii) How shall it raise the necessary capital?
(iii) What techniques shall be adopted, and what shall be the scale of operations?
(iv) Where shall production be located?
(v) How shall goods be distributed to the consumer?
(vi) How shall resources be combined?
(vii) What shall be the size of output?
(viii) How shall it deal with its employees?

We consider the first five problems in the remainder of this chapter; the rest are examined in chapters 6 and 8.

5.2 WHAT TO PRODUCE

(a) The first approach

Other things being equal, a firm will produce those goods which enable it to make the greatest return on capital. However, in practice, this usually means that it has to choose a line of production within the limited range of its specialist knowledge. Let us assume that the firm is manufacturing light farm machines and that it is contemplating producing lawnmowers.

Since it is likely that some firms are already producing lawnmowers, the market economy throws up two guidelines. First, there is the current price of mowers. The firm would have to estimate its own costs for producing similar mowers, the number it could expect to sell at this price, and its likely profits, and thus calculate the return on capital employed. Second, the accounts of companies have to be filed with the Registrar of Companies, and the profit earned by public companies is publicised in the financial pages of leading newspapers and specialist journals. If existing producers of lawnmowers were shown to be earning a high rate of profit, the prospects for a new competitor would look favourable.

(b) Market research

Where the proposed market is new or different from that for existing products, the above indicators are not so useful. Here the firm must fall back on some form of market research.

Initially, it may be producing similar goods, e.g. light agricultural machinery, and some indications of potential demand may come from wholesalers, retailers or even customers in conversation with the firm's representatives. Such suggestions can be cross-checked with those of other distributors (see p. 99).

Where the reaction is generally favourable, more thorough market research can be carried out, probably through a specialist market-research organisation. Market research can cover desk research, field studies and test marketing.

Desk research examines the broad determinants of the potential demand by using (i) published material, e.g. government statistics, and (ii) the firm's own sales records. As we saw in chapter 3, these determinants are price and the various conditions of demand. More specialist facts could be obtained from relevant periodicals and trade journals, e.g. *Gardeners' World* (where circulation figures indicate the number of keen gardeners). Membership figures for the Royal Horticultural Society could also be used.

More precise information on potential sales necessitates a planned, consumer-orientated *market-research programme* in potential markets. This would cover many aspects of market behaviour, particularly consumer reaction to the product – especially with regard to its quality, packaging, delivery dates and after-sales service, and to price cuts.

Before a national or major sales campaign is undertaken, some form of *test marketing* would probably be carried out so that modifications could be made to correct any deficiencies. For instance, such a test might reveal that certain features of the product were unnecessary, thus permitting greater standardisation. Moreover, not all potential customers have identical preferences. The firm would therefore consider (i) a 'marketing mix' – producing different models at different prices – and (ii) varying sales methods and channels of distribution (see below).

5.3 **RAISING THE NECESSARY CAPITAL**

(a) The need for liquid capital
In order to employ factors of production, a firm has to have finance. This is usually divided into (i) working capital and (ii) fixed capital.

(i) *Working capital* is for purchasing 'single-use' factors – labour, raw materials, petrol, stationery, fertilisers, etc. – more or less the factors we refer to in chapter 6 as 'variable factors'. Finance for working capital can be obtained from a variety of sources: banks, trade credit, finance companies, factor houses, tax reserves, inter-company finance, and advance deposits from customers.

(ii) *Fixed capital* covers factors which are used many times – factories, machines, land, lorries, etc. Some finance for fixed capital is therefore required initially for advance payments on factory buildings, machinery and so on before the firm is earning revenue, though it may be possible to convert fixed capital into working capital by renting buildings, hiring plant and vehicles or buying on deferred payments through a finance company. Normally, however, fixed-capital requirements are larger than those for working capital. Moreover, lenders recognise that they part with their money for a longer period and accept a greater risk. Thus finance for fixed capital tends to be more difficult to raise than for working capital.

(b) The long-term capital of a company
Sources of finance for the sole trader and partnership were reviewed earlier. Here we consider how a new company raises long term capital by: (i) selling shares and (ii) borrowing.

(i) *Shares*
A 'share' is exactly what the name implies – a participation in the provision of the capital. Shares may be issued in various units, usually from 5p upwards, purchasers deciding how many they want. Such an investment, however, involves two main risks. First, profits may be disappointing, and the price of the share may fall. Second, share prices in general may be falling just when the owner wishes to sell. To minimise these risks, investors usually buy shares in different companies, together with debentures and government bonds having a fixed rate of interest.

(1) ORDINARY SHARES
The dividend paid to the ordinary shareholder depends mainly upon the profitability of the company. However, the ordinary shareholder's dividend ranks last in order of priority, and if the company should be forced into liquidation the ordinary shareholder is repaid only after other creditors

have been paid in full. Thus the ordinary share is termed 'risk capital'. In return each ordinary shareholder has a say in the running of the company, voting according to the number of shares held. At a general meeting directors can be appointed or removed, changes made in the company's methods of raising capital and conducting business, and auditors appointed. Thus, because they take the major risks and decisions regarding the policy of the company, the ordinary shareholders are the real 'entrepreneurs'. In practice, however, their rights are rarely exercised. Usually few shareholders take the trouble to attend meetings, while unless the company is large the directors may control a high proportion of the shares and so be in a strong position. Indeed this may be achieved by making all new shares 'non-voting "A" shares'. Thus directors tend to be self-perpetuating.

(2) PREFERENCE SHARES

If the investor prefers a slightly reduced risk, he can buy a preference share entitling him to a dividend payment (but fixed at a given percentage) before the ordinary shareholder. Should the company be forced into liquidation, the preference shareholder usually ranks above the ordinary shareholder when it comes to the redemption of capital. Preference shares may be 'cumulative': if the company cannot pay a dividend one year, arrears may be made up in succeeding years before ordinary shareholders receive any dividend.

Since 1965 preference shares have lost popularity because of their unfavourable tax treatment (see below).

(ii) *Borrowing*

The long-term loans of a company are usually obtained by issuing 'debentures', redeemable after a specified period. These bear a fixed rate of interest (about 14%), which, being a first charge on the company's profit, means a lower risk to the investor of there being no return. Moreover, should the company fail, debenture-holders are paid first. In fact 'mortgage debentures' are secured on a definite asset of the company. Where the company is unable to meet its interest charges or to redeem the loan when due, the debenture-holders can force it into liquidation.

Thus the purchaser of a debenture takes less risk should the company fail. But because he is merely lending money he enjoys no ownership rights of voting on management and policy. On the other hand, a company whose profits are subject to frequent and violent fluctuations is not well-placed to raise capital through debentures. The method is best suited to a company making a stable profit (adequate to cover the interest payments) and possessing assets, such as land and buildings, which would show little depreciation were the company to go into liquidation.

A company having a large proportion of fixed-interest loans to ordinary shares is said to be 'highly geared'. Such a company will be able to pay high dividends when profits are good, but unable to make a distribution when profits are low. Where profits are expected to rise in the future, therefore, a company may prefer to raise capital for expansion by issuing debentures if the cost of doing so is not too high.

But it is the present-day corporation tax which provides the main impulse in this direction. Debenture interest (but not preference-share interest) is an accepted cost for the purpose of calculating tax. Thus it reduces taxable profits. On the other hand, if finance is raised by shares, there is no prior interest charge, and profits (which are subject to tax) are higher by that amount. This tax advantage has, since the introduction of corporation tax in 1965, led companies to finance capital expansion as far as possible by fixed-interest loans rather than by the sale of shares. Preference shares are now rarely issued.

(c) Financing the expansion of a company

One reason why small firms predominate is the difficulty of financing expansion. If a firm cannot retain sufficient profits or raise finance by mortgaging buildings, the only alternative is to seek additional investors. This usually means converting to a public company. The public can then be asked to subscribe for additional shares or debentures.

But the high costs of a public issue make it uneconomic to raise less than £150,000. This means that the difficult stage in the expansion of a firm occurs when its capital is in the region of £50,000, for it is still too small to contemplate a public issue. The gap may be bridged in three main ways. First, a stockbroker may be able to arrange for a life-insurance company or an investment trust to purchase shares or debentures, since such institutions are less concerned with the illiquidity of such stock. Second, in the new-issue market both issuing houses and merchant bankers arrange or provide medium-term capital to bridge the gap prior to making a public issue. Third, capital may be available through certain specialised finance corporations. For agriculture there is the Agricultural Mortgage Corporation (which lends on the security of land and buildings) and for film-making the National Film Finance Corporation. For small firms Charterhouse Development Ltd and Credit for Industry Ltd are among those who will help with long-term finance. More important is the Industrial and Commercial Finance Corporation, a body financed by the joint-stock banks, which provides capital for businesses – not necessarily companies – too small to make a public issue. But in order to obtain a loan the firm has to pass a searching investigation regarding its present financial position and business prospects. Larger loans are provided by the Finance Corporation for Industry. Finally, the National Enterprise Board may finance development of approved projects and provide technical advice.

Where a large amount of capital is required, say above £150,000 it is usual to obtain a stock-exchange quotation. This is only given by the Stock Exchange Council to a public company which has been subjected to a thorough examination. Once the introduction has been completed, the capital required can be raised by a stock-exchange 'placing', an 'offer for sale', or a 'public issue by prospectus'.

The first is the usual method when only about £150,000 is required, for the costs of underwriting and administration are less. An issuing house, stockbroker or investment company agrees to sell blocks of the shares privately to customers known to be interested in such issues.

For larger amounts up to £300,000, an offer for sale is a likely method. The shares are sold *en bloc* to an issuing house, which then offers them for sale to the public by advertisement. Although the issuing house makes a modest profit, underwriting costs are avoided.

When more than £300,000 is required, a public issue by prospectus is usual. Here the company's object is to obtain from the public in a single day the additional capital required. Hence it must advertise well and price its shares a little on the cheap side. The advertisement is in the form of a prospectus which sets out the business, history and prospects of the company together with its financial standing and the security offered.

The sale is usually conducted through an issuing house, which advises the company on the terms of the issue. Occasionally the public is invited to tender for the shares. Usually, however, a price is stated, in which case the issuing house will arrange for the issue to be underwritten by institutions such as merchant banks, who in return for a small commission will take any of the issue left unsold. Nevertheless such underwriters do not have to rely entirely on permanent investors, for speculators known as 'stags' are usually operating, who buy the shares in the hope of re-selling them quickly at a small profit.

In recent years there has been an increasing tendency to give existing shareholders the first option on new shares through a 'rights issue'. These are offered in proportion to the shares already held, usually at a favourable price.

5.4 THE DIVISION OF LABOUR

(a) Advantages of specialisation

In organising its factors of production, the firm will have to consider the advantages of specialisation, the fundamental principle of modern production. Here we examine it with particular reference to labour – although, as we shall see, it is equally applicable to machines, the distribution of goods to the consumer, localities and even countries.

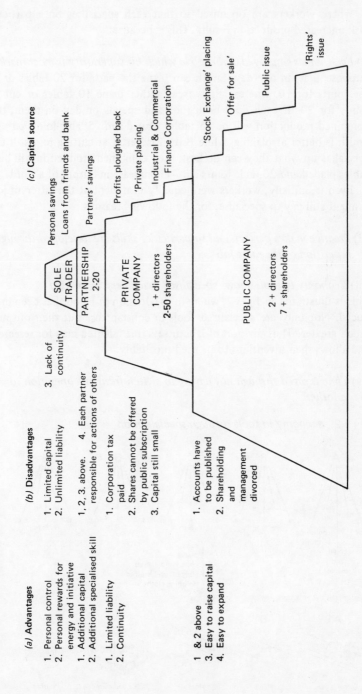

Fig 5.1 *private-sector firms*

(a) Advantages

1. Personal control
2. Personal rewards for energy and initiative

1. Additional capital
2. Additional specialised skill

1. Limited liability
2. Continuity

1 & 2 above
3. Easy to raise capital
4. Easy to expand

(b) Disadvantages

1. Limited capital
2. Unlimited liability

1, 2, 3. above.   4. Each partner responsible for actions of others

3. Lack of continuity

1. Corporation tax paid
2. Shares cannot be offered by public subscription
3. Capital still small

1. Accounts have to be published
2. Shareholding and management divorced

(c) Capital source

Personal savings
Loans from friends and bank

Partners' savings

Profits ploughed back

'Private placing'
Industrial & Commercial Finance Corporation

'Stock Exchange' placing

'Offer for sale'

Public issue

'Rights' issue

SOLE TRADER

PARTNERSHIP 2-20

PRIVATE COMPANY

1 + directors
2-50 shareholders

PUBLIC COMPANY

2 + directors
7 + shareholders

85

Where workers are organised so that each specialises on a particular task, increased production results. This is because:

(i) *Each man is employed in the job in which his superiority is most marked*
Suppose that, in one day, Smith can plane the parts for 20 tables *or* cut the joints for 10, whereas Brown can either plane 10 tables *or* cut the joints for 20. If each does both jobs and spends on day on them, their combined production will be 15 tables planed *and* 15 table-joints cut. But Smith is better at planing, while Brown is better at cutting joints. If they specialise on what they can do best, their combined production will be 20 tables planed *and* 20 table joints cut – an increase in output of a third.

Even if, initially, workers were equally proficient at the different jobs, it might still pay to specialise, for the following reasons.

(ii) *Practice makes perfect, and so particular skills are developed through repetition of the same job*

(iii) *Economy in tools allows specialised machinery to be used*
This is illustrated in fig 5.2, where in (b) division of labour has been introduced. Not only are specialised tools in constant use but their output is much greater. Thus division of labour sets free talented men for research – and allows their inventions to be used profitably.

(iv) *Time is saved through not having to switch from one operation to another*

Fig 5.2   *economy in tools through specialisation*

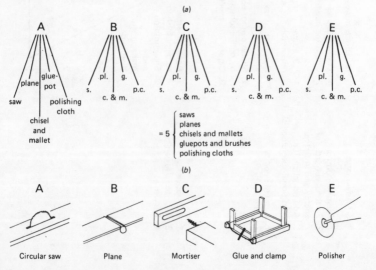

(v) *Less time is taken in learning a particular job*

(vi) *The employer can estimate his costs of production and output more accurately*

(b) Disadvantages of the division of labour

While the division of labour leads to lower costs of production, it may have disadvantages both for the worker and for society. The worker may find his job monotonous, and with some occupations such as paint-spraying there is a risk of occupational disease. Moreover, the skilled specialist may face redundancy if demand falls, while a strike by a few key workers can lead to widespread unemployment. Finally, standardised products tend to replace individual craft work.

(c) Limitations on the division of labour

Naturally the scope for the division of labour varies from one industry to another. Countries like Switzerland which have too few workers to permit much specialisation concentrate on manufacturing a narrow range of products. Again, in industries such as agriculture and building where the same operations are not taking place each day, many 'Jacks of all trades' are required. Moreover, an exchange system is essential: we must first unite in exchange before we can divide in production. Finally, the division of labour has to be related to current demand for the product. It is no use specialising in making something which nobody wants; conversely, minute division of labour is only possible when there is a large demand. The complex organisation of car production, for instance, rests on a mass demand for a standardised product made up from a multitude of small parts.

5.5 THE ADVANTAGES OF LARGE-SCALE PRODUCTION

As a firm's output increases, costs per unit may fall as a result of the advantages of large-scale production. These are often referred to as 'internal economies' to distinguish them from 'external economies', which arise indirectly from the growth of the industry (see p. 89).

(a) Internal economies
Internal economies are of five main kinds:

(i) *Technical economies*
In making a good, as distinct from distributing it, increased output permits more division of labour, greater specialisation of machines, the economy of large machines (e.g. a double-decker bus can carry twice as many passengers as a single-decker, though neither the initial cost nor running

costs are doubled) and the linking of processes (e.g. in steel-making, where re-heating is avoided).

Generally technical economies fix the size of the unit actually producing, e.g. a supermarket, rather than the size of the firm, which may consist of many units, e.g. Tesco. Where technical economies are great, the size of the typical unit will tend to be large – as, for example, in the production of cars, sheet steel, gas and electricity. Where, however, increased output merely means duplicating and re-duplicating machines, the tendency will be for the unit to remain small. For instance, in farming at least one combine harvester is necessary for about 500 acres. Thus farms tend to remain small, for as yet there are no great technical economies to be derived from large machines. Where few technical economies can be gained and yet the firm is large, consisting – as with chain stores – of many operating units, it is usually because other types of economy are possible, as follows.

(ii) *Managerial economies*

When output increases, division of labour can be applied to management. For example, in a shop owned and run by one man, the owner, although having the ability to order supplies, keep accounts and sell the goods, has yet to do such trivial jobs as sweeping the floor, weighing articles and packing parcels – tasks within the capability of a boy who has just left school. His sales, however, may not warrant employing a boy. The large business overcomes this difficulty: a brilliant organiser can devote all his time to organising, the routine jobs being left to lower-paid workers.

The function of management can itself be divided, e.g. into production, sales, transport and personnel. These departments may be further sub-divided – sales, for instance, being split into sections for advertising, exports and customers' welfare.

(iii) *Commercial economies*

If a bulk order can be placed for materials and components, the supplier will usually quote a lower price per unit, since this enables him also to gain the advantages of large-scale production.

Economies can also be achieved in selling the product. If the sales staff are not being worked to capacity, the additional output can be sold at little extra cost. Moreover, the large firm often manufactures many prodducts, so that one acts as an advertisement for the others. Thus Hoover vacuum-cleaners advertise their washing-machines, dishwashers and steam-irons. In addition a large firm may be able to sell its by-products, something which might be unprofitable for a small firm.

Finally, when the business is sufficiently large, the division of labour can be introduced on the commercial side, with expert buyers and sellers being employed.

Such commercial economies represent real gains to the community, reducing prices through better use of resources. On the other hand, where a large firm uses its muscle to *force* suppliers into granting it favourable prices, it will simply result in higher prices to other buyers.

(iv) *Financial economies*
In raising finance for expansion the large firm is in a favourable position. It can, for instance, offer better security to bankers – and, because it is well-known, raise money at lower cost, since investors have confidence in and prefer shares which can be readily sold on the stock exchange.

(v) *Risk-bearing economies*
Here we can distinguish three sorts of risk. First, there are risks which can be insured against, enabling large and small firms alike to spread risks.

Second, certain businesses usually bear some risk themselves, saving some of the profits made by the insurance company. Here the large firm has a definite advantage. London Transport, for instance, can cover its own risks, while a large bank can call in funds from other branches when there is a run on the reserves in a particular locality.

The third kind of risk is one that cannot be reduced to a mathematical probability and thus cannot be insured against – risk arising from changes in demand for the product or in the supply of raw materials; this is usually referred to as risk arising from 'uncertainty'. To meet fluctuations in demand the large firm can diversify output (like the Imperial Tobacco Company) or develop export markets. On the supply side, materials may be obtained from different sources to guard against crop failures, strikes, etc.

(b) External economies
While the firm can plan its internal economies, it can only *hope* to benefit from external economies which arise as the *industry* grows.

First, the concentration of similar firms in an area may produce mutual benefits: a skilled labour force; common services, such as marketing organisations; better roads and social amenities; technical schools catering for the local industry; product reputation; ancillary firms supplying specialised machinery, collecting by-products, etc. The firm must take into account such economies when deciding where production shall take place, for the lower costs may outweigh any diseconomies which arise through traffic congestion, smoke, etc. (see pp. 94–5).

Second, external economies can take the form of common information services provided either by associations of firms or even by the government.

Finally, as an industry grows in size, specialist firms may be established to provide components for all producers. Since such firms can work on a large scale, these components are supplied more cheaply than if the original producer had to manufacture his own.

5.6 THE SIZE OF FIRMS

(a) Horizontal, vertical and lateral combination

The advantages of large-scale production provide firms with a strong impetus to combine.

Horizontal integration occurs where firms producing the same type of product combine. Thus British Motor Holdings merged with Leyland Motors to form British Leyland.

Vertical integration is the amalgamation of firms engaged in the different stages of production of a good. Thus British Motor Holdings took over Fisher & Ludlow, a producer of car bodies. Vertical integration may be 'backward' towards the raw material, or 'forward' towards the finished product.

Fig 5.3 *horizontal and vertical integration*

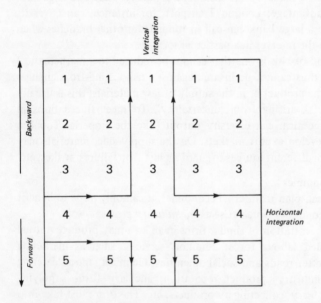

Both the above can lead to lower costs per unit, and therefore to increased profits. Thus horizontal integration can allow greater specialisation, commercial economies and a saving on administrative overheads. Vertical integration facilitates linked processes and reduces risk by increasing direct control over the supply and quality of raw materials and components. Moreover, all parts can be manufactured to an integrated design, and there is direct control over the distribution of the final product (see below).

Lateral integration occurs where a firm increases the range of its products. Concentration on one product may make a firm vulnerable to a change in fashion, a switch in government policy or a recession. Thus the firm diversifies, often by taking over other firms producing completely different products. Imperial Tobacco, for instance, includes among its interests Golden Wonder Crisps, while P & O is engaged in road transport and construction through its subsidiary companies.

Apart from increasing profits through economies of scale, integration can achieve other objectives, such as prestige and security of profits. One other aim, however, must not be overlooked – monopoly power. This is discussed in chapter 6.

Integration may result from internal development or combination with existing firms. Combination may be secured by a complete takeover, when a company buys all the shares of a smaller firm and absorbs it completely, or by the formation of a holding company in which the parent company owns enough shares of a subsidiary company to give it effective control, though the smaller company preserves its identity and enjoys considerable independence of action. Many large companies, e.g. Unilever, GEC and Great Universal Stores, hold such controlling interests in subsidiary companies.

(b) The predominance of the small firm

In spite of the advantages enjoyed by the large firm, we must not conclude that every firm has to be large to be competitive. Indeed the small firm still predominates in all forms of production. In agriculture two-thirds of all holdings are less than fifty acres in size, while in retailing nearly three-quarters of all firms consist of only one shop. Even more remarkably, the same is true of manufacturing, where one would have thought that technical economies of scale would be all-important. Table 5.1, which shows the size of the establishment – the factory or workshop – in manufacturing,

Table 5.1 *Size of manufacturing establishments in the United Kingdom, 1973*

Employees	Number of firms	Percentage of total firms	Number of employees (000s)	Percentage of total employed
1–10	50,000 (est.)	45	250 (est.)	3
11–99	45,888	42	1,487	20
100–999	12,740	12	3,487	46
Over 1,000	1,113	1	2,402	31
TOTAL	109,741	100	7,626	100

reveals two important features: (i) the small establishment is typical of manufacturing in the UK, over four-fifths employing less than 100 people; (ii) these small units employ only one-fifth of the labour force.

Any explanation of this predominance of the small firm has to deal with two salient facts: (i) small firms are especially important in certain industries, such as agriculture, retailing, building, and personal and professional services; (ii) variations in the size of firms exist even within the same industry. Both result from the nature of the conditions of demand and supply.

(i) *Demand*

Large-scale production may be only *technically* efficient; it is not *economically* efficient unless a large and regular demand justifies it.

The market may be small because demand is local (e.g. for personal services and the goods sold by the village store), or limited to a few articles of one pattern (e.g. for highly specialised and individually designed machine-tools) or because transport costs are high (e.g. for bricks and perishable market-garden produce), or because product differentiation divides it artificially (see p. 125).

Where demand fluctuates (e.g. in construction), the overhead cost of idle specialised equipment is heavy – but the smaller the firm, the less the burden.

(ii) *Supply*

Even if demand is large, factors on the supply side may make for small firms. While in certain industries, e.g. retailing and building, it is possible to start with little capital, the difficulty of obtaining further funds and the taxation of profits are obstacles to expansion. Furthermore, government monopoly policy may prevent mergers (see p. 133). Alternatively, where vertical dis-integration is possible, firms need not expand internally but simply employ specialist firms for advertising, research, supplying components and selling by-products. Important, too, is the fact that many small owners do not have the drive to expand or the ability to manage a large concern. Or, as in farming and retailing, they will work long hours (that is, accept a lower rate of profit) simply to be their own bosses.

Above all, as the size of the firm increases, management difficulties occur. If management is vested in heads of department, problems of co-ordination arise and rivalries develop. This means that one person must be in overall command – yet people with such capabilities are in very limited supply. In certain industries these difficulties may soon occur. Rapid decisions are required where demand changes quickly, e.g. in the fashion trades, or supply conditions alter, e.g. through the weather in agriculture. Or care may have to be given to the personal requirements of customers,

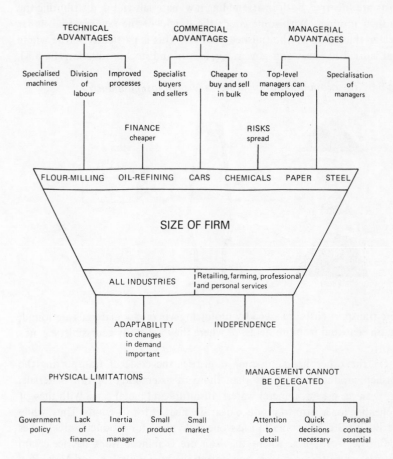

Fig 5.4 *factors influencing the size of the firm*

e.g. in retailing and services. This may require the close supervision of management, and thus the firm has to be small.

5.7 THE LOCATION OF PRODUCTION

In deciding where to produce, a firm has to weigh the advantages of a particular locality against the rent or land costs it will have to pay there compared with elsewhere.

(a) Location advantages
The advantages of producing in a particular locality can be classified as: (i) natural, (ii) acquired and (iii) government-sponsored.

(i) *Natural advantages*
Costs are incurred both in assembling raw materials and in distributing the finished product. With some goods the weight of the raw materials is far greater than that of the finished product. This is particularly true where coal is used for heat and power, e.g. in iron and steel production (fig 5.5).

Fig 5.5 *the production of pig-iron – a 'weight-losing' industry*

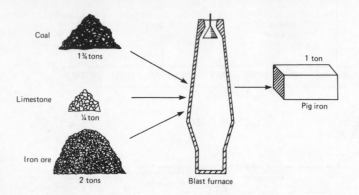

Here transport costs are saved by producing where raw materials are found, e.g. on coal- and iron-ore fields, or where they are easily accessible, e.g. near a port.

On the other hand, in some industries the costs of transporting the finished product are greater than those of assembling the raw materials, e.g. with ice-cream, mineral waters, furniture and metal cans. With these it is cheaper for a firm to produce near the market for its goods. Thus, while the British Steel Corporation has one main plant for producing steel tubes at Corby, Northants, where the iron ore is mined, Walls has ice-cream factories close to most large concentrations of population, and Metal Box manufactures its containers in over forty factories throughout Britain.

Suitability of climate may also affect location. Thus Lancashire's humid atmosphere helped the cotton-spinning and weaving processes. Indeed in agriculture climate is usually decisive, given satisfactory soil conditions.

Under 'natural advantages' we can also include an abundant supply of cheap labour. This may be important in attracting certain industries, e.g. shipbuilding to Malta.

(ii) *Acquired advantages*
Improved methods of production, the development of transport, inventions and new sources of power may alter the relative importance of natural advantages and so change an industry's location. Thus, as high-

grade iron-ore fields have become exhausted and improved techniques have reduced coal consumption, it is now cheaper to transport the coal than the iron ore to produce pig-iron, and so the industry has shifted from the coalfields to the low-grade iron-ore fields of the east Midlands. Similarly, improved transport may upset the relative pulls. By transporting coal and iron ore to Dagenham, the Ford Motor Company can produce pig-iron at a *consumption* centre. Finally, new inventions, such as humidifiers and water-softeners, can make an industry less dependent upon a particular locality.

Yet we must not over-stress the importance of the above changes. Even when natural factors have disappeared, an industry often remains in the same region because of the 'man-made' advantages it has acquired, e.g. steel or cotton. Such advantages were mentioned earlier when we studied external economies of concentration. A skilled labour force, communications, marketing and commercial organisations, nearby ancillary industries (to achieve economies of scale or to market by-products), training schools and a widespread reputation for the products of the region all help to lower the costs of production, thereby making the locality attractive to new firms.

(iii) *Government-sponsored advantages*
Unemployment in such highly localised industries as coal, cotton and ship-building, and environmental problems (traffic congestion, pollution, housing stress) in regions attracting new and expanding industries, have led the government to offer firms financial inducements to set up plants in Development Areas (see chapter 19).

(b) The level of rents in different areas
Location advantages have to be weighed against the cost of land (or, where it is hired, rent). This cost varies from one locality to another and is determined by the market mechanism. Since other firms, possibly from other industries, may be looking for the same site advantages, competition will fix the price of land at the highest which the keenest firm is prepared to pay. This will be the firm which puts the greatest value on the land's advantages compared with those of land elsewhere. Thus, early in its history it seemed that the cotton industry might settle on Clydeside, for this had all the natural advantages of south-east Lancashire. But it also had deep water – and shipbuilding firms were prepared to pay extra for this advantage. For cotton manufacturers this extra cost exceeded any disadvantage of being in Lancashire. Thus shipbuilding firms settled along the Clyde, and cotton firms in Lancashire.

In the final analysis, therefore, it is not the absolute advantages of a district which decide where a firm locates, but the advantages relative to those of other districts. Thus an industry whose outlay on unskilled labour forms a high proportion of its production costs would, other things being equal, be able to bid more for land in an area of cheap labour than one whose spending on such labour was minimal. And in town centres we see the same principle at work – shops oust other businesses, and houses are converted into offices.

(c) Other influences on location

A firm will normally choose the site where the advantages are greatest compared with its cost. But even for a comparatively new industry, where natural advantages are important, we cannot assume that they will be decisive. Thus it is largely historical accident which accounts for the presence of the British Leyland plant at Cowley on the outskirts of Oxford, for the old school of William Morris came up for sale just as the production of cars at his original cycle works was being expanded.

Moreover, electricity has now practically eliminated dependence on a coalfield site. Yet firms may still go to the original areas because of the advantages acquired over time. Others may choose to be nearer their markets. Some 'footloose' firms have even located in certain districts, particularly south-east England, largely because the managing directors (or their wives) have preferred living there!

The various factors influencing location are summarised in fig. 5.6.

Fig 5.6 *factors influencing the siting of a business*

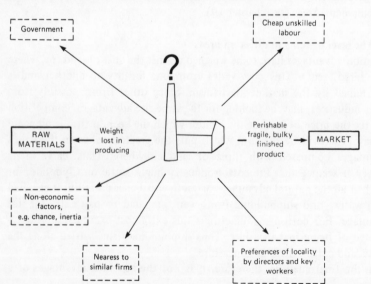

5.8 THE DISTRIBUTION OF GOODS TO THE CONSUMER

(a) The scope of production
A manufacturer has to decide how to get his finished goods to the consumer. He may undertake the task himself. But if he does so, he must employ salesmen, run delivery transport, carry stocks, advertise his product, organise exports, advise customers, establish servicing centres and give credit. Experts for these highly specialised functions can only be employed if output is large enough. Moreover, the manufacturer's main ability lies in organising production rather than selling.

Thus the principle of the division of labour is usually applied. Just as the manufacturer buys raw materials and components from other producers, so specialist firms get his goods to the consumer – there is *forward* vertical dis-integration. We will simplify our account of this selling process by grouping such firms into 'wholesalers' and 'retailers'. Fig 5.7 shows how they fit into the various stages in the production of chocolate.

(b) The wholesaler
The wholesaler buys goods in bulk from producers and sells them in small quantities to retailers. In doing so he helps production.

Fig 5.7 *the role of the wholesaler and retailers in the 'production' of chocolate*

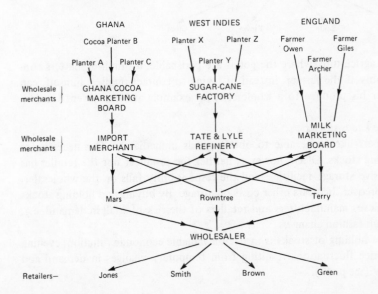

98

(i) He economises in distribution

Because shops usually stock a variety of goods, they can order supplies only in small quantities. Thus it is not economical for each producer to sell directly to them, for this would mean employing many salesmen, packing separate parcels and making deliveries to each shop in turn. Thus in fig 5.8a, 16 contacts and deliveries are necessary if 4 chocolate firms directly supply 4 retailers, compared with the situation in fig 5.8b, where each producer deals only with a wholesaler, reducing the total journeys to 8.

Fig 5.8 *economising in distribution through the wholesaler*

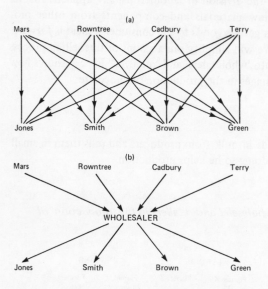

In agriculture, where the goods are perishable, it simplifes matters considerably if the farmer, instead of trying to contact retailers himself, can deliver his produce to a wholesaler, for example at New Covent Garden.

(ii) He keeps stocks

Shoppers like to be able to obtain goods immediately. This necessitates carrying stocks. Often, however, neither the producer nor the retailer has extensive storage facilities, and the responsibility falls on the wholesaler.

Moreover, he bears other costs of storage. By buying and holding stocks he relieves manufacturers and retailers of the risk of a fall in demand, e.g. through fashion changes.

The holding of stocks is in itself a valuable economic function, evening out price fluctuations resulting from temporary changes in demand and supply (see p. 49).

(iii) *He arranges imports from abroad*

Foreign manufacturers can rarely be bothered to ship small parcels to individual retailers abroad or to undertake the foreign-currency transactions involved. They prefer to deal with a wholesaler, an import merchant with established trade connections.

(iv) *He carries out certain specialised functions*

Not only does the wholesaler advertise goods but, in order to make selling easier, he may process goods – pasteurising milk, cooking beetroots, blending tea, refining sugar, and grading commodities such as wheat and cotton.

(v) *He is a channel for information and advice*

Suggestions which customers make to the retailer are passed on to the wholesaler, who, if he sees that they reflect the general view, conveys them to the manufacturer. Thus the latter can improve his product and anticipate fashion changes.

(vi) *He assists in the day-to-day maintenance of the good*

With many products, particularly vehicles and machinery, the wholesaler relieves the manufacturer of the task of providing an efficient maintenance, repair and spare-part service.

(c) The retailer

The retailer performs the last stage of the productive process, for it is he who puts the goods in the hands of the actual consumer. His work is to have the right goods in the right place at the right time.

(i) *He stocks small quantities of a variety of goods*

What the 'right good' is depends on the customer, for different people have different tastes. It is therefore necessary to stock a variety of goods so that customers can choose and take delivery there and then. Thus the retail shop is basically a showroom, particularly where goods are bought infrequently.

The size of the stocks carried will depend on many factors: the popularity of the product, the possibility of obtaining further supplies quickly, the perishability of the good or the likelihood of its going out of fashion, the season, the possibility of future price changes and, above all, the costs (chiefly bank interest charges) of carrying stocks.

(ii) *He takes the goods to where it is most convenient for the customer*

Taking the goods to the customer usually means that the retailer sets up his shop within easy reach, e.g. in a town centre. However, with goods in everyday use, such as groceries, small shops are often dotted around residential districts. Where customers are very dispersed, the retailer may even be a 'travelling shop'.

While customers take most goods away with them, the retailer arranges delivery if transport is essential, e.g. for furniture, or if the customer likes the extra convenience of delivery, e.g. of the morning milk.

(iii) *He performs special services for customers*
In the course of his main business the retailer performs many services to build up customer goodwill. Where the good is not in stock he will order it, and in other matters where contact with the manufacturer is necessary he often acts for the customer, e.g. by returning the goods for repair.

With many goods, too, such as fishing tackle, photographic equipment, musical instruments and machinery, he can often provide specialised advice.

Finally, goods may be sent on approval, or credit facilities arranged through hire purchase, special credit accounts, etc.

(iv) *He advises the wholesaler and manufacturer of customers' preferences*

(d) Types of retail outlet
Retailing might be widely defined as including all shops, mail-order firms, garages, launderettes and betting shops, and indeed any business selling

Fig 5.9   *retail sales %, Great Britain, 1977*

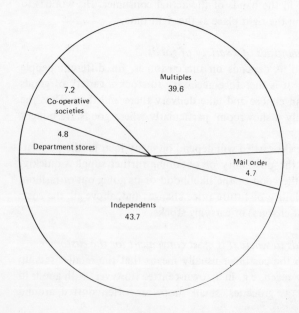

Multiples
39.6

7.2
Co-operative
societies

4.8
Department stores

Mail order
4.7

Independents
43.7

products or services to the consumer. However, it is usual to confine the meaning of 'retailing' to shops and mail-order outlets. These can be classified as follows.

(i) *Independents*
These are mainly small shops with no branches, and they account for nearly a half of total shop sales. Yet, in spite of their advantages of individual attention to customers, handy locations for quick shopping trips, and the willingness of owners to accept a lower return in order to be their own bosses, these independents are steadily losing ground to the larger stores.

A major bid to avert the decline has come through the voluntary chains, such as Spar, Mace and Wavy Line, whose members account for over a third of the independent shops. Shops in these chains retain their independence, but buy in bulk from wholesalers and use common advertising and display techniques.

(ii) *Multiples*
These can be defined arbitrarily as organisations of ten or more shops. Some, such as Mothercare and Dixon's Photographic, sell a particular type of good. Others, such as Woolworth, Boots and Marks & Spencer, sell a fairly extensive range of products. Together, multiples account for about 40% of all retail sales. Their chief advantages are economies of bulk buying and centralised control, the elimination of the wholesaler, quick recognition through standardised shop-fronts, and a reputation established through brand names.

(iii) *Supermarkets*
These may be defined as self-service shops with a minimum selling area of 2,000 sq. ft. While in their organisation they are mainly multiples, their share of the food trade warrants separate attention. In 1977 they accounted for half the grocery trade and nearly a third of total food sales.

The field is led by the main retail grocery chains, e.g. Tesco, Sainsbury, Associated Dairies and Fine Fare. Their strength lies in economies of scale, low labour costs, an attractive display of merchandise, and bulk buying and selling under their own labels (e.g. Sainsbury cornflakes and Tesco coffee). As a result they have gained ground rapidly through highly competitive prices. Indeed many have extended their activities to self-service selling of goods showing higher profit margins, e.g. clothing and hardware.

(iv) *Hypermarkets*
Urban congestion, inadequate parking space and rising rents have made high-street sites increasingly expensive. The American and, to an increasing extent, the European answer has been the large (over 40,000 sq. ft) out-of-

town shopping centre, or 'hypermarket', to cater for the car-borne weekly shopper.

However, in the UK this development has been slow, largely because planning consents have not been readily given, since out-of-town shopping may have an environmental cost in downtown decay or intrusion on the countryside.

(v) Department stores

Competition from multiples has forced department stores to vary their traditional pattern of having separate departments under the control of a responsible buyer (often described as 'many stores under one roof') in favour of bulk-buying by a central office. This, together with extended credit facilities, has allowed them to retain nearly 5% of the market.

The main groups are Debenhams, House of Fraser, the John Lewis Partnership, Great Universal Stores and United Drapery Stores.

(vi) Co-operatives (see pp. 77-8).

(vii) Mail order

During the 1960s mail-order business secured an increasing share of retail sales. Since then, however, much higher postal charges have reduced its rate of expansion. In 1977 mail-order business accounted for nearly 5% of the retail market.

The five major companies in this field – Great Universal Stores, Littlewoods Mail Order, Grattan Warehouses, Freemans and Empire Stores – sell by agency and illustrated catalogues, purchases usually being arranged through weekly interest-free payments. Over a half of all their sales are accounted for by women's clothing and household goods.

(e) Factors determining the retail outlet

The trend away from small, independent shops towards larger organisations, notably the multiples and supermarket chains, reflects a greater emphasis on competition through price rather than by better service. The larger firms are in a strong position to cut prices. Not only do they obtain the advantages of bulk buying but they may also induce manufacturers to supply goods under the retailer's own brand label at a price below that of the national brand. Moreover, large retailers catering for a whole range of shopping, e.g. food, can attract customers into their stores by 'loss-leaders'.

Economic factors helping this trend are:

    (i) *Increased income*, which has led to a swing in expenditure towards the more expensive processed foods and consumer durable goods.

    (ii) *An increase in car ownership*, which has enabled people to move from the city centre to the outer suburbs. Shops have followed, not only to be near their customers but also to obtain larger sites with parking facilities, lower rents and less congestion.

The car has also made customers more mobile, enabling them to travel to good shopping centres where they can purchase all their requirements at a single shop.

(iii) *An increase in the numbers of married women going to work*, which has promoted the demand for convenience foods and labour-saving devices. It has also led to a reduction in the number of shopping expeditions, a trend helped by the wider ownership of refrigerators and freezers.

These factors are likely to remain important in the future. It seems probable, therefore, that new supermarkets will take the form of discount stores or hypermarkets selling a wider range of products, the profit margins of which are larger than those on groceries. Moreover, the more favourable response to planning applications is enabling new stores to be developed outside towns, while cash-and-carry warehouses are now available to consumers who can buy in quantity.

Such changes are likely to be at the expense of the medium-sized business, for the smaller local retailers can offer 'convenience' services.

(f) The future of the middleman

Wholesalers and dealers who come between the manufacturer and the retailer or consumer are often referred to as 'middlemen'. They are frequently criticised on the grounds that they take too large a share of the selling price. It is argued that, if the manufacturer sold direct to consumers, prices could be reduced.

But, as we have seen, wholesalers relieve producers of essential functions, allowing them to obtain the advantages of specialisation in marketing products. Such forward vertical dis-integration is the cheapest way of getting goods to the consumer.

However, this does not mean that all criticism of middlemen is unjustified. Sometimes their profit margins are too high. This may occur through continuing with antiquated methods or by a single middleman's playing off one small producer, such as a farmer, against another (hence the formation of producers' co-operatives).

In recent years a tendency for the wholesaler to be eliminated has been due to: (i) the growth of large shops, which can order in bulk; (ii) the development of road transport, which reduces the necessity of holding large stocks; (iii) the desire of manufacturers to retain some control over retailing outlets in order to ensure that their products are pushed or a high standard of service is maintained; and (iv) the practice of branding many products, which eliminates many specialised functions. In other cases, however, the elimination of the wholesaler has been confined to sales of high-value goods, such as furniture and television sets; to circumstances where the producer and retailer are close together, as with the market gardener who supplies the local shop; and to cases where the manufacturer does his own retailing.

To some extent the wholesaler has responded to this challenge by developing in two main directions: (i) by establishing the cash-and-carry warehouse, sometimes called 'the retailers' supermarket'; and (ii) by becoming the organiser of a voluntary chain of retailers, who are supplied and to some extent controlled by him.

Selling direct to consumers by the manufacturer occurs chiefly where: (i) he wishes to push his product (e.g. beer or footwear) or to ensure a standard of advice and service (e.g. with sewing-machines); (ii) the personal-service element is important (e.g. with made-to-measure clothing); (iii) he is a small-scale producer–retailer, often selling a perishable good (e.g. cakes and pastries) or serving a local area (e.g. with printing); (iv) so wide a range of goods is produced that a whole chain of shops can be fully stocked (e.g. Maynard sweets, Manfield shoes); or (v) the good is highly technical or made to individual specifications (e.g. machinery).

SUPPLY: (ii)
COSTS AND
PROFITABILITY

6.1 COMBINING RESOURCES

(a) Classification of factors of production

In order to examine the problems connected with employing resources it is helpful to classify them according to particular characteristics.

Land refers to the resources provided by nature, e.g. space, sunshine, rain and minerals, which are fixed in supply.

Labour refers to the effort, physical and mental, made by human beings in production. It is this 'human' element which distinguishes it from other factors, for it gives rise to problems regarding psychological attitudes and unemployment.

Capital as a factor of production consists of producer goods and stocks of consumer goods not yet in the hands of the consumer. While consumer goods directly satisfy consumers' wants, e.g. loaves, bicycles, TV sets, producer goods are only wanted for making consumer goods, e.g. buildings, machines, raw materials. Capital is treated as a separate factor of production in order to emphasise: (i) the increased production which results from using it, (ii) the sacrifice of present enjoyment which is necessary to obtain it (see chapter 9), and (iii) the fluctuations of economic activity which may result from changes in its rate of accumulation (see chapter 16).

Enterprise is the acceptance of the risks of uncertainty in production – risks which, as we saw earlier, cannot be insured against. They arise because the firm spends in advance on raw materials, labour and machines, and the extent to which such costs are covered depends on the demand for the product when it is sold. Tastes may have changed or a rival may be marketing the good at a lower price than anticipated. The reward for uncertainty-bearing is profit – unless it is negative: loss. Whoever accepts such a risk is a true entrepreneur – the farmer working on his own account, the person who buys ordinary shares in a company, or the citizen of a state, who ultimately has to bear any losses made by a nationalised industry.

(b) The problem of combining resources

The problems peculiar to the different types of factors of production are considered in chapters 7–9. Here we are concerned with the more general problem of how much of each a firm will hire. In other words, how will the firm allocate its spending in order to obtain the greatest possible output from a given outlay? For example, the same amount of concrete can be mixed by having many men with just a shovel apiece or by having only one man using a concrete-mixer. Can we discover any general principle governing the firm's decision? We can begin by seeing what happens to output when one factor is held fixed while the amount of another factor is increased.

(c) The law of diminishing (or non-proportional) returns

Assume: (i) production is by two factors only, land and labour; (ii) all units of the variable factor, labour, are equally efficient; (iii) there is no change in techniques or organisation.

Table 6.1 shows how the output of potatoes varies as more labourers work on a fixed amount of land. Until 3 men are employed, the marginal product of labour is increasing – the third labourer, for instance, adding 19 cwt. Here there are really too few labourers for the given amount of land. Thereafter the marginal product falls, the fourth labourer adding only 13 cwt, and so on; total output is still increasing, but at a diminishing rate. The maximum return per labourer occurs when there are 4 labourers to the plot. If we increase the number of labourers to eight, the maximum return per labourer can only be maintained by doubling the amount of land. When 11 labourers are employed they start to get in one another's way, and from then on total output is declining absolutely.

Again it must be emphasised that units of the variable factor are homogeneous. The marginal product of labour does not fall because less efficient labourers have to be employed. Diminishing returns are the result of more labourers being employed on a fixed amount of land.

Nor does the law formulate any *economic* theory; it merely states physical relationships. While the physical productivity of an extra labourer is important to a farmer in deciding how many men to employ, it will not *determine* his decision. He must also know the relative costs of factors; that is, he requires economic data as well as technical facts.

(d) The practical applications of the law of diminishing returns

The law is significant both in our everyday life and in the theoretical analysis of the economist.

First, it helps to explain the low standard of living in many parts of the world, particularly the Far East. Increasing population is cultivating a

Table 6.1 *Variations in output of potatoes resulting from a change in
labour employed*

Number of men employed on the fixed unit of land	Total output	Output (cwt) Average product	Marginal product
1	1	1	1
2	8	4	7
3	27	9	19
4	40	10	13
5	$47\frac{1}{2}$	$9\frac{1}{2}$	$7\frac{1}{2}$
6	54	9	$6\frac{1}{2}$
7	60	$8\frac{4}{7}$	6
8	65	$8\frac{1}{8}$	5
9	69	$7\frac{2}{3}$	4
10	71	$7\frac{1}{10}$	2
11	71	$6\frac{5}{11}$	0
12	66	$5\frac{1}{2}$	−5

Notes
(a) *Total output* is the total output (cwt) from all factors employed.
(b) *Average product* refers to the average output per man. It therefore equals

$$\frac{\text{total output}}{\text{number of men employed}}$$

(c) *Marginal product* refers to the marginal output (cwt) to labour, and equals the addition to total output which is obtained by increasing the labour force by one man. That is, marginal output equals total output of (n + 1) men minus total output of n men.
(d) There is a fundamental relationship between average product and marginal product. Marginal product equals average product when the latter is at a maximum (fig 6.1). This relationship is bound to occur. So long as the marginal product is greater than average product, the return to an additional labourer will raise the average product of all labourers employed. On the other hand, as soon as the marginal product falls below average product, the additional labourer will lower the average product. Hence when average product is neither rising nor falling, that is, at its maximum, it is because marginal product equals average product.

This relationship can be made clearer by a simple example. Suppose Botham has played 20 innings and that his batting average is 60 runs. Now if in his next innings he scores more than 60, say 102, his average will increase – to 62. If, on the other hand, he scores less than 60, say 18, his average will fall – to 58. If he scores exactly 60 in his twenty-first innings, his average will remain unchanged at 60.

108

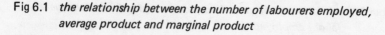

Fig 6.1   *the relationship between the number of labourers employed, average product and marginal product*

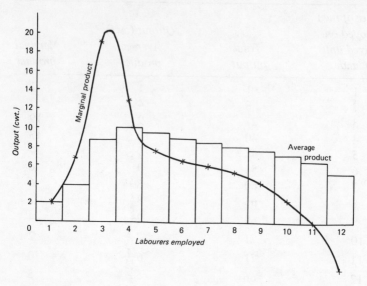

fixed amount of land. Marginal product, and thus average product, are falling; so, therefore, is the average standard of living.

Second, it shows how a firm can adjust the marginal physical products of factors by altering the proportion in which they are combined. Thus few labourers to the plot gave a high return per labourer; after 4 labourers, the average product began to fall. So the law is often referred to as 'the law of varying proportions'. The firm will choose that combination of factors which yields the maximum output from a given outlay, as follows.

(e) The optimum combination of variable factors

So far we have assumed that there are just two factors, land and labour, and that land is fixed. But suppose that there is another variable factor, say capital. Now the farmer will have to decide how he will combine labour with capital.

How much of each he employs will depend upon its productivity relative to its price, since he will alter the combination until, for the last pound spent on both labour and capital, he obtains the same amount of product. Suppose, for instance, the last pound's worth of labour is yielding more potatoes than the last pound spent on capital. It will obviously pay the farmer to transfer this pound from capital to buying more labour, for this will increase his total physical yield.

But labour and capital are obtained in different units, their units being different in price. Thus we cannot directly compare the productivity of one man with that of one unit of capital, say a mechanical hoe; we must allow for their respective prices. If the cost of one man is only one-third of the cost of a mechanical hoe, then the marginal product of a man need only be one-third of the hoe's to give the same yield for a given expenditure. Thus the farmer will be in equilibrium in combining factors when:

$$\frac{\text{Marginal product of labour}}{\text{Price of labour}} = \frac{\text{Marginal product of capital}}{\text{Price of capital}}$$

A corollary of this is that, like the housewife in purchasing her goods, the entrepreneur will tend to buy more of a factor as its price falls, and less as it rises. Suppose the wage-rate rises but the marginal product of labour remains unchanged. The fundamental relationship stated above has now been destroyed. To restore the position it is necessary to raise the marginal product of labour and to lower that of capital by combining less labour with more capital: in short, a rise in wages without a corresponding increase in the productivity of labour will, other things being equal, tend to bring about the replacement of labour by machines.

6.2 THE COSTS OF PRODUCTION

(a) Opportunity costs and profit
Suppose a man sets himself up as a shopkeeper selling sweets. He invests £1,000 of his savings in the business, and in the first year his receipts are £20,000 and his outgoings £11,000. The accountant would say that his profits over the year were £9,000. The economist, however, would disagree.

The reason for this is that the economist is not so much concerned with money costs as with 'opportunity cost' – what a factor could earn in its best alternative line of production. This concept of cost has a bearing on (i) the economist's concept of 'profit', and (ii) how long production should continue when total costs are not covered.

(b) 'Implicit costs'
The £11,000 money outgoings of the shopkeeper above can be regarded as 'explicit costs'. But when we look at costs as alternatives forgone we see immediately that the shopkeeper has certain 'implicit costs' – the rewards his own capital and labour could earn elsewhere. If, for instance, his capital could be invested at 12%, there is an implicit cost of £120 a year. Similarly with his own labour. His next most profitable line, we will assume, is to be a shop manager earning £5,880 a year. Thus a total of £6,000 in implicit costs in addition to the explicit costs should be deducted from his receipts.

(c) Normal and super-normal profit

But we have not finished yet. The shopkeeper knows that, even in running a sweet shop, some risk arises through uncertainty – a risk which he avoids if he merely works for somebody else. The shopkeeper must therefore anticipate at least a certain minimum profit, say £1,000 a year, before he will start his own business. If he does not make this minimum profit, he feels he might as well go into some other line of business or become a paid shop manager. Thus another type of cost (which we call 'normal profit') has to be allowed for – the minimum return which keeps a firm in a particular industry after all other factors have been paid their opportunity cost. Normal profit is a cost because, if it is not met, the supply of entrepreneurship to that particular line of business dries up.

We have, therefore, the following costs: explicit costs, implicit costs and normal profit. Anything left over after all these costs have been met is 'super-normal' profit. In terms of our example, we have:

		£	£
Total revenue			20,000
Total costs:	explicit	11,000	
	implicit	6,000	
	normal profit	1,000	
			18,000
Super-normal profit			2,000

(d) Fixed costs and variable costs

For the purposes of our analysis, we shall classify costs as either *fixed* or *variable*.

Fixed costs are those costs which do not vary in direct proportion to the firm's output. They are the costs of indivisible factors, e.g. buildings, machinery and vehicles. Even if there is no output fixed costs must be incurred, but for a time, as output expands, they remain the same.

Variable costs, on the other hand, are those costs which vary directly with output. They are the costs of the variable factors, e.g. operative labour, raw materials, fuel for running the machines, wear and tear on equipment. Where there is no output, variable costs are nil; as output increases so variable costs increase.

In practice it is difficult to draw an absolute line between fixed and variable costs: the difference really depends on the length of time involved. When current output is not profitable, the entrepreneur will have to contract production. At first overtime will cease; later, workers will be paid off. In time, more factors, e.g. salesmen, become variable, and if receipts still do not justify expenditure on them they too can be dismissed. A factor becomes variable when a decision has to be taken on whether it shall be replaced, for then its alternative uses have to be considered. Eventually machines need renewing; even they have become a variable cost. A decision may now be necessary on whether the business should continue.

The distinction between fixed and variable factors and costs is useful in two ways. First, in economic analysis it provides a means of distinguishing between differences in the conditions of supply which result from changes in the time period. The *short period* is defined as a period when there is at least one fixed factor. While, therefore, supply can be adjusted by labour working overtime and more raw materials being used, the time is too short for altering fixed plant and organisation. Thus the firm cannot achieve its best possible combination for a given output. In the *long period* all factors are variable; they can therefore be combined in the best possible way. Thus supply can respond fully to a change in demand.

Second, as we shall see later, the distinction is fundamental when the firm is considering whether or not to continue producing. In the long period all costs of production, fixed and variable, must be covered if production is to continue. But in the short period fixed costs cannot be avoided by ceasing to produce; they have already been paid for, simply because it was necessary to have some 'lumpy' factors even before productions could start. Only variable costs can be saved; and so, provided these are covered by receipts, the firm will continue to produce. Anything that it makes above such costs will help to recoup its fixed costs.

(e) Changes in costs as output expands

In our discussion of the law of diminishing returns we referred to quantities of factors and yields in physical terms. But in deciding how to maximise profit, the firm will be concerned with those quantities translated into money terms. It can then see directly the relationship between costs and receipts at different outputs and is thus able to decide what output will give the maximum profit (see table 6.2). Our first task, therefore, is to consider how costs are likely to change as output increases. We shall assume perfect competition in buying factors of production – the demand of each firm is so small in relation to total supply that any change in demand will not directly affect the price of those factors.

In the short period there are, by definition, bound to be fixed factors. And when considering the law of diminishing returns we found that when a variable factor was added to a fixed factor the marginal product might increase for a time but would eventually diminish. How will this affect costs as output expands?

Let us assume that two factors are being used, one of them fixed. If each unit of the variable factor costs the same, but the output from additional units is increasing, the firm is obtaining an increasing amount of output for any given addition to expenditure. In other words the cost of each additional unit of output is falling as output expands. On the other hand, if the marginal product of the variable factor is diminishing, the cost of an additional unit of output is rising. This cost of an additional unit of output is known as *marginal cost* (MC).

The above conclusions are represented diagrammatically in fig 6.2, where average product = total product of x units of the variable factor/x and average cost = total cost of n units of output/n.

Fig 6.2   *the relationship between returns and costs*

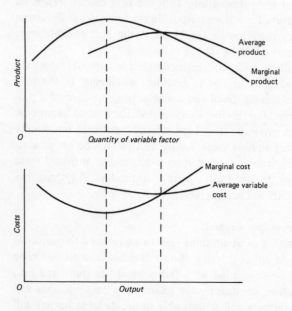

(f) Cost schedules

Table 6.2 illustrates this relationship between output and costs. The figures, which have been kept as simple as possible, are for an imaginary firm, Rollermowers Ltd, manufacturers of lawnmowers. Fixed costs (FC) amount to £1,000, and, as variable factors are added, output expands. At first there is an increasing marginal product; as a result MC is falling. This has its effect on average total cost (ATC) until approximately 75 units are being produced. From then onwards, as the fixed factors are being worked more intensively, diminishing returns cause the ATC curve to rise. These figures can be plotted on a graph (fig 6.3).

The following relationships between the curves should be noted:
  (i)   AFC and AVC added vertically give ATC.
  (ii) The MC curve cuts both the AVC and ATC curves when they are at a minimum, the same reason applying as in table 6.1, note (d).

113

Table 6.2 *Costs of Rollermowers Ltd* (in £)

Output per week (units)	Fixed cost (FC)	Total variable cost (TVC)	Total cost (TC)	Marginal cost (MC)	Average fixed cost (AFC)	Average variable cost (AVC)	Average total cost (ATC)
0	1000	—	—		—	—	—
				20			
10	1000	200	1200		100	20	120
				14			
20	1000	340	1340		50	17	67
				10			
30	1000	440	1440		$33\frac{1}{3}$	$14\frac{2}{3}$	48
				10			
40	1000	540	1540		25	$13\frac{1}{2}$	$38\frac{1}{2}$
				$13\frac{1}{2}$			
50	1000	675	1675		20	$13\frac{1}{2}$	$33\frac{1}{2}$
				$18\frac{1}{2}$			
60	1000	860	1860		$16\frac{2}{3}$	$14\frac{1}{3}$	31
				24			
70	1000	1100	2100		$14\frac{2}{7}$	$15\frac{3}{7}$	30
				30			
80	1000	1400	2400		$12\frac{1}{2}$	$17\frac{1}{2}$	30
				39			
90	1000	1790	2790		$11\frac{1}{9}$	$19\frac{3}{8}$	31
				51			
100	1000	2300	3300		10	23	33
				66			
110	1000	2960	3960		$9\frac{1}{9}$	$26\frac{8}{9}$	36
				84			
120	1000	3800	4800		$8\frac{1}{2}$	$31\frac{2}{3}$	40

Notes
(1) TC of n units = FC + VC of n units.
(2) MC is the extra cost involved in producing an additional unit of output. That is, MC of the nth unit = TC of n units – TC of n – 1 units. Here output is shown in units of 10, so that this difference in total costs has to be divided by 10.
(3) AFC of n units = $\dfrac{FC}{n}$.
(4) AVC of n units = $\dfrac{TVC \text{ of } n \text{ units}}{n}$.
(5) ATC = $\dfrac{TC \text{ of } n \text{ units}}{n}$.

Fig 6.3 *cost curves*

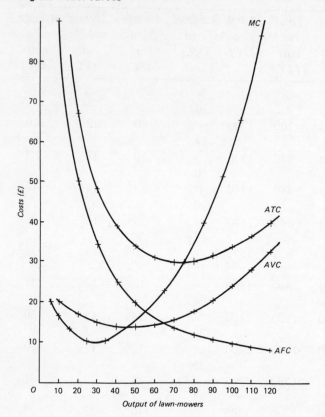

6.3 HOW MUCH TO PRODUCE: OUTPUT OF THE FIRM UNDER PERFECT COMPETITION

In order to ascertain whether a firm is maximising profits, we have to know (i) the price at which it can sell different outputs and the price at which it can buy different quantities of factors, and (ii) whether it is free to enter another industry where it can make higher profits. Both questions involve us in a study of the extent to which competition prevails.

First we shall assume that the conditions of 'perfect competition' – the highest form of competition – apply. Later we show how relaxing these conditions leads to imperfect competition, forms of which prevail in real life.

(a) The conditions necessary for perfect competition

For perfect competition to exist the following conditions must hold:

(i) A large number of relatively small sellers and buyers

If there are a large number of sellers relative to demand in the market, any one seller will know that, because he supplies so small a quantity of the total output, he can increase or decrease his output without having any significant effect on the market price of the product. In short he takes the market price as given, and can sell any quantity at this price.

This is illustrated in fig 6.4, where (a) shows market price OP determined by the demand for and supply of the goods of the industry as a whole. But the industry supply, we will assume, comes from a thousand producers, each of about the same size. Each producer therefore sells such a small proportion of the total market supply that he can double his output from ON to OM or halve it from OM to ON without affecting the price – fig 6.4b.

Fig 6.4   the firm's demand curve under perfect competition

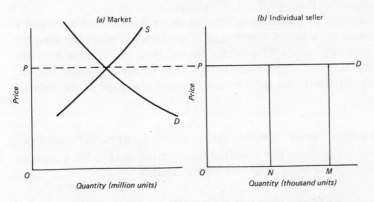

Fig 6.5   the firm's demand curve under perfect and imperfect competition

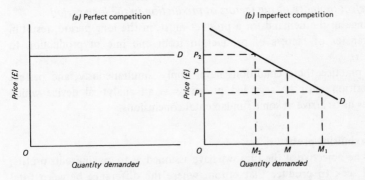

In other words, in perfect competition a seller is faced with an infinitely elastic demand curve for his product. If, in our example, he charges a higher price than OP, nobody will buy from him; if he charges less than

OP, he will not be maximising his revenue, for he could have sold all his output at the higher price, OP.

In contrast, the producer in fig 6.5b sells such a large proportion of the market supply that a change in his output affects the price he receives for his product. When he supplies OM, the price is OP. If he increases his supply to M_1, the price falls to OP_1. Similarly, if he decreases his supply to OM_2, the price rises to OP_2. Alternatively such a producer can decide on the price he charges, leaving it to the market to determine how much is sold at that price. But he cannot fix both price and quantity at the same time.

(ii) *Homogeneous product*
Buyers must regard the product of one producer as being a perfect substitute for that of another, and purchase solely on the basis of price, switching to a competitor if one producer raises his price.

Such identity of product does not exist where there is a real or imaginary difference (e.g. a special wrapping or brand name) or where reasons other than price (e.g. goodwill) influence buyers. Here an individual producer can raise his price without necessarily losing all his customers. In short, product differentiation leads to some downward slope in the demand curve.

(iii) *A perfect market, especially perfect knowledge of market conditions*
The above conditions give a perfectly competitive market. For a situation of perfect competition to exist we must also have:

(iv) *Free entry of new firms into the market*

(v) *Perfect mobility of the factors of production in the long period*
A change in the demand for a product must, in the long period, result in the transfer of factors of production from one line of production to another.

In practice these conditions never apply simultaneously, and perfect competition must be regarded primarily as an analytical device which enables us to arrive at some fundamental conclusions.

(b) Maximising profit
Since the objective of the firm, we have assumed, is to maximise its profits, it will seek to produce that output where the difference between total revenue and total costs is greatest. The firm, therefore, will be concerned with two broad questions: (i) How much will it obtain by selling various quantities of its product? (ii) How much will it cost to produce these different quantities?

At first sight it may seem that maximum profit will occur at the minimum average cost output. But this is unlikely to be so. The real question which the entrepreneur will be continually asking is: 'If I produce another unit, will it cost me less or more than the extra revenue I shall receive from the sale of it?' That is, he concentrates his attention at the margin: if an extra unit of output is to be profitable, *marginal revenue* (the revenue received from the last unit of output) must at least equal *marginal cost* (the cost of producing the last unit of output).

Under perfect competition the producer will obtain the market price for his goods, whatever his output. In other words, marginal revenue (MR) equals price, with the price line horizontal (figs 6.5 and 6.6). On the other hand, although under perfect competition the firm can buy increasing quantities of its factors at a given price, the MC curve eventually rises because of diminishing returns.

Fig 6.6 *the equilibrium output of the firm under perfect competition*

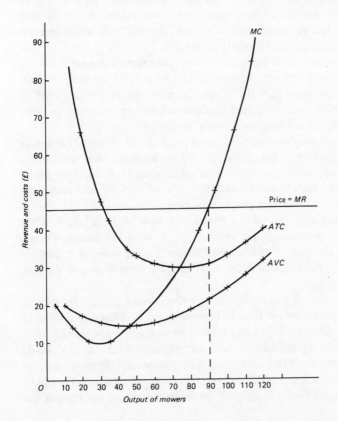

(c) The equilibrium output of Rollermowers

Let us return to our imaginary firm. Assume that the market price of mowers is £45. We can impose this MR curve on the cost curve diagram (fig 6.6).

Now at any output where MR (price) is above MC, Rollermowers can increase profits by expanding output. Or, if MC is above MR, contracting output will increase profits. The equilibrium output, therefore, is where MR (price) equals MC (that is, 90 lawnmowers) provided current revenue covers current costs.

'Current revenue' is simply the number of goods currently produced times their price. But, as we have seen, 'current costs' depend upon whether we are dealing with the short or the long period.

(d) The short-period 'shut-down' price

A firm will only *start* to produce if it expects that total revenue will be sufficient to cover (i) the cost of fixed factors, (ii) the cost of variable factors, e.g. labour, raw materials, and (iii) normal profit.

We will imagine that the firm does think it can make a go of it. It buys highly specific machinery (fixed costs) which, we will assume for the sake of simplicity, has no value to any other firm, together with labour and raw materials (variable costs), and starts producing.

But as time goes by it finds that its original expectations are not being fulfilled. Although the cost of variable factors is being covered, the firm sees that, unless price rises the margin between the two is too small to provide sufficient cash to replace machines when they wear out. In other words the business as a whole will prove unprofitable.

But what will our firm save by stopping production forthwith? Obviously its variable costs, for these vary directly with output. But what of its machines, which, since they have no alternative use, have no resale price? These are fixed factors which have already been paid for, and ceasing to use them now cannot recoup past expenditure.

Consequently our firm takes a philosophic view of the situation. It has some perfectly good machines which, if used, will add nothing to costs. So, provided the cost of the variable factors is being covered, it goes on producing. Anything earned above such cost will help to recoup the cost of the fixed factors.

How can we tell if variable costs are being covered? Simply by looking at the AVC curve. If we take Rollermowers as an example, a price of £13.50 for a mower would just enable it to produce in the short period. Here MC would equal MR and, with an output of 45 units, TVC would just be covered. Any price lower than this, however, would mean that, for any output where MC = MR, total receipts (price times output) would be less than TVC (AVC times output). Rollermowers could not make a 'go' of it even in the short period; and so we can call £13.50 the 'shut-down' price.

(e) The firm's short-period supply curve

A firm's MC curve is its short-period supply curve. At any price below £13.50 per mower, Rollermowers will stop production, because TVC are not covered. At higher prices, however, it will produce an output where price equals MC, as follows:

Price (£)	Output (units)
13.50	45
18.50	55
24	65
30	75
39	85, and so on.

This schedule is graphed in fig 6.7.

6.4 THE INDUSTRY'S SUPPLY CURVE

(a) The short-period supply curve

In the short period, no new firms can enter the industry because, by definition, they cannot obtain fixed factors. The supply curve of the industry, therefore, is obtained simply by adding the output of all existing firms at each given price.

Suppose, for the sake of simplicity, that the industry consists of four firms, the other three being less efficient than Rollermowers. Their outputs (starting from minimum AVC) are given under A, B and C in table 6.3.

Table 6.3 *Short-period supply schedule*

Price (£)	Output (units)				
	Firm A	*Firm B*	*Firm C*	*Rollermowers*	*Total*
13.50	—	—	—	45	45
18.50	—	—	45	55	100
24	—	45	55	65	165
30	50	55	65	75	245
39	55	65	75	85	280

This is shown graphically in fig 6.7. The MC curves of the four firms are summed horizontally to obtain the short-period supply curve of the

Fig 6.7 *the short-period supply curve of the industry*

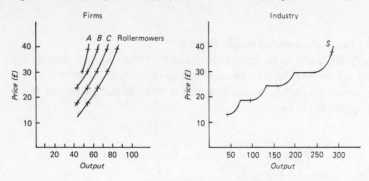

industry. This rises from left to right, showing that more is supplied the higher the price.

It will be observed that the supply curve derived above is not smooth, but stepped. This is because we have taken only four firms. If there had been many firms, each differing only slightly in efficiency, we would have had a smoother curve.

(b) Supply in the long period

In the long period a firm will still produce where MR = MC, but total costs must be covered.

Fig 6.8 *the effect of competition on the abnormal profits and output of Rollermowers Ltd*

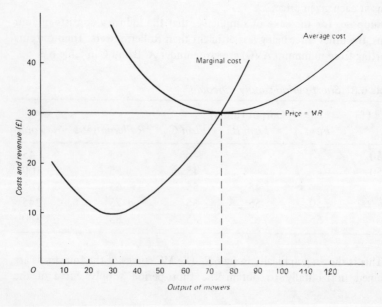

As regards the industry, however, any super-normal profits being made will attract new firms, for these can now obtain plant. Moreover, competition will force all firms, both old and new, towards the most efficient size. As a result supply increases and the price of the product falls until super-normal profits are eliminated (fig 6.8).

The above argument would produce a horizontal supply curve. In practice, however, it has to be modified. First, while there may be some external economies as the industry expands, there is a major diseconomy – higher rewards have to be paid to attract factors from other industries. Second, entrepreneurs are unlikely to be equally efficient in looking ahead when making their decisions, and some firms will always be doing better than others. The situation, therefore, is that even in the long period there is likely to be an upward-sloping supply curve. The extent to which this happens is indicated by elasticity of supply.

6.5 ELASTICITY OF SUPPLY

(a) Definition

Consider fig 6.9. For a rise in price from OP to OP_1, supply extends from OM to OM_1 with S_1 and to OM_2 with S_2. At price OP, therefore, S_2 is said to be more elastic than S_1.

More precisely, the elasticity of supply of a good at any price or at any output is the proportional change in the amount supplied in response to a small change in price divided by the proportional change in price. In the supply schedule on p. 54, for instance, when the price of eggs rises from 10p to 12p supply expands from 32,000 to 40,000. Elasticity of supply is therefore equal to:

$$\frac{\frac{8}{32}}{\frac{2}{10}} = \frac{5}{4} = 1.25$$

As with elasticity of demand, we say that supply at a given price is elastic if elasticity is greater than 1, and that it is inelastic if elasticity is less than 1. There are two significant limiting cases.

(i) *Elasticity of supply equal to infinity*

The main uses of this concept are: (1) where there is perfect competition in buying factors of production; and (2) where production takes place at constant cost. In both cases the supply curve is horizontal – fig 6.10a.

(ii) *Supply absolutely inelastic*

Here a good is fixed in supply whatever the price offered – fig 6.10b. This applies to rare first editions and old masters, and by definition to fixed factors in the short period (see p. 118).

122

Fig 6.9 *elasticity of supply*

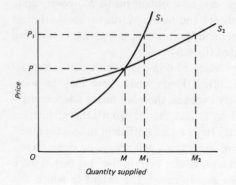

Fig 6.10 *extremes of elasticity of supply*

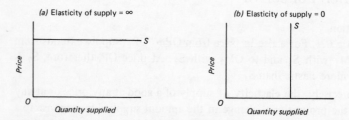

(b) Factors determining elasticity of supply

Elasticity of supply is determined by: (i) the period of time under consideration; (ii) the relationship between the individual firms' minimum-supply points; and (iii) the cost of attracting factors from alternative uses. We shall consider each in turn.

(i) *Time*

We distinguish three main periods:

(1) MOMENTARY EQUILIBRIUM

Here the supply is fixed, and elasticity of supply = 0. An example is Christmas trees on Christmas Eve. With many goods, some increase in supply can take place by either drawing on stocks, or switching factors of production from one product to another (where a firm makes two or more different products).

(2) SHORT-PERIOD EQUILIBRIUM

Usually varying supply requires a change in the factors of production employed. But this takes time – and the period differs for each factor. In the short period, as we have seen, it is possible to adjust supply only by altering the variable factors (raw materials, labour, etc.).

(3) LONG-PERIOD EQUILIBRIUM

Other factors – the fixed factors, e.g. land already sown and capital equipment – can be altered in the long period, allowing supply to adjust fully to a change in price. Thus elasticity is greater in the long period. For example, in fig 6.9, S_1 could well represent the short-period supply curve, and S_2 the long.

(ii) *The relationship between the firms' minimum-supply points*

The supply curve is obtained by aggregating the supply of individual firms. If these firms each offer a supply to the market at more or less the same minimum price, supply will tend to be elastic at that price. Similarly, as price rises, the greater the number of firms coming in, the greater is the elasticity of supply.

(iii) *The cost of attracting factors of production*

In order to expand production additional factors have to be attracted from other industries. For an industry as a whole, this means that higher rewards will have to be paid. What we have to ask, therefore, is how much of a factor will be forthcoming in response to a given price rise. In other words, what is the elasticity of supply of factors of production? And, of greater significance, what influences determine this elasticity?

In answering this question we can first consider what happens when one particular industry, e.g. office-building, wishes to expand. Let us concentrate on one factor: labour. With increased demand for building labourers, wages rise. But they rise not only for the office-building industry but for all other industries employing such labourers – house-building, road-construction, public works, etc. How will it affect these industries?

First, they will try to substitute other factors, e.g. cement-mixers, bull-dozers, etc., for the labour which now costs more. Is such substitution physically possible? If so, how elastic is the supply of these alternative factors? Will their prices rise sharply as demand increases? If physical substitution is fairly easy and the supply of alternative factors is elastic, it will mean that a small rise in wages will release much labour for the office-building industry.

Second, higher wages will lead to increased costs in building houses, constructing roads, etc. The supply curve of these products, therefore, moves to the left; and, the higher the proportion of wages to total costs, the further will it move. The extent to which this leads to a reduced proportion of these alternative goods will depend upon the elasticity of demand for them. If elasticity is high, the small rise in the price of the good will cause a considerable contraction of demand, and labour will be released for office-building. If, on the other hand, demand is inelastic, even a considerable rise in wages will have little effect on the output of houses, etc., and the increase in the supply of labour to office-building will be correspondingly small.

We see, therefore, that the two main influences affecting the elasticity of supply of a factor to a particular industry are (1) the extent to which other factors can be substituted, and (2) the elasticity of demand for the alternative goods it produces.

(c) Practical uses of the concept of elasticity of supply

(i) *The elasticity of supply of a good is a major factor in determining how much its price will alter when there is a change in the conditions of demand*

This can be seen by considering the likely effect on the price of cane sugar, in the short and long period, of an increase in the demand for sugar.

We can assume a fairly inelastic demand curve for sugar. The original price is OP (fig 6.11). Demand then increases from D to D_1. The supply of

Fig 6.11   *changes in the price of cane sugar over time in response to a change in demand*

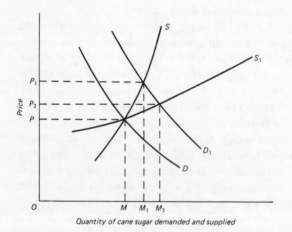

Quantity of cane sugar demanded and supplied

cane sugar in the short run is inelastic, for supply can be expanded only by adding labour, fertilisers, etc. Price therefore increases to OP_1. But in the long period more land can be planted with sugar-cane. Supply is now more elastic, and is represented by the curve S_1. The long-run price falls to OP_2.

(ii) *The elasticity of supply is significant with regard to taxation*

First, where the supply of a good is inelastic, the Chancellor of the Exchequer can impose a tax on the producer without its having a great effect on the amount of the good offered for sale. Suppose, for instance, that a man owns a field which is suitable only for sheep-grazing, and that the most any farmer will pay him for the use of this field is £10 a year, which the owner accepts. Now suppose that the government puts a tax of £5 a year on this type of land. This means that the owner will have to pay the tax out of his own pocket, for the farmer will pay no more, and the land cannot be put to any other use. In fact the government could tax almost all the rent away before it would make any difference to the number of sheep being grazed on it. However, if all the rent went on tax, the owner might leave the land standing idle (see p. 165).

Second, the relative elasticities of demand and supply determine the proportion of a selective indirect tax borne by the producer as compared with the consumer (see p. 336).

6.6 MONOPOLY

(a) Imperfect competition

Where any of the conditions of perfect competition are not fulfilled, some form of 'imperfect competition' results and the firm's demand curve is downward-sloping:

(i)   A seller may be so large that the quantity he supplies affects the price.

(ii) Products may not be homogeneous, because product differentiation or goodwill allows a producer to raise his price somewhat while still retaining some customers.

(iii) Lack of knowledge, barriers to entry or immobility of factors of production result in imperfect elasticity of demand or supply.

Consumers, for instance, may not have complete knowledge of prices ruling elsewhere - as, for example, in retail markets. Thus sellers can raise their prices without losing all their custom.

There are many 'shades' of imperfect competition. At one extreme we have a single producer of a product, e.g. British Oxygen; at the other, the only difference from perfect competition is that firms each produce a slightly different brand, e.g. toothpaste. The first situation we call 'monopoly', the second 'monopolistic competition'. In between we can have just a few sellers of the same or of a slightly different product - 'oligopoly'. In this case, each seller has to take into account the reactions of rivals to his own pricing policy. For instance, if he raises his price, will rival firms follow his lead and do likewise, or will they keep their prices unchanged in order to win over some of his customers? Each different assumption gives

Fig 6.12 *market forms*

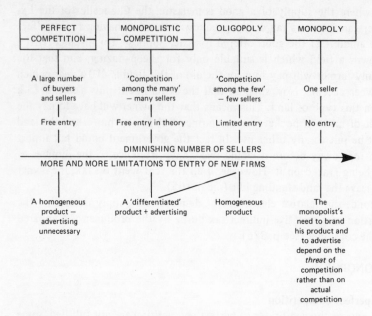

its own solution to the equilibrium output of the industry.

The broad market forms are shown in fig 6.12. We restrict our study to an examination of monopoly.

(b) Sources of monopoly power

While to some extent all goods are substitutes for each other, there may be essential characteristics in a good or group of goods which give rise to gaps in the chain of substitution. If one producer can so exclude competitors that he controls the supply of a good, he can be said to be a 'monopolist' - a single seller.

In real life there is seldom complete monopoly. But one producer may dominate the supply of a good or group of goods. In the UK any firm which accounts for a quarter (in value) of the market supply is considered to be a monopoly (see p. 134).

Possible sources of a monopolist's power to exclude competitors are:

(i) *Immobility of the factors of production*

Such immobility means that existing suppliers cannot be challenged by new entrants. It may arise through:

(1) *Legal prohibition of new entrants* - as with public utilities, where many firms would create technical difficulties, e.g. gas, electricity, water and telephone services.

(2) *Patents, copyrights and trademarks*, where the object is to promote invention and the development of new ideas.

(3) *Government policy of establishing single buying and selling agencies*, e.g. marketing boards.

(4) *Control of the source of supply by one firm*, e.g. minerals, specialist workers (e.g. Dior dress designers), trade unions and professional associations.

(ii) *Ignorance*

A monopoly may persist largely through the ignorance of possible competitors. They may not know about the super-normal profits being made by the existing firm, or they may be unable to acquire the necessary know-how, e.g. for involved technical processes.

(iii) *Indivisibilities*

Whereas the original firm may have been able to build up its size gradually, new firms may find it difficult to raise the large capital required to produce on a scale which is cost-competitive, e.g. with cars, drugs, computers.

In some cases, too, the efficient scale of plant may be so large relative to the market that there is only room for one firm. This applies to many of the public utilities, e.g. transport, water, electricity generation.

(iv) *A deliberate policy of excluding competitors*

Restriction of competition falls into two main groups. On the one hand we have the sources of monopoly power described so far. These have, as it were, resulted indirectly rather than from any deliberate action by producers. Such 'spontaneous' monopolies must be contrasted with 'deliberate' monopolies – those which are created specifically to restrict supply.

It is essential to distinguish between the two when formulating policy. While the 'spontaneous' monopolies may still abuse their fortunate position in order to make high profits, to a large extent they are inevitable, and usually policy should seek to control rather than destroy them. On the other hand, monopolies solely designed to follow restrictive practices detrimental to the consumer should, where possible, be broken up. In practice, however, it is often difficult to draw a distinct line between the two. While firms may increase production or combine in order to reduce costs through economies of scale, the effect may still be that competitors are forced out.

Deliberate action to exclude competitors takes various forms. Firms producing or selling the same good may combine, or a competitor may be subject to a takeover bid. Monopolies are often formed in the sale of services. Trade unions are primarily combinations of workers formed with the object of obtaining higher wages (see chapter 7). Certain professions, such as medicine and the law, have their own associations which regulate qualifications for entry, professional conduct, and often the fees to be charged.

Some practices designed to exclude competitors are highly questionable – vicious temporary price-cutting, agreements in submitting tenders, intimidation of rivals' customers by threats to cut off the supply of another vital product, etc.

(c) The effect of the downward-sloping demand curve on marginal revenue

Consider fig 6.13. In (a) the producer is selling under conditions of perfect competition. His marginal revenue is equal to the full price, since all units sell at this. Thus, for the fourth unit, MR is the shaded area A.

Fig 6.13   *marginal revenue under conditions of perfect and imperfect competition*

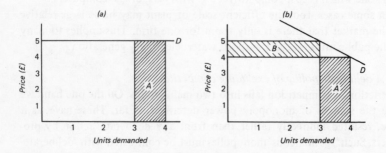

In (b), however, the producer is selling under conditions of imperfect competition. If he wishes to sell a fourth unit, he must lower his price from £5 to £4. But this lower price applies not only to the fourth unit but also to the first three units. Thus his net addition to receipts is equal to what he gets for the fourth unit, A, less what he loses on the three previous units, B. Under imperfect competition, therefore, MR is always less than price at any given output.

(d) The relationship between the costs, revenue and output of a monopolist

Let us consider another imaginary manufacturer of lawnmowers, Airborne Mowers Ltd. To simplify, we shall assume that it has identical cost curves to those of Rollermowers, but differs in that it has a patent for its particular mower, thereby excluding competitors. In short, Airborne Mowers is a monopolist. Since its output is also the market supply, the number of the mowers which it puts on the market affects the price. Thus if it produces only 20 mowers a week, each will sell at £79; if total output is increased to 90, the price drops to £44.

Airborne Mowers has the same problem as Rollermowers – to decide which output yields maximum profit. But it has an extra complication on the revenue side – as output increases, price falls for the *whole* of the output. The result can be seen in marginal receipts (table 6.4). These figures are plotted in fig 6.14.

By inspection we can see that the maximum profit is made when 65 Airborne mowers are produced each week. At this output, MR = MC (both £24), as in perfect competition. But MR is no longer equal to, but is less

Table 6.4 *Costs, receipts, and profits of Airborne Mowers* (in £)

Output per week (units)	Total	Costs Average total	Marginal	Price per unit	Receipts Total	Marginal	Profits
0	1000	–	–	–	–	–	–1000
			20			84	
10	1200	120		84	840		–360
			14			74	
20	1340	67		79	1580		240
			10			64	
30	1440	48		74	2220		780
			10			54	
40	1540	$38\frac{1}{2}$		69	2760		1220
			$13\frac{1}{2}$			44	
50	1675	$33\frac{1}{2}$		64	3200		1525
			$18\frac{1}{2}$			34	
60	1860	31		59	3540		1680
			24			24	
70	2100	30		54	3780		1680
			30			14	
80	2400	30		49	3920		1520
			39			4	
90	2790	31		44	3960		1170
			51			–6	
100	3300	33		39	3900		600
			66			–16	
110	3960	36		34	3740		–220
			84			–26	
120	4800	40		29	3480		–1320

130

Fig 6.14   *the equilibrium output of a monopolist*

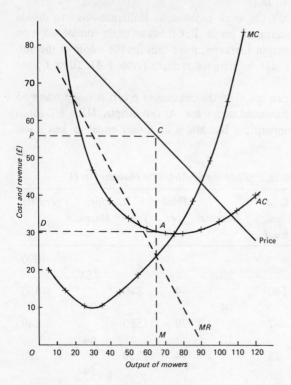

than price (£56.50). Total weekly receipts are £3,672.50 and total costs £1,982.50 (by interpolation), giving a maximum profit of £1,690.

Alternatively we can use the price and ATC at an output of 65 units to calculate profit. In fig 6.14, total receipts equal the rectangle OMCP (output times price) = 65 × £56.50; total cost equals the rectangle OMAD (output times average cost) = 65 × £30.50. Thus profit is the difference between the two: the rectangle DACP equals 65 × £26, i.e. £1,690.

(e) Monopoly and perfect competition: policy difficulties

Monopoly is an emotive word; it is often assumed that in seeking to maximise his profit the monopolist will always follow policies harmful to the consumer. The argument runs as follows.

Where there is perfect competition, output for all firms in the industry will take place where price equals MC, i.e. at OM (fig 6.15). In other words, production is carried to the point, OM, where the cost of producing an extra unit, MP, just equals the value which consumers place on that extra unit in the market.

Fig 6.15 *output under perfect competition and monopoly*

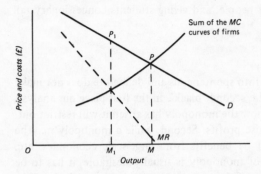

Now suppose a cartel formed from all the individual firms becomes responsible for selling the product. In order to maximise profits the cartel will sell an output where MC = MR, i.e. OM_1, at price MP_1. Thus consumers get less of the product and at a higher price than under perfect competition. In short, factors of production are not fully allocated according to the wishes of consumers.

Yet, although it may contain much truth, the argument is not infallible.

First, it rests on the assumption that the competitive industry's supply curve will be the same as the MC curve of the monopolist. But this is unlikely to be so. A single firm may be able to obtain economies of scale not open to the comparatively small firms which comprise the competitive industry. In addition its investment may be higher, since it need not fear over-capitalisation of the industry as similar investment is carried out by rival firms.

It is probable; therefore, that the monopolist will, at the relevant market output, have lower costs than firms producing under perfectly competitive conditions. Indeed, even though the monopolist is maximising profits, the consumer may obtain more of the product and at a lower price than under perfect competition.

Second, the argument ignores influences on the growth of firms over time, especially investment in research and innovation. Thus we have to ask whether firms are more likely to spend on research and innovate if by being given monopoly powers they can be assured of the rewards. In short, is monopoly more conducive to growth than perfect competition? We cannot develop the argument here, but the mere existence of the Patent Act suggests that there is some truth in it. On the other hand there have been instances where monopolies have bought up patents so that they would *not* be developed in competition with them.

Third, if a monopolist can keep separate the parts of his market where elasticities of demand differ, he may, by charging different prices, supply certain clients who would be ruled out by a single price, e.g. by charging lower surgery fees to poor people, and giving students concessionary rail fares.

(f) The control of monopoly

The division of monopolies into spontaneous and deliberate does not make the first group 'white' or the second 'black'. In the first place our analysis has shown that no matter how the monopoly has arisen it will restrict output if its aim is to maximise profits. Second, while a monopoly may be 'deliberate' there may still be benefits from large-scale economies, etc. Thus, while some control of monopoly is usually desirable, it has to be applied according to the facts of the case, its benefits being weighed against its possible economic and social disadvantages – restriction of output, waste of resources in maintaining the monopoly position (e.g. by advertising), lack of enterprise through the absence of competition, exertion of political pressure to secure narrow ends (e.g. by trade unions), and a redistribution of wealth from consumers to the monopolist.

As a result monopolies in the UK are regulated rather than prohibited. Yet any policy faces difficulties. An exact assessment of the public benefits and disadvantages resulting from a monopoly is impossible. Very often, too, the decision as to whether a monopoly is useful or anti-social depends on circumstances and therefore varies from one period to another (note the fostering of monopolies in the depression of the 1930s). Moreover, if legislation is proposed the term 'unfair competition' has to be closely defined in rigid legal terms, whereas for purposes of control it really requires an elastic interpretation based on economic issues. Last, government policy in another field may affect a possible monopoly situation. Thus tariff protection, by restricting competition from abroad, fosters monopolies in the home market.

Broadly speaking, policy can take three main forms:

(i) State ownership

When it is important not to destroy the advantages of a monopoly, the problem may best be solved by the state's taking it over completely; the public then appears to be effectively protected. Without the incentive of the profit motive there should be no tendency for state-owned monopolies to seek high profits. Should, however, such profits be made, they would eventually be passed on to the public in lower prices and reduced taxation.

In practice, however, profits may be masked by inefficiency in operation. Consequently provision must be made for the prices charged to be examined by an independent council and for efficiency checks to be carried out by independent experts.

(ii) *Legislation and administrative machinery to regulate monopolies*
This method is usually employed when it is desired to retain monopolies
because of their benefits but to leave them under private ownership.

The Monopolies and Restrictive Practices Act 1948 (since amended) set
up a Monopolies Commission to investigate monopoly situations. Upon
the commission's report, a ministerial order could declare certain practices
illegal. Subjects investigated have included the supply of electric lamps,
household detergents, colour film, wallpaper, drugs, breakfast cereals,
bricks and duplicating equipment; tendering practices by builders in the
Greater London Area; collective discrimination; and restrictive practices in
the professions.

(iii) *Breaking up or prohibition of the monopoly*
Where the monopoly is, on balance, detrimental to consumers, policy can
take the form of breaking it up or prohibiting it by legislation. Thus the
state could reduce the period for which patents are granted or make their
renewal more difficult. Alternatively it could outlaw attempts to eliminate
competition, whether by unfair practices, the formation of cartels or
restrictive agreements. Total prohibition was the policy at one time
followed in the U.S.A.

In the UK an investigation by the Monopolies Commission led to the
Restrictive Trade Practices Act 1956. This (1) allowed manufacturers and
traders to enforce *individual* resale price maintenance through the ordinary
civil courts; (2) banned the *collective* enforcement of resale price maintenance through such practices as private courts, stop lists and boycotts;
(3) required other restrictive pacts, such as common-price and level tendering, to be registered with a new Registrar of Restrictive Trading Agreements,
appointed by the crown; and (3) set up a new Restrictive Practices Court.
The court sits as three-member tribunals, each consisting of at least one
judge and two lay members; for a practice to be allowed it must be justified
as being 'in the public interest' according to one of seven closely defined
'gateways'. The tribunal's decision is made on a majority basis.

But the 1956 act still permitted individual suppliers to enforce resale
price maintenance for their own products. This was amended by the
Resale Prices Act 1964, which made minimum-resale-price maintenance
illegal, except for goods approved by the court. For such approval to be
granted, the resulting benefits to consumers must outweigh any detriments.

The Monopolies and Mergers Act 1965 strengthened and extended the
legislation on monopolies. A merger or proposed merger can be referred
to the Monopolies Commission where it would lead to a monopoly or
would increase the power of an existing monopoly. The act also increased
the government's powers to enforce the findings of the commission (for
example, by allowing it to prohibit mergers or dissolve an undesirable
monopoly).

The Fair Trading Act 1973 introduced a new concept with regard to monopoly and consumer protection. Unlike the earlier Monopolies Acts, whose primary concern was whether monopolies might be harmful to economic efficiency, and not in the public interest for that reason, the object of this new act was stated to be to 'strengthen the machinery of promoting competition'. The act:

(i)   created an Office of Fair Trading under a Director-General. Not only did the Director-General take over the functions of the Registrar of Restrictive Trading Agreements, but he now also has the responsibility for discovering probable monopoly situations or uncompetitive practices. Thus the Office of Fair Trading provides ministers with information and advice on consumer protection, monopoly, mergers and restrictive practices.

(ii) empowered the renamed Monopolies and Mergers Commission to investigate local as well as national monopolies and extended its powers of enquiry to the nationalised industries and even to restrictive labour practices (though with limited follow-up powers).

(iii) reduced and criterion for a monopoly situation to a one-quarter (minimum) market share.

PART III
FACTORS AND THEIR
REWARDS

THE DETERMINATION
OF FACTOR REWARDS

7.1 INTRODUCTION

(a) Sharing the national 'cake'

Factors of production co-operate together to produce the national product. Each of these factors is owned by somebody. How much of the cake each individual in the country obtains depends upon (i) how much of the factors he owns, and (ii) the reward each factor receives.

Differences in individual incomes, therefore, depend upon both inequalities of ownership and inequalities in earnings. It is the latter which are the subject of this chapter.

(b) Factor rewards in a given industry, occupation or district

Here we are concerned solely with the reward to factors in a given industry, occupation or district. That is, we examine how the price of a factor service is determined in a particular market. Analysis by ordinary demand and supply curves is therefore possible. (Later, [in chapter 14], when we consider the economy as a whole, it is necessary to speak of labour, wages, capital, investment and the rate of interest in broad terms and substitute a general approach for this particular analysis.)

7.2 THE THEORETICAL DETERMINATION OF FACTOR REWARDS

The theory which follows applies to all resources. However, it is usually illustrated in terms of labour and the wage-rate, and we shall adopt this practice.

The wage-rate is the price of labour and, like other prices, it is determined in a free market by demand and supply.

(a) Demand

The demand for labour is made up of the individual demands of all the firms using it. It is a *derived demand* in that it depends upon the sale of the product it makes. The actual price which a firm is willing to pay for a worker depends upon the addition to receipts which will result. We can be more precise by developing our analysis of the law of diminishing returns. Let us assume that (i) there is perfect competition in the market where the product is sold, and (ii) there is perfect competition in buying labour – each firm is so small that it cannot, by varying its demand, alter the wage-rate which it has to pay.

The analysis of the law of diminishing returns was conducted in terms of physical yields – cwts of potatoes. But when engaging labour, the firm is more interested in what the product sells for. What it asks, therefore, is how much total receipts will increase if an additional worker is employed. The value of this extra contribution is known as the *marginal revenue product* (MRP).

The MRP depends not only on the marginal physical product, but also on the price at which the product sells. Under perfect competition, the producer can sell any quantity at a given price. Hence the MRP is equal to the marginal physical product times the price of the product. Thus, in table 6.1, by taking the marginal physical products and assuming that potatoes sell at £10 per cwt, we can arrive at the MRP. For example, when 2 labourers are employed the total physical product is 8 cwt, which at £10 a cwt yields a total revenue of £80, and so on. (See p. 107.)

The farmer in our example will employ an extra worker so long as the MRP exceeds the cost, that is, the wage-rate. Thus, if the wage-rate were £65 per week, he would engage 6 workers because the value of the product of the sixth man was £65, and this just covered his wages. If fewer men, say 5, were employed, he could add more to receipts than to costs by taking on another worker, for the MRP of £75 would exceed the wage-rate (£65). On the other hand, if 7 men were employed, the farmer would be paying the seventh man £5 more than he contributed to receipts.

Of course it might be questioned whether the firm can always estimate the MRP of a factor of production. Thus, with certain workers, such as clerks, teachers and policemen, there is no definite physical product. How then can their marginal physical product, and thus the marginal revenue product, be measured? The answer is simply that it cannot be – but that does not alter the fact that, in practice, a firm behaving rationally and not 'empire-building' does proceed to engage workers as though it can so estimate.

The MRP at different wage-rates, therefore, gives the demand curve of the individual firm for labour (fig 7.1). The *industry's demand curve* is the sum of the demands of the individual firms (curve D, fig 7.2). This would be a simple horizontal addition if the price of the product remained unchanged. But it is much more realistic to assume that, as firms engage more labour, the extra output will lead to a fall in the price of the product. The

Fig 7.1 *the firm's demand curve for labour*

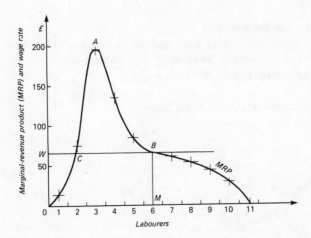

result will be that the industry's demand curve for a factor will fall more steeply than the curve obtained by a straightforward addition of firms' marginal-revenue-product curves.

(b) Supply
The supply of labour will depend upon:

(i) *The response of existing labour to a higher wage rate*
In the short period, an industry may find that a wage increase may result in *less* labour being supplied, the higher income enabling workers to enjoy more leisure, as in coal-mining. In the long period, however, higher wages should attract labour from other industries, occupations or localities, so that the long-period supply curve follows the shape of the S curve in fig 7.2.

(ii) *The cost of attracting workers from alternative uses or localities*
In the long period, a higher wage will attract labour from other industries and occupations. The extent to which a given wage increase attracts workers depends upon the elasticity of demand for the products in these alternative sources. If demand is inelastic, higher wages can be offered to hold on to labour, and thus the supply of labour will expand little in response to the wage rise (see p. 125).

(iii) *The mobility of labour*
In the theoretical long period, a higher wage rate should attract labour from alternative uses or localities. But, because labour experiences particu-

140

lar difficulties in moving, the 'long period' is delayed indefinitely (see chapter 8).

(c) Demand, supply, and the wage-rate

The reward of a factor, in this case the wage-rate, is determined by the interaction of demand and supply. Thus, in fig 7.2, with demand curve D and supply curve S the wage rate is OW.

Fig 7.2 *the determination of the price of a factor*

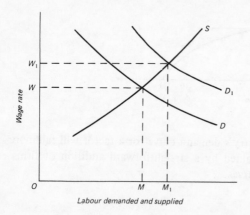

The wage-rate can rise through an increase in the MRP or a decrease in the supply of labour to the market. The MRP can rise through an increase in physical productivity or through a higher selling price of the product. Both would lead to a shift in the demand curve to the right, say from D to D_1 (fig 7.2). As a result, the wage rate rises to OW_1 and the number of men employed increases from OM to OM_1. Higher labour productivity leads to higher employment, other things being equal. Similarly, a decrease in the supply of labour to a particular industry, e.g. because of the attraction of other industries, would have the effect of raising the wage-rate, but with fewer unemployed.

(d) The effect of imperfect competition on factor rewards

The above discussion assumed that there was perfect competition both in the sale of the product and in engaging factors of production. But in the real world such competition may not exist. If, for instance, the firm is selling its product under imperfect competition, the price received will fall as output increases. This means that the marginal revenue product of an extra labourer will be less than the marginal physical product multiplied by its price, since the lower price applies to all previous units produced.

Similarly, a firm may be the only employer of a factor in a locality, so that, as this firm demands more, the factor price rises not only for the additional factor but for all previous factors. Thus the marginal cost of employing such factors is higher than their market price. In both instances the demand for the factor will be less than it would have been had competition prevailed.

Finally trade unions may exert a monopoly power in the sale of labour, a subject discussed in chapter 8.

LABOUR AND WAGES

8.1 THE NATURE OF THE LABOUR FORCE

(a) Special features of labour

Labour is the effort, both physical and mental, made by human beings in production. It is the 'human' element which is important.

Because people have feelings and emotion their response to economic forces is different from that of machines. First, whereas a machine which proves profitable can be reproduced fairly easily and quickly, the overall supply of labour does not depend upon its earnings. Other factors are more important in deciding how many children parents have (see p. 144). Second, the effort of labour is not determined solely by the reward offered. The method of payment may affect effort, while raising wages may result in less work being offered. Above all, a contented worker will produce more than an unhappy one; thus job satisfaction or loyalty to a firm, rather than a high rate of pay, may be decisive in inducing an employee to work overtime. Third, labour does not move readily, either occupationally or geographically, in response to the offer of a higher reward. Often such 'immobility' results from strong human contacts. Fourth, workers can combine together in trade unions. Finally, if unemployed for long periods, workers deteriorate physically and mentally.

Both firms and government must have policies which take account of these special characteristics. Training schemes are essential to improve the skill of workers and thus their productivity. Firms must pay particular attention to psychological and social factors in an effort to secure a contented labour force. Furthermore, they must endeavour to co-operate with the workers' trade-union representatives. Above all, firms have to comply with the constraints imposed by government policy.

The government is vitally concerned with labour. It lays down the requirements of the employment contract, supervises working conditions and prescribes the terms under which a worker may be dismissed. Moreover, it exerts pressure in wage negotiations in order to avoid inflationary wage increases. Most important, it pursues a variety of policies aimed at securing a high and stable level of employment.

This chapter examines these special features, though postponing the problem of full employment to chapter 18.

(b) The supply of labour

The total supply of labour in an economy depends upon:

(i) *The size of population*

The size of the population sets an obvious limit to the total supply of labour. But while it is influenced by economic factors, e.g. through the birth rate and immigration, it is doubtful, especially in more advanced economies, whether economic factors are of paramount importance.

(ii) *The proportion of the population which works*

The working population, the proportion of the population which forms the labour force, is determined chiefly by age distribution, social institutions and customs, the participation rate of married women and the wages offered, and to a lesser extent by the numbers who can live on unearned incomes.

(iii) *The amount of work offered by each individual labourer*

Higher rates of pay usually induce a person to work overtime, the increased reward encouraging him to substitute work for leisure. But this is not always so. A higher wage-rate enables the worker to maintain his existing material standard of living with less work, and he may prefer extra leisure to more goods.

Nevertheless, as we shall see, more significant than the overall supply of labour are the obstacles to mobility which divide up the labour market.

8.2 THE DETERMINATION OF THE RATE OF PAY

(a) Methods of rewarding labour

Some people are self-employed – window-cleaners, plumbers, solicitors, etc. As such they are really entrepreneurs, securing the rewards when demand is high but accepting the risks of working for a low return. Nevertheless, most workers contract out of risk, accepting a wage which is received whether or not the product of their labour is sold – although some element of risk-bearing may be incorporated in the wage agreement, e.g. by commission payments, bonus schemes and profit-sharing arrangements.

In what follows, reference will be mainly to the wage-rate – the sum of money which an employer contracts to pay a worker in return for services rendered. This definition includes salaries as well as wages, and makes no distinction between time- and piece-rates.

Earnings are what the worker actually receives in his pay-packet (his 'take-home' pay) *plus* deductions which have been made for insurance, income tax, superannuation, etc. In practice earnings over a period often exceed the agreed wage-rate, additions being received for overtime working, piece-rates and bonus payments.

Where the nature of the work allows workers to be paid on a piece-rate basis as an alternative to time-rates, the firm has to consider their respective merits.

(i) *Time-rates*
Time rates are more satisfactory than piece-rates where:
(1) a high quality of work is essential, e.g. in computer programming;
(2) the work cannot be speeded up, e.g. in bus-driving and milking cows;
(3) there is no standard type of work, e.g. in car repairs;
(4) care has to be taken of delicate machinery, e.g. in hospital medical tests;
(5) output cannot be easily measured, e.g. in teaching and nursing;
(6) working long hours may undermine health, e.g. in laundry work;
(7) the labour is by nature a fixed factor which has to be engaged whatever the output, e.g. clerical and selling staff;
(8) periods of temporary idleness necessarily occur, e.g. in repair work.

On the other hand, time-rates have certain disadvantages:
(1) There is a lack of incentive for better workers.
(2) Supervision of workers is usually necessary.
(3) Agreements can be undermined by working to rule and 'go-slow' tactics.

(ii) *Piece-rates*
Where output is both measurable and more or less proportionate to the amount of effort expended, piece-rates are possible. It is not essential that each individual worker's output can be measured exactly. So long as the output of his group can be assessed he can share in the group's earnings.

The advantages of piece-rates are:
(1) Effort is stimulated.
(2) The more efficient workers obtain higher rewards.
(3) The need for constant supervision and irksome time-keeping is eliminated.
(4) Interest is added to dull, routine work.
(5) Workers can proceed at their own pace.

(6) A team spirit is developed where workers operate in small groups.

(7) Workers are encouraged to suggest methods of improving production.

(8) The employer's costing calculations are simplified.

(9) Output is increased, and the more intensive use of capital equipment spreads overheads.

We see, therefore, that piece-rates have advantages for both employee and employer. Moreover, the lower prices which result benefit the community as a whole. Nevertheless, for the following reasons they are often disliked by trade unions:

(1) Workers may over-exert themselves.

(2) Where piece-rates have to be varied according to local conditions or different circumstances, e.g. capital per employee, negotiations for a national wage-rate are difficult.

(3) Variations in piece-rates from one place to another undermine union solidarity.

(4) The union may lose control over the supply of labour, and this makes it difficult to take strike action or to apportion work in periods of unemployment.

(5) Piece rates are subject to misunderstanding, e.g. an employer who instals a better machine may be accused of cutting the rate if he does not attribute all the increased output to the effort of labour.

(6) Workers may resist being shifted from tasks in which they have acquired dexterity (and which therefore produce high piece earnings) even though the current needs of the factory organisation require such a transfer. Thus employers find that piece-rates lead to a loss of control over their employees, and many prefer to pay high time-rates to avoid this.

(iii) *Combined time- and piece-rates*

When deciding the basis of the wage-rate, both employees and employers want certain guarantees. Workers have a minimum standard of living to maintain, and they desire protection against variations in output which lie outside their control, e.g. weather conditions. On the other hand, employers providing expensive equipment must ensure that it is used for a minimum period of time. Thus piece-rates are usually incorporated in a wider contract which provides for some basic wage and a stipulated minimum number of hours.

(b) The wage-rate

In chapter 7 it was shown how, under conditions of perfect competition, demand and supply determine the wage-rate. Take the wages of plasterers, for instance. The demand for plasterers depends upon the price at which houses sell (a derived demand) and the productivity of plasterers. The supply of plasterers is the number offering their services at different wage-rates. This will vary with the length of time under consideration. But in the long period more will be forthcoming the higher the wage-rate, since they will be attracted from lower-paid areas or occupations.

For example, if the conditions of demand and supply are different in different parts of the country, the wages of plasterers will differ. If there were perfect geographical mobility, plasterers would move from low-wage districts to high-wage districts, until eventually a common equilibrium wage-rate would be established. Similarly, where different wage-rates existed for different occupations, perfect occupational mobility would eventually eliminate these differences.

In practice, geographical and occupational mobility are not perfect, so that differences in wage-rates persist. A typist earns more in London than in Norwich; a doctor earns more than a docker. In short, immobilities result in the labour market's being divided into a number of separate smaller markets according to locality and occupation. It is necessary, therefore, to examine the obstacles to mobility in more detail.

(c) Obstacles to the mobility of labour
A worker may be required (i) to shift his job from one industry to another, (ii) to change his occupation, or (iii) to move his home to a different district. Often conditions dictate that all three types of change take place at the same time, but this is not necessarily so. Each presents its own obstacles to changing jobs, and gives rise to the 'immobility of labour'.

(i) *Obstacles between industries*
Provided that it does not involve a change of occupation or district, a worker can usually move his job from one industry to another fairly easily. Clerks, typists, storemen, lorry-drivers and porters, for example, are found in most industries. But middle-aged and older workers may experience difficulty. Prejudice or tradition in certain industries may also prove to be obstacles. Women, for instance, would find it difficult to become taxi-drivers in London. Moreover, loyalty to a firm may prevent a worker from looking elsewhere even though he has suffered a cut in wages (obviously this does not apply if he is unemployed).

(ii) *Obstacles to a change of occupation*
In changing occupations there may be obstacles to entering a new one.
  (1) A high natural ability is required in certain occupations.
  (2) Training may be costly and take time.
  (3) Stringent conditions are sometimes prescribed by trade unions and professional associations.
  (4) The new job may be repugnant; and, equally, some occupations,

e.g. the church, art and acting, are so fulfilling that workers are not drawn into other occupations by the offer of higher wage-rates.

(5) Workers may be too old to learn new jobs.

(6) Workers may prefer to remain unemployed or in alternative occupations rather than accept a wage below a recognised minimum.

(7) In spite of legislation, there is still discrimination on account of sex, colour, social class or religion.

(8) Workers may be ignorant of wage-rates and opportunities in other occupations.

Of the above, the greatest obstacle to occupational mobility is natural ability. In this respect it should be noted that there can be more mobility between occupations, e.g. storeman and clerk, requiring the same level of innate ability than between, for example, doctors and dockers, where there are marked differences in the natural ability and training required. The first is sometimes termed 'horizontal' occupational mobility; the second, where there are non-competing groups of workers is called 'vertical' mobility.

(iii) *Obstacles to a change of district*

When it comes to moving from one part of the country to another, workers have to overcome both real and psychological obstacles. These include: the costs of moving; the difficulty of securing accommodation elsewhere on comparable terms, particularly for council and rent-controlled tenants; social ties involving friends, clubs, church, etc.; family ties, such as children's education; imperfect knowledge of vacancies or wages paid in other localities; and prejudice against certain parts of the country (people at present generally prefer to live in the south-east rather than in the industrial north).

Such immobility of labour means that wage-rates can often be more easily explained by supply conditions rather than by demand. Even if there is competition between employers, differences in supply produce differences in the wage-rates between occupations, and between localities even for the same occupation. Thus solicitors earn more than their clerks because, on the demand side, the services of solicitors are valued more highly and, on the supply side, the supply of solicitors is small compared with clerks, for more natural ability and longer training are required.

Immobility is also one of the major causes of unemployment, and in chapter 19 we consider some of the ways in which the government tries to reduce occupational and geographical immobility.

8.3 TRADE UNIONS AND COLLECTIVE BARGAINING

(a) The determination of the conditions of employment in the real world

While demand and supply are the underlying determinants of an occupation's basic wage-rate, the actual wage and the conditions of employment are strongly influenced by government intervention, imperfect competition in the labour market and the trade-union activity.

The government influences the wage-rate through: (i) its minimum-wage regulations in certain industries (see p. 150); (ii) the legal protection it affords to workers with regard to conditions of work, e.g. stipulating a written statement of the conditions of employment, prohibiting discrimination on account of sex or race, protecting employees against unfair dismissal, providing for redundancy payments and regulating conditions for health and safety at work; and (iii) guidelines for wage settlements which it may lay down from time to time in its efforts to combat inflation (see chapter 20).

Imperfection in the labour market arises where one firm is the major employer in a locality (see above). But mainly it is due to trade unions, which (through the closed shop) can establish what is virtually a monopoly in the supply of a given type of labour. We therefore analyse the economic background to trade-union activity with reference to its strength in negotiating wage increases.

(b) Objectives of trade-union activity

Trade unions have many functions, the most important of which are: (i) providing educational, social and legal benefits for members; (ii) improving standards of work; (iii) obtaining pay increases; and (iv) co-operating with governments in order to secure a workable economic policy and to improve working and living conditions generally. The remainder of this chapter is concerned with (iii).

(c) The process of collective bargaining

Collective bargaining is the settlement of conditions of employment by employers negotiating with the workers' trade unions. For its smooth working, certain conditions should be fulfilled. First, it must be pursued with good sense on both sides. This is enhanced where the industry has a tradition of good labour relations and where there is some accepted objective measure to which wage-rates can be linked (e.g. the Index of Retail Prices, wage-rates paid in similar trades, the level of profits in the industry). Second, both sides should be represented by strong organisations. Where all employers are linked in an association, there is no fear of outsiders stealing a march by negotiating independent wage bargains, while, if the union can speak for all its members, employers know an agreement will be honoured. Unofficial stoppages damage the union's reputation, and to avoid them there must be regular contact between employer and union and prompt investigation of grievances on the shop-floor. Third, there must be an understood procedure for settling disputes. While this must not be so prolonged as to fray patience, it should exhaust all possibilities of reaching agreement before a strike or lock-out is called.

In short the procedure of collective bargaining covers (i) negotiation and (ii) the settlement of disputes.

(i) *Negotiation*

Broadly speaking the machinery for negotiation falls into three categories:

(1) VOLUNTARY NEGOTIATION

Generally the government has left it to the unions and employers' organisations to work out their own procedures, and today voluntary machinery covers 65% of the insured workers of Great Britain. Because union organisation varies, the recognised procedure differs between industries and trades. Indeed it may contain no provision for arbitration when a wage-claim is rejected, as in the engineering and shipbuilding industries.

(2) JOINT INDUSTRIAL COUNCILS

Most industries have some national joint council or committee which, without outside assistance, thrashes out agreements. Usually it follows the system of Joint Industrial Councils, composed of representatives of employers and workers in the industry. These consider regularly such matters as the better use of the practical knowledge and experience of the workpeople, general principles governing the conditions of employment, means of ensuring workers the greatest possible security of earnings and employment, methods of fixing and adjusting earnings, technical education and training, industrial research, improvement of processes and proposed legislation affecting the industry. Although Joint Industrial Councils are sponsored by the government, they are not forced upon any industry, and some important industries, such as iron and steel, engineering, shipbuilding and cotton, which had already developed their own procedure for negotiation, have not formed Joint Industrial Councils. Nevertheless, in 1979 there were some 400 Joint Industrial Councils or bodies of similar character.

(3) WAGES COUNCILS

In some industries and trades where the organisation of workers or employers or both is either non-existent or ineffective, the government has had to intervene. This started in 1909 when Trade Boards were set up to fix minimum time- and piece-rates for the 'sweated' trades, such as bespoke tailoring, where home-workers were being paid exceptionally low wages. Subsequently these boards were increased in number, and in 1945 were re-named Wages Councils and given extended powers. In 1979 there were 43 such Wages Councils, covering the clothing, textile, food-and-drink and metalware industries, together with distribution, catering, road haulage and other services. The councils are appointed by the Secretary of State for Employment and are each composed of equal numbers of employer and worker representatives, together with not more than three independent members. Their task is to fix minimum remuneration and conditions regarding holidays, and a minimum week, which, if the minister approves, become the subject of a Wage Regulation Order, enforceable by law. In addition they may advise the minister on problems affecting labour in the industry.

In agriculture, wages are fixed by machinery similar to the Wages Council system. Thus about 15% of insured workers are covered by schemes of statutory wage regulation, as opposed to the 65% for whom negotiation is on a voluntary basis.

(ii) *Settlement of disputes*
Where the negotiating machinery fails to produce an agreement, it is a help if agreed procedures exist for ending the deadlock. Three methods can be employed: conciliation, arbitration or special inquiry.

(1) CONCILIATION
In 1974 the Secretary of State for Employment set up an *independent* Advisory Conciliation and Arbitration Service (ACAS), controlled by a council whose members are experienced in industrial relations. When efforts to obtain settlement of a dispute through normal procedures have failed, ACAS can provide conciliation if the parties concerned agree.

(2) ARBITRATION
ACAS can, at the joint request of the parties to a dispute, appoint single arbitrators or boards of arbitration chosen from a register of people experienced in industrial relations to determine differences on the basis of agreed terms of reference.

Alternatively the Terms and Conditions of Employment Act 1959 allows claims that a particular employer is not observing the terms or conditions of employment established for the industry to be referred compulsorily to an industrial court for a legally binding award.

(3) INQUIRY AND INVESTIGATION
The Secretary of State for Employment has legal power to inquire into the causes and circumstances of any trade dispute and, if he thinks fit, to appoint a court of inquiry with power to call for evidence. Such action, however, is chiefly a means of informing parliament and the public of the facts and causes of a major dispute, and is taken only when no agreed settlement seems possible.

The minister's power of inquiry also allows for less formal action, by way of setting up committees of investigation, when the public interest is not so general.

Neither a court of inquiry nor a committee of investigation is a conciliation or arbitration body, but both may make recommendations upon which a reasonable settlement of a dispute can be based.

(d) The extent to which trade unions can secure wage increases

This brings us to the questions of how and to what extent unions can secure increases in wage-rates by collective bargaining. We shall assume that the trade union is a 'closed shop' with 100% membership, making it virtually a monopolist in selling its particular type of labour.

Broadly speaking there are three ways in which a trade union can secure a wage increase:

(i) *It can support measures which will increase the demand for labour*

An increase in the demand for labour will come about if the MRP curve rises, either through an improvement in the physical productivity of the workers or through an increase in the price of the product. Thus the National Union of Mineworkers not only supports the National Coal Board's exhortation to miners to improve output per man-shift, but backs the campaign advertising the advantages of solid fuel for central heating.

Fig 8.1 *the effect on the wage-rate of a change in marginal revenue productivity*

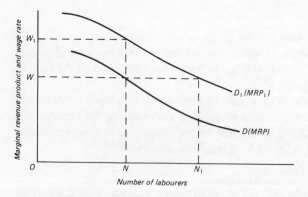

The situation is illustrated in fig 8.1. As marginal revenue productivity rises from MRP to MRP_1, wages of existing workers, ON, rise from OW to OW_1. Alternatively, if there were unemployment, extra men, NN_1, could be employed at the previous wage-rate.

(ii) *It can restrict the supply of labour, allowing members to compete freely in fixing remuneration with employers*

Where a trade union or professional association can limit entry it may also stipulate a minimum wage-rate or scale of charges. But it need not do so. The supply of plumbers and electricians, for instance, is restricted by apprenticeship regulations, but many work on their own account and *negotiate* their own rewards. Similarly, solicitors, doctors, surgeons, accountants and surveyors are restricted by the necessary professional qualifications, but suggested scale fees are not rigidly charged.

We can therefore analyse this method of securing a wage increase by the simple demand-and-supply approach (fig 8.2). If the trade union reduces the supply of workers in an occupation from S to S_1, the wage-rate rises from OW to OW_1.

Fig 8.2 *the effect on the wage-rate of trade-union restriction of the supply of labour*

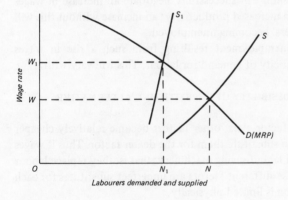

(iii) *It can fix a minimum wage rate*

Where wages are raised by restricting entry, the trade union does not have to worry about unemployed members. It works simply on the principle that, assuming demand remains unchanged, greater scarcity leads to a higher reward.

Most trade unions, however, are faced with a more difficult problem. While they may secure higher wage-rates for their members, their success may be double-edged if, as a result, many members are sacked. What we really have to ask, therefore, is: *Under what conditions can a trade union obtain higher wages for its members without decreasing the numbers employed?*

Once again we have to consider conditions of competition.

154

(i) *Perfect competition in both selling the product and buying labour*

In the short period, even if there is perfect competition, a firm may be making super-normal profits. Here a strong trade union could, by threatening to withhold all its labour, force the employer to increase wages to the point where his super-normal profits disappear.

But this could not be permanent. The long-period equilibrium position is one in which there are no super-normal profits and the wage-rate is equal to the MRP. A higher wage will represent a rise in costs. Some employers will now be forced out of business (see p. 121) and remaining firms will have to reduce their demand for labour until once again the wage-rate is equal to the MRP. Thus in fig 8.2 we will assume that OW is the original wage-rate fixed by competition and ON the number of men employed – the trade-union membership. Suppose the trade union stipulates a minimum wage of OW_1. In the long period employment will then be reduced to ON_1. Given a downward-sloping MRP curve, this will always be true. Where there is perfect competition both in selling the product and in buying labour, a trade union can successfully negotiate an increase in wages only if there has been increased productivity: an increase without this will merely lead to members' becoming unemployed.

The amount of unemployment resulting from such a rise in wages depends upon the elasticity of demand for labour. This will vary with:

(1) THE PHYSICAL POSSIBILITY OF SUBSTITUTING ALTERNATIVE FACTORS

As the price of one factor rises, other factors become relatively cheaper and the tendency is to substitute them for the dearer factor. Thus if wages rise firms try to instal labour-saving machinery; that is, they replace labour by capital. But because different factors are imperfect substitutes for each other, such substitution is limited physically.

Fig 8.3 *possibility of substitution between labour and capital*

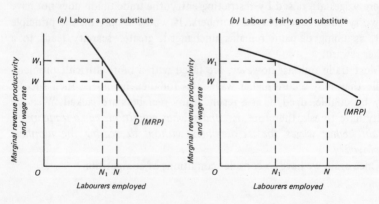

The degree to which substitution is possible is shown by the slope of the marginal productivity curve. Where labour is added to another factor, but is a poor substitute for it, marginal productivity falls steeply; where it is a fairly good substitute, marginal productivity falls more gently. Thus in fig 8.3a labour is not a good substitute for the fixed-factor capital, and marginal revenue productivity falls steeply. Demand for labour is therefore inelastic, and a wage rise of WW_1 leads to only NN_1 men becoming unemployed. Compare this with fig 8.3b, where labour and capital are better substitutes. Here the same wage fall leads to much more unemployment.

It should be noted that, since the possibility of substitution increases over time, the longer the period under consideration the greater will be the change in the labour force.

(2) THE ELASTICITY OF SUPPLY OF ALTERNATIVE FACTORS

Under conditions of perfect competition the cost of a factor to an individual firm will not rise as the firm's demand for that factor increases (see p. 121). But when we are analysing a rise in the wage-rate of the workers of an *industry* we must recognise that the whole industry will now be demanding the alternative factors in order to substitute them for labour. This increased demand will raise the price of the alternative factors, again limiting the extent to which substitution is carried out. Thus if the supply of the alternative factor is perfectly elastic, only the physical considerations referred to above will affect the demand for it; if, on the other hand, supply is inelastic, it is likely that the quick rise in its price will soon make it uneconomic to substitute it for labour.

(3) THE PROPORTION OF LABOUR COSTS TO TOTAL COSTS

The proportion of labour costs to total costs has two effects. First, if labour costs form only a small percentage of total costs, demand for labour will tend to be inelastic, for there is less urgency in seeking substitutes (see p. 71). Second, if labour costs form a small percentage of total costs, as in steel production, a rise in wages will produce only a small movement to the left of the supply curve of the product. The opposite applies in each case.

(4) THE ELASTICITY OF DEMAND FOR THE FINAL PRODUCT

A rise in the wage-rate shifts the supply curve of the product to the left. Hence the market price of the good rises. We have to ask, therefore, how much demand for the good will contract as a result. The answer depends upon the elasticity of demand.

If demand is elastic, D_{el} in fig 8.4, the quantity of the good demanded will contract considerably, from OM to OM_1. This will mean a large reduction in the numbers employed. On the other hand, if demand is in-

Fig 8.4 *the extent to which demand for the product contracts as a result of a wage increase*

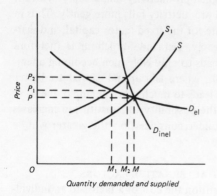

Quantity demanded and supplied

elastic, D_{inel}, there will be no great contraction – only to OM_2. Here people are willing to pay a higher price for the good, OP_2, and this will cover the increase in wages.

Elasticity of demand depends mainly on the availability of substitutes. Thus demand in export markets is usually more elastic than in the home market, for with the former there are often many competing alternative sources of supply from foreign firms. Consequently, if an industry sells a high percentage of its output abroad, e.g. scientific instruments and machine-tools, the trade union is limited in its ability to secure wage increases.

(ii) *Imperfect competition*

If there is imperfect competition in selling the product or in hiring labour, the firm is likely to be making super-normal profits. Here it may be possible for the trade union to wring increased wages from the employer without loss of employment. Since it is a monopolist in the supply of labour, the union can insist that the firm shall employ *all* or none of its members at the new wage-rate. Thus the firm may be forced to employ workers beyond the point where MRP = MC. The difference would come from super-normal profits, with the firm working on the principle that 'half a loaf is better than no bread'.

In these circumstances there is a whole range of possible wage-rates between the minimum which workers will accept and the maximum which employers are prepared to give rather than lose all their labour. The success of the trade union will depend, therefore, upon (1) the extent to which it can maintain its monopoly position by preventing employers from engaging blacklegs – non-union workers, or other substitute labour – and (2) the bargaining ability of its leaders relative to that of the employers. On the one side the union leaders have to estimate how high they can push the wage-rate without employers' allowing a strike to take place; on the other the employers must judge the lowest rate acceptable without a strike. As each is by no means certain of the other's strength, bluff will play a large part in the negotiations. Such factors as a large order-book for the firm's products, costly capital equipment's standing idle, or a wealthy strike fund, will obviously strengthen the union's hand. Should a strike actually take place, it is usually because of misjudgment by one side; it is doubtful whether either really gains in the long run by strike action. Thus the strike is a form of 'blood-letting', allowing one or both sides to re-assess the position before further negotiations take place.

CAPITAL, LAND AND ENTREPRENEURSHIP

9.1 CAPITAL

(a) What is capital?

A schoolteacher earns, say, £120 a week. She also has £520 in the National Savings Bank, yielding her £26 per annum interest (50p a week). We can say, therefore, that her total income is £120.50 a week, or £6,266 per annum; her capital assets are £520.

Thus we see that, whereas *income* is a *flow of wealth* over a *period of time, capital* is a *stock of wealth* existing at any one *moment of time.*

This broad definition of capital, however, has slightly different meanings when used by different people. The ordinary individual, when speaking of his capital, would include his money assets, holdings of securities, and house, and possibly many durable goods, such as his car, television set, cine-camera, etc. (sometimes referred to as 'consumer's capital'). The businessman would count not only his real assets (such as his factory, machinery, land and stocks of goods) but also any money reserves ('liquid capital') held in the bank, and titles to wealth (such as share certificates, tax-reserve certificates and government bonds).

But the economist considers capital chiefly as a form of wealth which contributes to production. In other words, he is concerned with capital as a *factor of production* – that is, as something real and not merely pieces of paper. It is the factory and machines, not the share certificates (the individual's entitlement to a part of the assets), which are vital to him.

This has two effects. First, in defining capital, he concentrates his attention on all producer goods and any stocks of finished consumer goods not yet in the hands of the final consumer. Second, in calculating the 'national capital', he has to be careful to avoid double-counting. Titles to capital – shares, bonds, savings certificates, National Savings, Treasury bills and other items of the national debt – must be excluded. Share certificates merely represent the factories, machinery, etc., which have already been counted. Government debt refers to few real assets, for most has been expended on shells, ships, and aircraft in previous wars. The only exception regarding titles to wealth is where a share or bond is held by a foreign national, or conversely, where a British national holds a share or bond representing an asset in a foreign country. We then have to subtract the former and add the latter when calculating national capital. Foreign shares or bonds held by British nationals, for example, can always be sold to increase our real resources.

Fig 9.1 *'capital' in the economy*

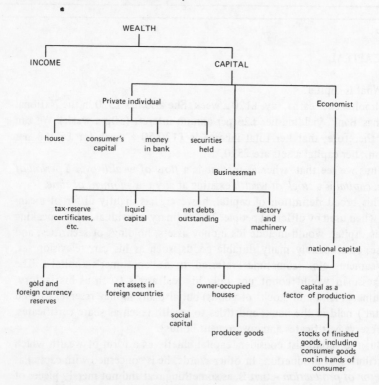

Naturally, 'social capital' (roads, schools, hospitals, municipal buildings, etc.) which belongs to the community at large is just as much capital as factories, offices, etc. And, in order to be consistent, owner-occupied houses have to be included, for they must be treated in the same way as houses owned by property companies.

(b) Capital as a factor of production

When the economist refers to 'capital', it is usually in the sense of *wealth which has been made by man for the production of further wealth*. This is because capital plays such an important part in increasing production and therefore in improving living standards. It is in this sense that the term is used from now on.

Increased production occurs because capital – tools, machines, irrigation works, communications, etc. – greatly assists people in their work. Indeed, with modern electronic equipment, machines often take over the work itself. As the use of capital increases, there are three possible gains. First, more current goods can be produced. Between 1969 and 1978 the output of agriculture, forestry and fishing increased by 13%. But over that period the number of employees in that area fell by 19%. There was thus an increased output per employee, due almost entirely to the introduction of more efficient machines. Second, instead of simply producing more current goods, people can be released to produce new goods. And, third, people can, as an alternative to more goods, enjoy increased leisure.

(c) The accumulation of capital

If capital is so important in adding to our well-being, why do we not have more of it? The answer is simply that we can accumulate capital only by postponing current consumption. In everyday language, more jam tomorrow means less jam today. The accumulation of capital represents an opportunity cost over time – consumption now or greater consumption later? A simple example will make this clear.

Suppose a peasant farmer has been tilling the ground with a primitive spade. By working 12 hours a day he can cultivate 2 acres. Obviously, if he had a plough which could be drawn by his oxen, it would help him considerably. How can he obtain it? Three ways are open to him:

  (i)   He could reduce the land he cultivates to 1½ acres, using the 3 hours saved on tilling to make the plough.
 (ii)   He could reduce his leisure and sleeping time from 12 to 8 hours, using the extra 4 hours to make the plough.
(iii)   He could decide not to consume some of the produce already harvested, exchanging it instead for the plough.

Whichever method is chosen entails some present sacrifice. With (i) and (iii) the farmer has less to eat, lowering his standard of living. With (ii) he has to go without some leisure. In short he has to draw in his belt or work harder. But the reward comes when he has the plough: with 12 hours' work a day he can now cultivate 4 acres, thereby doubling his standard of living.

One other point emerges from this illustration: the more fertile his land, the easier it is for the farmer to increase his income. If, because of the poverty of the soil, 16 hours were required to dig his 2 acres, our farmer would have found it more difficult to obtain his plough. He could not reduce his consumption below the subsistence level; nor could he go without essential sleep. Similarly, countries with extremely low living-standards are in a vicious circle which can only be broken by economic aid from richer countries or by enforced five-year plans which ruthlessly cut current consumption, as in the USSR, China and Cuba.

(d) Maintaining capital intact

Naturally our farmer will have to devote time to repairing the plough. So long as it is capable of cultivating 4 acres, we can say that capital is being 'maintained intact'. If it is replaced by a better plough which allows more acres to be cultivated, or another plough is added, capital is being 'accumulated'. Where capital is not maintained, it is being 'run down' or 'depreciated'.

In practice it is unusual for the same people to devote so much time to producing consumer goods and so much to the production of capital. Instead, production is organised by applying the principle of the division of labour – some people specialise in consumer goods and others in capital goods.

9.2 INTEREST

Investment, that is adding to capital goods or stocks, usually first involves obtaining liquid capital. Interest, expressed as a rate, is the price which has to be paid for this liquid capital. What we shall examine here is the rate of interest which has to be paid for liquid capital in a *particular* use or industry. We shall *not* discuss what determines the *general* level of interest in the economy.

The *demand for liquid capital* arises because it is necessary or advantageous to use capital in production. The farmer who sows his seed in the autumn and harvests his crop in the summer is using capital in the form of seed. Similarly, a manufacturer needs capital in the form of a factory and machines because, given sufficient demand, it is cheaper to produce in this way.

Now, as we saw when examining the farmer's decision to make a plough, the accumulation of capital can come about only by postponing present consumption. This can be done directly by the producer himself. The farmer could have obtained his seed by putting aside a part of the previous year's harvest; the manufacturer can buy his machines by retaining, rather than distributing, some of his profits. However, such retentions may be inadequate for the capital needed. In this case, funds might be borrowed from other people who have saved.

The actual demand of the farmer or manufacturer would depend upon the marginal revenue productivity of such capital. For instance, if the addition to profit which a farmer thinks will be received during the year for adding an extra ton of fertiliser costing £100 is £120, he would be willing to borrow the money for the fertiliser so long as the interest he had to pay was not more than £20 – that is, 20%. The 'marginal-revenue-productivity-of-capital' curve will show the different amounts of capital which the farmer will find it profitable to borrow at different rates of interest.

The sum of the demand curves for liquid capital from all firms in an industry gives the demand curve for the industry, though some allowance should be made for a fall in the price of the good produced by the capital equipment (see p. 138).

The *supply* of liquid funds for a particular use can only be obtained by bidding them away from alternative uses. How much has to be paid for a given quantity relative to other uses will depend upon: (i) whether lenders consider more or less risk is involved; (ii) the period of the loan – people prefer to lend for a short period rather than a long one; and (iii) the elasticity of demand for other products employing capital.

Generally speaking, however, we can expect more liquid capital to be forthcoming the higher the rate of interest offered. We therefore have an upward-sloping supply curve, and the market rate of interest is fixed by the interaction of the demand and supply curves (as in fig 7.2).

Once again, however, we must point out that this is only a partial explanation of the determination of a rate of interest. It does not tell us why, for instance, £10 million of liquid capital should be forthcoming at 10% rather than at 6% or 14%. This will depend upon the general level of interest rates. Analysis of what determines that level is, however, outside the scope of this book.

9.3 LAND AND RENT

(a) The determination of 'commercial rent'

To the economist, the terms 'land' and 'rent' have a special meaning. This is just as well, for in everyday speech each can imply different things. Thus, if I buy land for farming it will probably include buildings, fences, a water supply and a drainage system, all of which are really capital. Similarly, I can rent things other than land – a house, a television set, a gas meter, building equipment, shooting rights, etc. Rent in this sense simply means a periodic payment for the use of something. It can be termed 'commercial rent'.

Usually, however, rent does refer to payment for the use of a piece of land, and before we consider 'land' and 'rent' in their special economic sense, we must ask what determines how much rent is paid to a landlord.

The problem is similar to the determination of the return on any factor service. The demand for land depends on its marginal revenue productivity, and the curve slopes downwards from left to right for the reasons given in chapter 7.2. On the supply side, land, like labour, can usually be put to alternative uses – building factories or houses, growing wheat or barley, raising cattle or sheep, and so on. A given piece of land will be transferred to its most profitable use. If, for instance, the price of cattle rises and that of wheat falls, some land will be transferred from arable to pasture farming. Thus the supply curve for land in a particular use slopes upwards from left to right. The interaction of the demand and supply curves will give the rent actually paid (as in fig 7.2).

Of course, this assumes (i) that the landlord can vary the rent charged any time the demand for and supply of his particular type of land alters, and (ii) that land can be transferred fairly quickly to a different use. The first assumption is complicated by the fact that rents are usually fixed for a period of years. Only when the contract expires is the landlord free to adjust the rent. The second assumption implies that we are concerned only with the long period in our analysis. But what of the short period, when land is a fixed factor? An analysis of this situation is basically what we are concerned with in the remainder of this chapter.

(b) Ricardo's views on 'land' and 'rent'

To explain the special meaning which economists today give to the terms 'land' and 'rent', we have to examine the views of Ricardo, a classical economist of the early nineteenth century. He was concerned not with the rent paid to land for a particular purpose, but with the rent paid to land as a whole. Moreover, he was referring to land in the economist's sense – as the resources provided by nature (see chapter 6) – and, as such, its total supply was fixed.

In this respect, he argued, land was different from the other factors of production, labour and capital, where more would be supplied the higher the price and, if no price at all were offered, there would be no supply. But with land as a whole – in the sense of space and natural resources – the same amount is available whatever the price offered. An increase in price cannot bring about an expansion of supply; and if the price fell to zero the same amount would still be available. Thus land as a whole has no supply price.

The return to land, therefore, was merely a 'residual' –the difference between, on the one hand, what was received for the product, and, on the other, the payments of wages and interest to labour and capital respectively. If the price received for the product was high, there would be more left over as rent; if the price was low, there would be less for rent. Rent did not determine the price of the good produced; instead, the opposite was true – rent was determined by price.

(c) The nature of the return to a fixed factor

Although there were certain blind spots in Ricardo's exposition of what
determined price, he did point out an essential truth – that the return to a
factor fixed in supply (that is, where supply is absolutely inelastic) will
vary directly with variations in the price of the good produced by it. We
can illustrate this more clearly by a simple example.

Let us assume: (i) a given plot of land on which only potatoes can be
grown; (ii) that only land and labour are necessary to grow potatoes; and
(iii) that the supply of labour for growing potatoes is perfectly elastic
because only a small proportion of the total labour force is required.

Fig 9.2 *the effect of the price of a product on the rent of land*

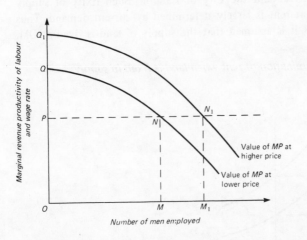

The return to this plot of land will depend entirely on the price of
potatoes. This can be seen from fig 9.2. When the marginal revenue product
of labour is shown by the curve QN, at a wage of OP, OM men are employed. The value of the total product is OMNQ; the wage-bill is OMNP
and the return to the plot of land PNQ. If now the price of potatoes
increases, the marginal-revenue product of labour rises to $Q_1 N_1$. OM_1 men
are now employed at a wage-bill of $OM_1 N_1 P$. (Each worker still receives
the same wage, OP, because the supply of this type of labour is perfectly
elastic). But the return to the given plot of land has increased to $P N_1 Q_1$.
The opposite would apply if the price of potatoes fell.

Certain practical conclusions follow from the above analysis:

(i) Because the plot of land will grow only potatoes, it will be cultivated so long as the value of the total product is sufficient to pay
the wage-bill. In other words, at the lower price a lump-sum tax
on the plot up to QPN could be levied without affecting the out-

166

put. This is the basis of the much-proposed tax on land.

(ii) The return to land as we have analysed it above – rent in its economic sense – is purely a surplus. It arose because, by definition, our plot of land was confined to one particular use – growing potatoes. The supply of this land offered for sale or hiring will not be affected by a price, simply because nobody has any other use for it. In short, it has no opportunity or transfer cost.

(iii) Once land has been built on, it is largely specific to a given use, and the return to the land and building will be dependent on demand.

(iv) Because land is really space, it is impossible to increase the area of sites in city centres except by building upwards, e.g. as in Oxford Street and the City of London. Such fixity of supply means that rent is largely determined by current demand. Thus in fig 9.3 it is assumed that the supply of land is fixed at OM.

Fig 9.3 *the determination of rent when land is fixed in supply*

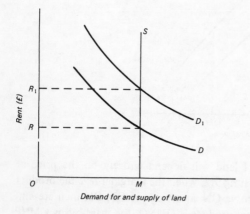

Demand for and supply of land

This means that the rent is determined by demand: an increase from D to D_1 raises rent from OR to OR_1. For instance, rents in Oxford Street depend upon the demand for shops there (which in its turn depends upon people's spending) and rents in the City of London depend on the demand for offices there (which in turn depend upon the level of trade).

(d) Economic rent
Economists have generalised Ricardo's concept of land to cover all factors which are fixed in supply. 'Economic rent' is the term used to describe the earnings of any factor over and above its supply price. Put in another way, it is any surplus over its transfer earnings – what it could obtain in its next

most profitable use (its 'opportunity cost', in our earlier terminology). How this idea can be applied generally will now be explained.

The actual rate of return to a factor is the price per period of time at which it is selling its services. For example, the return to a plasterer is his wage, say £90 per week. But what is the opportunity cost? Simply what has to be paid to retain it in its present use – that is, sufficient to keep it from going to the best alternative use. Take our plasterer, for instance. His next-best occupation may simply be plasterer's labourer, earning £45 per week. He would offer his services as a plasterer, therefore, at anything above £45 per week.

A second plasterer, however, may be a competent bricklayer, and as such earn £60 per week. He will only offer his services as a plasterer, therefore, if at least £60 per week is offered. And so we could go on. The supply curve of plasterers to the industry is thus an 'opportunity cost' curve (fig 9.4).

Fig 9.4   *economic rent (NB current rates are three times those shown)*

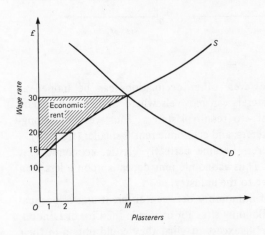

If in fig 9.4 we now insert the demand curve, we can obtain the current wage rate to the industry, £90, when OM plasterers will be employed. But all plasterers receive this wage-rate. Thus the first plasterer receives an economic rent of £45, the second £30, and so on. The total economic rent received by plasterers as a whole is shown by the shaded area.

(e) What determines the size of economic rent?

The size of economic rent earned by a particular type of factor depends upon the elasticity of supply of that factor and how the particular type of factor is defined.

(i) *The elasticity of supply*

Elasticity of supply is determined largely by the period of time under consideration and by immobilities, some of which cannot be eliminated even in the long period. Both will affect economic rent.

Let us assume that, in the short period, the supply of plasterers is fixed: there is insufficient time for them to move into alternative occupations or for others to move in. In short, there is no alternative occupation – they can either work as plasterers or not at all. Thus all their earnings are economic rent – fig 9.5a.

Fig 9.5 *economic rent and elasticity of supply*

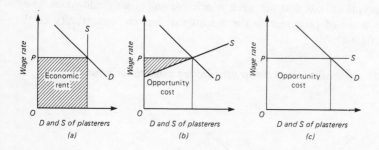

In the long period, however, other occupations can be trained as plasterers, and existing plasterers can move elsewhere. Sufficient has to be paid – the opportunity cost – to retain plasterers. Thus we have a long-period supply curve of plasterers, and economic rent is smaller (fig 9.5b).

If the supply of plasterers became perfectly elastic, economic rent would disappear (fig 9.5c). Thus economic rent depends upon a less than perfectly elastic supply curve to the industry.

Sometimes the degree of immobility between different uses or occupations persists indefinitely. Building sites for offices in the City of London, for instance, earn rents far in excess of what they could obtain in their best alternative use, say for houses. Simply because such sites are very limited in supply, competition for office accommodation has forced up the rents of these sites far beyond the possible price which houses could offer. A large part of their earnings, therefore, is 'economic rent'.

Sometimes, too, we refer to the 'rent of ability'. Many footballers, pop singers, film stars, barristers and surgeons have talents which, to all intents and purposes, are unique, for they cannot be duplicated by training others. Their high earnings, therefore, are almost wholly in the nature of 'economic rent'.

(ii) *The definition of an 'occupation', etc.*

If we adopt a wide definition of our factor, e.g. land as a whole, the distinction is between employing it or idleness, and thus the whole of its earnings is economic rent. This is what Ricardo had in mind.

If, however, our definition is narrower, e.g. covering only land for a particular use, such as growing wheat, then the opportunity cost (e.g. growing barley) will be larger and the economic rent smaller. Similarly, we could distinguish between cabinet-makers and carpenters, surgeons and doctors, and so on. Each would give a smaller 'economic rent' than if the distinction were simply between cabinet-makers and labourers, surgeons and teachers, etc.

(f) Quasi-rent

For fixed factors, particularly capital equipment, what the firm has to pay to retain them will vary according to the period of time.

In the short period, capital equipment is, by definition, fixed in supply. There is no transfer price. More capital equipment cannot be added; nor can existing equipment be diminished. The entrepreneur will continue to work his capital equipment so long as total earnings just cover the cost of his variable factors (see chapter 6). Any earnings above variable costs will be in the nature of a residual which helps towards the cost of the fixed factors. The size of this residual depends upon the price at which the product sells.

This can be seen immediately if we refer to fig 6.3. Were the demand for mowers to increase, the price would rise, say to £60, and production would be expanded to the point where once again price equalled marginal cost – that is, to 100 units. The increased cost of such production would be equal to the increase in total cost – that is, £510. But total receipts would have increased by £1,950, and so, through the fixed factors, the shareholders of Rollermowers earn an additional return – the increase in 'super-normal profit', equal to £1,440.

As time passes, however, we move into the long period. If the product has been selling at a high price, the high return to the capital equipment will induce firms to produce and instal additional equipment. On the other hand, if the price of the product was low, existing capital equipment will either be transferred to its next most profitable use or, when it wears out, simply not be replaced. In the long period, therefore, earnings of fixed factors are, under perfect competition, equal to their transfer cost: economic rent is eliminated.

To distinguish between economic rent which is more or less permanent and that which disappears over time, the latter is often referred to as 'quasi-rent'. It is not a true rent, for the high return earned by such factors leads to an increase in their supply, and this eliminates the economic rent they earn. True rent refers only to factors which are fixed in supply; even if their earnings are high, identical factors are not forthcoming, and so economic rent persists.

9.4 ENTREPRENEURSHIP

(a) The identity of entrepreneurship and risk-bearing

For production to take place, resources must be brought together and set to work. Whoever undertakes this task is often described as 'the entrepreneur'. Usually, however, economists give a narrower meaning to the term.

Organising production can be broken down into two parts. First, there is the task of co-ordination – setting the resources to work. Second, there is accepting the risk of buying factors to produce goods which will only be sold in the future – when receipts may not cover costs.

In practice it is not always easy to separate co-ordination and risk. A farmer, for instance, not only manages and runs his farm, but also accepts the risk involved in deciding what to produce. On the other hand, in a joint-stock company most co-ordination is left to a paid board of directors, with a manager under them. Here the risks of the business are borne by the ordinary shareholders; with a public corporation, they are carried by the taxpayers. Neither takes a part in running the business, except in a most remote way.

The function of co-ordination, therefore, can be fulfilled by a paid manager. In this respect, management is simply an exceptionally highly skilled form of labour. Thus we narrow our concept of enterprise to 'bearing those risks of the business associated with ownership'.

(b) The nature of risks

A business is always open to the risk of fire, accidents, burglary, storm damage, etc. But these risks are calculable. A mathematician can work out, for instance, the chances of a building's catching fire during the year. While he cannot say which building will be destroyed, he knows that on average, say, one out of every 10,000 will be. Such risks, therefore, can be insured against. They are then reduced to a normal cost – what the firm has to pay to contract out of the risk involved.

Certain risks, however, cannot be calculated according to the law of averages. Nobody, for instance, can forecast with certainty how many cold drinks will be sold in Britain next summer. That will depend on the weather. Similarly, it might be thought that a new 'mini' car will sell well. But again, there is a chance that it will not. The risk that demand will be different from that estimated cannot be reduced to a mathematical probability. Such a risk, therefore, cannot be insured against; it must be accepted by those persons whose money is tied up in producing goods for an uncertain demand.

These uninsurable risks are inherent in a dynamic economy. Modern methods of production take time. When an entrepreneur engages resources, therefore, it is an act of faith – faith in his estimate of the demand for the product some time ahead. But demand can never be completely certain. People have freedom of choice, and their tastes may change. Many of the factors affecting demand fluctuate even over a relatively short period of time. Things are similar on the supply side. Techniques do not stand still; new methods discovered by a rival may mean that, by the time a firm's product comes on the market, it is undersold by a cheaper or better substitute.

Thus there is always some degree of uncertainty, and this involves risk. It is a risk which must be shouldered by those who back with their money the decision as to what shall be produced. The true entrepreneurs, therefore, are those who accept the risks of uncertainty-bearing.

9.5 PROFIT

(a) How profit differs in nature from other rewards
The reward of uncertainty-bearing is 'profit'. But profit differs from the earnings of other factors. First, it may be negative. Whereas wages, rent and interest are paid as part of a contract at the time of hiring, profits are received in the future, and then only if expected demand materialises. Thus its size is uncertain. Where the entrepreneur has been far too optimistic, a loss is made. Second, profit fluctuates more than other rewards, for it feels the immediate impact of booms and slumps. In a boom, profits rise faster than wages, while in a slump they fall more severely.

(b) Differences in the meaning of the term 'profit'
It is essential to distinguish four different concepts of 'profit'.

(i) Profit in its everyday meaning
To the accountant, profit means simply the difference between total receipts and total costs (see p. 109). But, because the economist defines cost in terms of alternatives forgone, he would amend this idea of profit by deducting, first, the return which would have been received on capital had it been used elsewhere, and second, the value of the entrepreneur's skill in the best alternative line of business.

(ii) Normal profit under perfect competition
Because uncertainty cannot be eliminated from a dynamic economy, there must be a return to induce people to bear uncertainty. This is true

even in the long period. Thus there must be a rate of profit – the price which equates the demand for and supply of entrepreneurship. In the long period under perfect competition, any rent element from profit is eliminated. We then have normal profit – the cost which has to be met if the supply of uncertainty-bearing is to be maintained.

Two modifications should be noted. First, industries differ as regards the uncertainty involved. Where fashions or techniques change frequently, for instance, uncertainty is greater. This would tend to reduce the supply of entrepreneurs in such industries at any given level of normal profit, and thus for them normal profit must be higher. Second, the elimination of the rent element in profit in the long period is only possible if entrepreneurs of equal ability are available. In practice this is not so. Thus there will always be some entrepreneurs earning a rent of ability (super-normal profit) even in the long period, simply because their forecasts and decisions are more accurate.

(iii) *Super-normal profit*

Under perfect competition the entrepreneur is able to make super-normal profit for a period because new firms cannot enter the industry. Certain factors such as key workers and machines are for a time fixed in supply, and entrepreneurs already possessing them will make super-normal profit. In other words such profit is really the return to fixed factors in the short period; it is the 'quasi-rent' earned by such factors.

(iv) *Monopoly profit*

With monopoly, competitors can be excluded. Certain factors, e.g. diamond-mines, know-how, patents and copyrights, are fixed to the monopolist. Even in the long period, competitors cannot engage such factors, and so super-normal profits persist. The profits of the monopolist, therefore, are closer to economic rent than to quasi-rent.

(c) The role of profit in a private-enterprise economy

'Profit' tends to be an emotive word, and firms which make large profits are often frowned upon. But usually there is little justification for this, since it is through profits – and losses – that the market economy works. We must emphasise, however, that we are discussing only profits under competitive conditions. But, given such conditions, profit fulfils the following functions:

(i) *Normal profits induce people to accept the risks of uncertainty*

Because uncertainty is implicit in a dynamic economy, a reward – normal profit – is essential for entrepreneurs to undertake production. Thus normal profit is a cost, as essential as the payment of wages. The level will vary with the industry; thus it will be higher for oil exploration than for selling petrol.

(ii) *Super-normal profit indicates which industry should expand and which should contract*

When a firm produces a good which proves to be popular with consumers, it probably makes super-normal profit. This indicates that output should be expanded. On the other hand losses show that consumers do not want the good, and production should contract.

(iii) *Super-normal profit encourages firms to increase production*

Profits not only indicate that consumers want more of a good; they are also the inducement to firms to produce those goods. As we saw in chapter 6, super-normal profits act as the spur for existing firms to increase capacity and for other firms to enter the industry. On the other hand, when losses are being incurred, firms go out of production and the industry contracts. Thus losses are as important as profits in the operation of the market economy.

(iv) *Super-normal profit provides the resources for expansion*

An industry making super-normal profit can secure the factors necessary to expand. First, profits can be ploughed back, while shareholders will respond to requests for further capital, usually through rights issues. New firms can enter the industry, because investors will subscribe to a company intending to operate where the level of profits is relatively high. Second, profits allow expanding firms to offer higher rewards to attract factors. In this way resources are moved according to the wishes of consumers.

(v) *Profits ensure that production is carried on by the most efficient firms*

In a competitive industry the firm making the largest profit is the one whose costs are lowest. It will have an incentive to expand production and, if necessary, can afford to pay more for factors to do so. Less efficient firms must copy its methods to retain factors. In any case the increased output of the more efficient firm will eventually lower the price of the product. As a result inefficient firms make losses: profits have become negative.

To sum up, profits and losses are the means by which the process of natural selection occurs in the market economy. Where there is competition it is wrong to regard profits as being somehow immoral. The exception is monopoly profits, which are not eliminated even in the long period. Entry into the industry is not free; consequently profits are not competed away. It may be that such monopoly profits stimulate research and allow an industry to expand. But where scarcity has been deliberately brought about, they simply represent an economic rent earned at the expense of consumers by the monopolist owners. Thus an efficient allocation of resources according to the wishes of consumers does not take place.

PART IV
PUBLIC-SECTOR
PRODUCTION

THE ALLOCATION OF RESOURCES THROUGH THE PUBLIC SECTOR

10.1 THE CASE FOR PUBLIC-SECTOR PRODUCTION

(a) Defects of the market economy in allocating resources

In the market economy, supply responds to price signals. The main strengths of this method of allocating resources are (i) that, through demand, individual preferences are indicated by their effect on the price of a good; and (ii) that, through the profit motive, resources are used efficiently in supplying goods. Chapters 3–6 have explained how both are achieved, and how some inefficiencies, e.g. those of monopoly power, may be corrected by government action.

In certain circumstances, however, such market intervention is inadequate. First, community goods, such as defence and street-lighting, cannot be supplied through the price system since it is impossible to exclude free-riders. Second, public goods, such as parks and roads, where there is no reduction in the quantity available for others when one person has more (that is, marginal cost is nil), are not fully used when charges are levied. Third, either through ignorance or miscalculation of future benefits, people – even those with sufficient income – may devote an inadequate proportion of it to purchasing merit goods, such as education. Fourth, a project may be so large that only the government can provide the capital required, particularly where there is some doubt if revenue will cover total costs, e.g. in coal-mine modernisation, Concorde, atomic energy. Fifth, external costs and benefits may be so widespread that only the government can take full account of them, e.g. new-town development, new-airport construction.

(b) Forms of public-sector organisation

Where any of the above conditions hold, it is necessary or likely that the good or service will be provided through the public sector. The actual form of organisation will vary between a government department, a local

178

authority, a nationalised industry and other quasi-government bodies – usually termed commissions, committees or councils. The respective merits of each form are discussed in chapter 11.

(c) The growth in importance of the public sector
Table 10.1 indicates the growth in the relative importance of the public sector in recent years. This growth has stemmed from two main sources –

Table 10.1 *Percentage distribution of the Gross Domestic Product and the labour force by sector, 1961–78*

	GDP		Labour force	
	Private sector	*Public sector*	*Private sector*	*Public sector*
1961	75.9	24.1	77.0	23.0
1963	75.3	24.7	76.9	23.1
1965	75.3	24.7	77.2	22.8
1967	74.1	25.9	76.3	23.7
1969	74.0	26.0	74.2	25.8
1971	73.3	26.7	72.9	27.1
1973	73.1	26.9	72.9	27.1
1975	69.1	30.9	70.8	29.2
1977	70.4	29.6	70.3	29.7
1978	71.0	29.0	70.4	29.6

Source: National Income and Expenditure (Blue Book).

(i) increased recognition of the weaknesses of the market economy in the modern complex economy, and (ii) greater political support for parties advocating some form of corporate state, e.g. socialism.

10.2 DEMAND AND NEEDS

(a) Differences between 'demand' and 'needs'
Whereas goods and services are supplied by private-sector firms in response to effective demand, government departments and local authorities provide goods and services according to 'needs', a social rather than an economic concept. 'Needs' are more difficult to assess than demand.

For example, in the private sector owner-occupied houses are built according to the price which people are able and willing to pay for them. Demand will depend upon the price of the house, the prices of other goods and services (particularly near-substitutes), the level of income, the distribution of wealth and all the other factors mentioned in chapter 3 as influencing the conditions of demand. Supply responds automatically to this demand; the number and type of houses supplied depends ultimately on the equilibrium price determined in the market.

In contrast, in providing housing according to needs the public-sector authorities regard housing as a social obligation. Consequently, price signals are either inadequate or non-existent. This increases the difficulties of decision-making. Consider the factors which have to be borne in mind in planning a housing programme based on needs. First, the authorities have to estimate the number of households seeking accommodation according to the sizes of the family units, the ages of their members, their location, their preferences as between houses and high-rise flats, and so on. Moreover, since houses are very durable, some consideration has to be given to future requirements. Second, the authorities have to decide arbitrarily on the standard of an adequate housing unit. Third, they have to get the dwellings built, either through a private contractor or by their own direct-labour building organisations.

(b) Subjective assessment of 'needs'

The task of estimating needs is made more difficult because there is no price system in operation to provide reliable criteria. Thus rents charged by local authorities are less than the open-market rent. This means that demand exceeds supply, and the only indication of need thrown up by this restricted-price system is the number of households waiting their turn on the housing list.

And, all the time, the authorities must be conscious of dealing with limited resources – more spent on housing may mean less available for the health services. In the last resort, therefore, the standard of goods and services provided on the basis of needs is determined by the political views of the central government and local councils.

10.3 PRICING POLICY IN THE PUBLIC SECTOR

The problem arises as to how goods and services provided by the public sector are to be paid for.

(a) Provision from the proceeds of taxation

With community goods, where free-riders cannot be excluded, no price can be charged, since nobody will pay when private rights to them cannot be granted, e.g. with defence, consular services and BBC radio and TV. Here the cost has to be covered entirely from taxation.

The same largely applies to public goods, where in economic terms marginal cost is nil (see p. 177). These will only be enjoyed to the maximum if no charge is levied, e.g. for crossing bridges, visiting public parks, etc.

With other goods and services, some charges can be levied. Indeed such charges promote economy in use, while there is an element of fairness in that those enjoying them contribute to their cost. Nevertheless, merit goods are usually subsidised from taxation, mainly in order to encourage people to consume more than they otherwise would if they had to pay the full economic price, e.g. for housing. Re-distribution of income, however, may also be an objective of such subsidies.

(b) Covering the cost by charges

The real difficulty for pricing policy arises with those goods where total costs are expected to be covered by charges on consumers. This applies particularly to the nationalised industries, which are generally expected to pay their way, taking one year with another. The snag is that if, to secure the optimum allocation of resources, production takes place up to the point where price equals marginal cost (the principle of marginal-cost pricing), total costs may not be covered. The reason is that fixed costs are so high, e.g. for railways and electricity supply, that a single price equalling marginal cost cannot generate sufficient revenue to cover total costs.

In practice the problem has been overcome in three ways:

(i) The difference has been covered by a *subsidy*, either directly, e.g. for city transport, or indirectly, through writing off accumulated deficits from time to time, e.g. for coal and railways.

(ii) A *standing charge* is levied irrespective of units consumed, e.g. for electricity. The standing charge goes to meet fixed costs; the price per unit consumed covers marginal costs.

(iii) The industry is allowed to exploit its monopoly position by *price discrimination*. This is possible where different customers, having different elasticity of demand for the product, can be kept separate, each being charged the price he is willing to pay. By 'charging what the traffic will bear', total revenue is increased. Such price discrimination is used by British Rail (e.g. cheap-day trippers and students are charged lower fares than commuters) and the Gas Corporation (where industrial users pay more than domestic consumers).

10.4 COST-BENEFIT ANALYSIS

(a) The economics of government decision-making

Government responsibility for defence, education, roads, airports, parks, health services, etc., means that it has to make decisions regarding the allocation of resources. In particular, all involve investment; but, since capital is limited, that investment has to be apportioned so as to obtain the greatest possible satisfaction. The type of question which has to be answered continually is: Should we build a new aircraft-carrier or develop a new all-purpose aeroplane for the RAF? How much should be spent on university education? Is investment in a new motorway justified? What is the best site for a new airport? Should land be purchased for the National Trust or should the money be spent on a rare work of art? How much can we afford to devote to kidney machines in view of the claims of cancer research? Should housing be provided by rebuilding or by improving existing houses?

The difficulty is that, since community, public and merit goods are provided free or considerably below market price, the indications of the desirability of investment which the price system usually provides are almost non-existent. Some allowance, too, has to be made for external costs and benefits. For instance, the usual cost-revenue criterion may be inappropriate when there is unemployment, for a road scheme which gives work to unemployed men reduces the real cost. Finally, the government can pay more attention to the wishes of unborn generations, allowing these to sway a decision in purchasing land for the National Trust or buying a painting for an art gallery.

Government decisions often depend upon subjective political considerations. For example, re-distribution of income is a factor in providing free education, while egalitarian and social reasons are prominent in requiring schools to be organised on comprehensive lines. But deciding all public-sector investment solely at the political level has serious defects now that the government has increased its involvement in the economy. First, the number and complexity of the decisions which have to be made make some decentralisation of decision-making desirable (something which is achieved automatically by the price system). Second, the one-man, one-vote method of electing governments does not weight votes according to the intensity of satisfaction gained or lost by a given investment. For instance, the simple-majority decision allows two voters marginally in favour of a new motorway to outvote one voter who would suffer considerably by it. Third, political decisions are essentially subjective, whereas economic efficiency in resource allocation requires that objective criteria be used as far as possible.

(b) The role of cost-benefit analysis (CBA)
Thus for much government decision-making a new technique, known as cost-benefit analysis (CBA), has been evolved. This works by identifying all the relevant benefits and costs of a particular scheme and then measuring them in money terms. This allows all the benefits and costs to be aggregated, as it were, in the form of a balance-sheet upon which the ultimate decision can be made.

For example, the benefits of a new motorway would obviously include the time saved in travel, fuel economies, reduced congestion in towns through which motor traffic formerly passed, fewer road accidents and the pleasure derived by the extra motorists who could now make day trips. Against this, however, would have to be set the cost of constructing the motorway, the additional noise suffered by nearby residents, the congestion on the feeder roads, the toll of animal life and so on.

It is obvious, however, that in giving a monetary value to such benefits and costs one can run up against serious theoretical and practical difficulties. Where market prices are available, the benefits and costs are fairly definite, e.g. the cost of building the motorway. But if no charges are made for the use of the motorway, how do we know the possible value of the benefits received? The number of motorists likely to use the road can be estimated, but how do we value the journey each makes, since some are travelling on business and others on leisure pursuits? Similarly with the reduction in accidents; we can estimate the saving to the hospital service, in police time, etc., but how do we value the physical suffering avoided? And the motorway may result in fewer deaths: what price do we put on the saving of human life? Similar problems arise in valuing such intangibles as noise, traffic congestion and the toll of animal life. It may be possible to obtain a price by analogy, e.g. the fall in the value of houses resulting from the noise, and the life-span earning-power of people dying in accidents, but no such calculation can be completely satisfactory.

At best, therefore, all CBA can do is to lay bare the issues, emphasising the possible margin of error in any figures given, so that some definite magnitudes of the various items which have to be considered are made available to the decision-makers.

Even so, CBA cannot be used where political decisions dominate. For instance, how much is spent by Britain on defence will depend upon subjective views as to how far Russia's expansionary aims are a threat to Britain and on the extent to which such expenditure can be trimmed in order to expand the social services. Similarly, comprehensive education is often advocated as a means of promoting a more integrated society, while local-authority housing may be provided in areas of high land values, e.g. Hampstead, in order to achieve a 'social mix'. While social factors can be identified, it is almost impossible to measure them satisfactorily.

Moreover, it may be difficult to apply CBA to certain decisions. Consider, for instance, a local authority which is spending £1 million on swimming facilities. The decision rests between: (i) one swimming-bath of Olympic standards which, while it could be used for local people, would also bring prestige to the town; (ii) three smaller swimming-baths, each capable of providing training facilities and holding galas; and (iii) six very small baths specifically designed to teach children to swim. The advantages of each are largely immeasurable by CBA since they embrace so many intangibles. As a result councillors decide subjectively (perhaps on political lines) at a council meeting.

Nor can a firm CBA decision be taken for a project which involves irreversible decisions, such as the survival of a species of animal or plant, since it is impossible to estimate the current cost of a decision which would deny future generations the opportunity to choose.

Finally, there is always the problem of deciding on the cut-off point and the 'time horizon' for the benefits and costs to be included. The viability of a project could rest on these, and there is always the temptation for interested parties to extend the cut-off point or the time-horizon in order to justify particular preferences.

Such problems, together with the practical difficulties of measuring intangibles, mean that CBA cannot be fully objective. Thus its role is limited to systematically presenting all the information relevant to a decision and to indicating the weight which can be placed on the accuracy of the calculations submitted. By doing so it ensures that the claims of rival pressure groups are assessed and all the relevant issues fully debated before the ultimate political decision is taken.

10.5 WAGE-CLAIMS IN THE PUBLIC SECTOR

(a) The increased bargaining strength of labour in the public sector
In the nationalised industries workers tend to be in a strong bargaining position. Not only are they highly organised in powerful unions, but the industries themselves are basic to the rest of the economy. Moreover, certain groups, e.g. power-station electricians and railway signalmen, are particularly able to press for high wage increases since demand for their services is inelastic (for the reasons given on pp. 154-6).

Even within the civil service and local government the growth of strong trade-union organisation has changed attitudes. At one time public officials would not consider strike action, but in recent years there have been 'guerrilla' strikes aimed at disrupting essential services in small sectors, e.g. VAT collection, hospital treatment and the distribution of telephone bills.

(b) The government's difficulties
The government faces three main kinds of difficulty. The first covers those industries where, on an economic assessment, wage-claims are exorbitant. Increased productivity, one of the main supporting grounds for increased wages, results from the installation of new machinery as well as from the skill or effort of labour. If wage-claims are met, labour costs may be too high relative to sales revenue. Not only does the return on capital suffer but it becomes impossible to accumulate sufficient reserves to provide for future development. British Leyland (now 90% publicly owned) is a prime

example. But the argument also applies to the steel and shipbuilding industries, where closures are only averted by government subsidies. Indeed, the coal industry would be in the same position were it not for the high price of oil, which allows coal prices to be raised. The dilemma facing the government is how to ensure that the rewards of capital investment are distributed equitably among workers in the industry, the taxpayers who provide the capital, and consumers (who should enjoy some advantage from lower prices).

The second difficulty arises within the traditional civil-service and local-government activities. Here wage rises have to be covered by taxation, and the obstacles to increasing taxation mean that wage increases for government employees fall behind those secured in the private sector. Eventually the exasperation of government employees finds expression in guerrilla strikes. In 1979 the government, faced with such workers' discontent, set up a Pay Comparability Commission to examine rates of pay in the public sector relative to those in the private sector.

The third difficulty occurs when the government is seeking to operate a prices-and-incomes policy. The temptation is to hold prices in the national-ised industries, and this eventually leads to financial difficulties. As regards incomes, while the government can only urge trade unions and private-sector firms to respect wage guidelines (that is, unless it is prepared to invoke statutory controls), it is under an obligation to adhere to the recommended norm in granting wage-claims in the public sector. When, as in 1979, private-sector firms disregard this norm in order to secure indust-rial peace, government employees resent what they feel is discrimination against them, and disruptive action follows.

It remains to be seen whether the discipline of monetary ceilings from which wage payments have to be met, which were imposed by the Con-servative government when it took office in 1979, will prove effective. The logic is that future wage increases will have to be absorbed by reducing the number of employees. Unless the work can be covered by the greater efficiency of a smaller work-force, public services will have to be curtailed.

ORGANISATIONS IN THE PUBLIC SECTOR FOR SUPPLYING GOODS AND SERVICES

11.1 THE GOVERNMENT DEPARTMENT

(a) The need for 'public accountability'
When the state provides goods and services, consideration has to be given to two fundamental principles which pull in opposite directions.

The first, 'public accountability', arises because British democracy requires that where the state is granted powers it shall be answerable, in some form or another, for the way in which those powers are exercised. The citizen requires some assurance that powers granted to the state to produce goods and services are not abused by authoritarianism, inefficiency or monopolistic exploitation.

The second principle is 'economic efficiency'. The difficulty is that, by insisting on strict public accountability, we may so tie the hands of those running the state services that they cannot operate efficiently.

(b) Accountability through the government department
The most efficient form of accountability is achieved when a government department produces the goods or services, for at its head is a minister who accepts full responsibility for its work. He is subject to examination in parliament, having to explain general policy in debate and to answer questions on even minor details of administration. Over finance, too, there is strict control: the Treasury ascertains that money is spent economically and within the limit authorised by parliament.

But this form of accountability has certain inherent snags. First, parliament is basically a forum for discussing major political issues rather than for dealing with administrative details. In any case, MPs are laymen without the necessary technical knowledge to supervise. Second, parliament would be overworked if it tried to exercise detailed control. Third, frequent questions in parliament on the decisions of civil servants can lead to their taking a 'play-for-safety' attitude or the line of least resistance. The opposition probes mainly with political ends in view; civil servants are therefore hardly likely to follow a bold, imaginative policy which, should it fail, could excite considerable criticism, when by taking an alternative middle-of-the-road line they can settle for a less troubled life. Fourth, Treasury control over finance is restrictive in character. Whereas private enterprise only requires proposed expenditure to be justified by overall profits, the Treasury insists that each individual item of service be provided at the lowest possible cost.

To sum up, accountability clashes with economic efficiency. Thus the government-department form of organisation is most appropriate for dealing with community and public goods which are basically non-commercial in that, because charges cannot be levied, their cost is covered by taxation; in providing merit goods, where only nominal charges are levied; and where functions are basically limited to supervision or control or both, e.g. in foreign affairs and tax collection.

11.2 LOCAL AUTHORITIES

(a) The advantages of local-authority provision
While some local authorities may provide trading services, e.g. municipally owned transport, their activities are mostly concerned with community, public and merit goods, e.g. environmental services, roads, parks, education and housing. Making local authorities responsible has certain advantages:

(i) *Those who run local services are local people responsive to local needs and attitudes*
In contrast, administration from Whitehall makes for uniformity throughout the country.

(ii) *It allows close contact between the governed and those who govern*
When administration is at the local level people can get in touch directly with those who make decisions and the officials who carry them out. This tends to eliminate the frustration and delay associated with bureaucracy.

(iii) *It facilitates continuity of policy*
Although councils are usually run on party lines, most decisions are of an administrative character, so that only on a few issues, e.g. comprehensive schooling, is there a political division. Generally, therefore, all councillors can work together to decide the best long-term policies for the community, something which might be hampered if services were administered by a central government subject to swings of the political pendulum.

(iv) *It provides for a division of power between Whitehall and town hall*
Thus a local protest, e.g. about a proposed airport or motorway, serves to remind the central government that its decisions must respect local feelings and loyalties.

(v) *Local authorities lighten the burden of administration*
This would otherwise put a severe strain on Westminster and Whitehall.

(b) The structure of local government in England and Wales
The local-government structure of England and Wales is almost identical but, although broadly parallel, those of Scotland and Northern Ireland have some differences. The general scheme is two-tier (fig 11.1).

Fig 11.1   *the structure of local government in England and Wales*

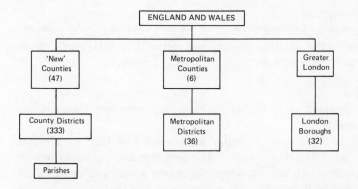

Outside the conurbations, England and Wales are divided into counties, which in turn are divided into county districts; and below these may be parishes (which provide minor local amenities, such as sports facilities and village halls, and may monitor planning applications being considered by the district councils).

In six conurbations – the complexes of towns centred on Liverpool (Merseyside), Manchester, Birmingham (West Midlands), Leeds-Bradford (West Yorkshire), Sheffield (South Yorkshire) and Newcastle-Sunderland (Tyne and Wear) – there is a special metropolitan system, whereby the districts have greater powers than elsewhere. In London, the other main conurbation, a similar structure operates through the Greater London Council and the 32 London boroughs.

(c) Functions of local authorities
Local councils provide their services on the authority of parliament. Most of their functions are *obligatory*, and action can be taken against them if

these are neglected. Others, such as libraries and trading services, are *permissive*: the authority undertakes them at its discretion.

The work of local authorities can be classified under five main headings:

(i) *Protection*
E.g. the police and fire services.

(ii) *Regulation and control*
E.g. the licensing of cinemas, the inspection of weights and measures and of food and drugs, and consumer protection.

(iii) *Personal*
Services for individuals directly, e.g. education, housing and the care of children and old people.

(iv) *Environmental*
The maintenance and improvement of people's surroundings by providing public-health and sanitary services (e.g. refuse disposal), roads, street-lighting, parks, museums, libraries, community centres, etc.

(v) *Trading*
Services provided on a commercial basis, e.g. passenger transport and entertainments.

Figure 11.2 sets out the major services and how they are allocated between the different authorities. As a general rule the *counties* provide those services which are best administered over a wide area or which are most economically provided on a large scale and therefore for a large population, e.g. education. The *county districts* are basically sanitation and housing authorities.

As already noted, the *metropolitan districts* perform many of the counties' functions. *London* broadly follows this metropolitan pattern.

(d) The local authority as a form of business organisation
Responsibility for carrying out the functions of the particular local authority rests with the *council*, the elected body.

But, apart from meeting infrequently, councils are normally too large to consider business in detail. Nor are any councillors the equivalent of the full-time ministers at Whitehall who take charge of departmental policy. In local government this function is performed by *committees* (fig 11.3). Certain committees are required by law to be appointed, e.g. those for finance, social services and education; the rest are decided by the council. Committees are usually given executive as well as advisory functions.

Fig 11.2 *the main services of local government*

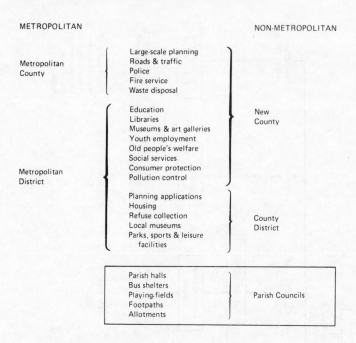

METROPOLITAN   NON-METROPOLITAN

Metropolitan County
- Large-scale planning
- Roads & traffic
- Police
- Fire service
- Waste disposal

New County
- Education
- Libraries
- Museums & art galleries
- Youth employment
- Old people's welfare
- Social services
- Consumer protection
- Pollution control

Metropolitan District

County District
- Planning applications
- Housing
- Refuse collection
- Local museums
- Parks, sports & leisure facilities

Parish Councils
- Parish halls
- Bus shelters
- Playing-fields
- Footpaths
- Allotments

The key figure in a committee is the *chairman*: not only is he in close and regular contact with the corresponding chief officer, but he instigates much of the committee's work; he is the nearest equivalent to the chairman or managing director of a company.

The policies decided upon by the council and its committees are put into effect by paid *permanent officers*. Since the only compulsory appointments are those of education officer and director of social services, councils have great flexibility in planning their management structure. In practice most appoint a chief executive, treasurer, engineer, surveyor, housing manager and parks superintendent, according to the services operated.

(e) Paying for local services
Every year the treasurer of each council submits an estimate of expenditure for the coming year to the finance committee, which considers these estimates and decides how the money is to be raised. By far the largest single item of spending is education (fig 11.4). Other major items are highways, police and social services. Spending is of two kinds, capital expenditure and current expenditure.

Capital expenditure is incurred on such items as new houses, schools, roads, etc. The benefits from these projects extend far into the future, and

190

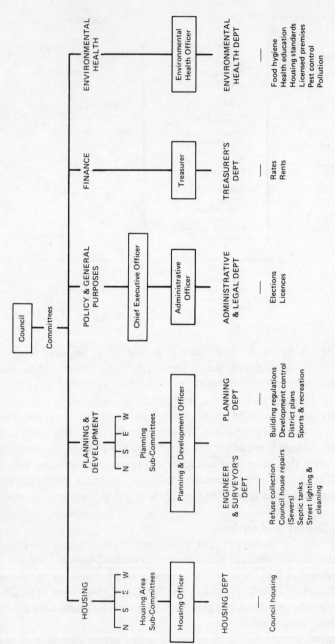

Fig 11.3 *the structure of a district council*

Fig 11.4 *local-authority revenue and expenditure, 1977*

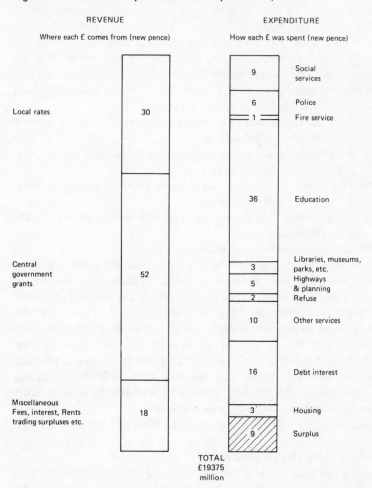

REVENUE

Where each £ comes from (new pence)

Local rates 30

Central government grants 52

Miscellaneous Fees, interest, Rents trading surpluses etc. 18

EXPENDITURE

How each £ was spent (new pence)

9 Social services

6 Police

1 Fire service

36 Education

3 Libraries, museums, parks, etc.

5 Highways & planning

2 Refuse

10 Other services

16 Debt interest

3 Housing

9 Surplus

TOTAL £19375 million

it would be unfair to throw their full cost onto the ratepayers of one particular year. Such expenditure is therefore covered by long-term loans which, together with the interest on them, are repaid over a number of years. Councils borrow mainly on the open market, but where they find this difficult they can obtain funds from the Public Works Loans Board, which is financed by central-government funds.

Current expenditure refers to the everyday spending necessary to run services (e.g. housing administration and repairs, teachers' salaries, student grants) and to pay interest charges. Obviously, if a council is to pay its way it must balance current expenditure with current income from charges, government grants and rates.

Charges have the advantage that those who benefit from the service pay at least a part of its cost, as with rents for housing, admission fees to swimming-baths and fines on overdue library books. But while some trading services make a profit (especially lotteries), most local-government activity is concerned with providing community, public and merit goods whose cost has to be covered mainly from taxation, either central or local.

Government grants, which now provide 52% of the revenue of local authorities, are made for the following purposes:

(i)   To offset the defects of the rating system by transferring more of the burden to general taxation.

(ii) To assist local authorities with services of national concern, e.g. roads, police, education and so on.

(iii) To ensure a minimum standard in the provision of such services.

(iv) To help the poorer authorities.

(v)   To encourage local authorities to provide services above the minimum required.

(vi) To assist in special emergencies, e.g. floods.

The basis upon which grants are made must achieve the above objectives without destroying local control or initiative, or committing the government to expenditure beyond the ceiling it feels it can afford. Thus, while grants based on a *percentage* of the service's cost or of so much per *unit* encourage local authorities to spend more than the bare minimum, they make it difficult for the government to control its own spending. The *general or block* grant – a single, annual lump sum to be used at the local authority's discretion – avoids this, but only at the risk of discouraging those authorities which are keen to improve and develop services. Their extra revenue has to be found from local sources.

The result is that today there are two main types of grant:

(i) *Grants in aid of specific services*

Calculating the grant on a percentage basis, e.g. police (50%), highways (50–75% according to the class of road), encourages high standards. On the other hand it necessitates careful central auditing to ensure that spending is not wasteful. Thus a grant of so much per unit, irrespective of whether standards above the minimum are provided (e.g. in housing), is easier to administer.

(ii) *The rate support grant*

This is a block grant to assist with other services and to help the poorer authorities. It is calculated on a formula embracing a number of factors such as the rate resources of the authority, the density of population and the numbers of young and old people in the area.

In addition some help is given by the Exchequer to reduce the 'domestic rate', i.e. the rate on dwellings, as opposed to that on commercial and industrial property.

Rates are levied to cover the amount by which spending exceeds revenue from charges and government grants. They are calculated as follows. All buildings and land within the authority's area are given a 'net rateable value' by valuation officers of the Board of Inland Revenue. The figure is the rent which might reasonably be expected from the property, less the cost of upkeep.

The rates which have to be paid by the occupiers of this property are calculated according to the total amount which has to be raised and the rateable value of the area. Suppose a district has a rateable value of £10 million, and that it has to raise £5 million towards its own spending and £1 million to cover the requirement (technically known as the 'precept') from the county council. This total of £6 million would be obtained by levying a 60p rate. This means that the occupier of a house rated at £300 would have to pay annual rates of £180, usually by two payments in advance each October and April or by a monthly scheme.

The rating system has certain advantages for financing local-government services:

(i) Because it is a tax reserved for local authorities, it strengthens their independence by providing an income free from the control of Whitehall.

(ii) The rate yield can be predicted accurately.

(iii) Evasion is difficult.

(iv) It is simple and cheap to administer.

(v) Most households make a contribution to local services, thereby encouraging responsibility.

On the other hand a system originating some four hundred years ago is bound to have weaknesses for providing finance on today's scale. The most important criticisms are:

(i) Until the introduction of the system of rate rebates in 1967 rates tended to bear more heavily on poorer families. People may live in a large house because they have a large family. In any case we consider that taxes should be progressive (taking a higher proportion of the rich person's income) and should make allowances for for family responsibilities.

(ii) Unlike those of most other taxes, the rate yield does not automatically increase with inflation or greater prosperity. Instead the rate poundage has to be increased, and the unpopularity of this deters councils from improving services by spending more on them. The deterrent effect is heightened by the fact that elections tend to be held soon after the rate is fixed each year.

(iii) Property improvement is discouraged because it increases the rateable value and thus the rate payments.

(iv) The poorer districts have a lower rateable value, yet these are likely to require higher spending on local services.

(v) The de-rating of agricultural land since 1929 is now an anomaly which adds to the rate burden of rural areas.

(vi) Assessments of rateable value cannot be completely objective, and the shortage of skilled valuers tends to delay periodic re-assessment.

The defects of the rating system have resulted in: (i) a demand for other local taxes, e.g. a local income tax, a sales tax and the retention of licence revenue, e.g. from motor vehicles; (ii) increased help by way of government grants; (iii) the introduction of rate rebates (90% covered by government grants) for people with small incomes; and (iv) certain local councils' running lotteries.

11.3 THE NATIONALISED INDUSTRIES

(a) Reasons for nationalisation

In addition to providing community, public and merit goods, the state has in recent years taken over the production of certain goods and services from the private sector, nationalising such industries as coal, gas and electricity supply, iron and steel, shipbuilding, aerospace and the Bank of England.

Nationalisation, however, does not automatically solve the problem of allocating resources; it simply means that the ultimate economic decisions are taken by the government. But in making those decisions the government can allow for external benefits and costs (e.g. by keeping the shipyards working at a loss because the men would otherwise be idle), overcome the temptation of a monopoly industry to maximise profits by restricting output (e.g. by producing up to the point where price, not marginal revenue, equals marginal cost) and re-distribute income through its pricing policy (e.g. by providing low-priced transport for senior citizens).

While the precise arguments for nationalisation depend upon the industry concerned, the following are those most generally advanced.

(i) *Single control over all firms in the industry enables the full advantages of large-scale production to be achieved*

Competition between firms may result in their working at less than optimum size. Uncertainty about rivals' plans may inhibit investment because of fear of over-investment by the industry as a whole. It may also lead to duplication of research and unnecessary design differences in both the capital equipment and the finished product. The National Coal Board, for instance, has developed a standard pattern of miner's safety helmet.

Similarly, nationalisation secures commercial and financial economies. Competitive advertising between firms (though not between industries) is eliminated, while, in borrowing, a state-owned industry can usually obtain finance more cheaply than a private firm.

(ii) *State ownership is essential for the necessary capital investment*

Private owners may not have the resources or may be unwilling to commit themselves to long-term capital outlays. Thus, for security and technical reasons, atomic energy has been developed by the state, while the railway modernisation programme would have been too risky for private enterprise. Moreover, losses may possibly be justified by external benefits, e.g. relief of unemployment, less congestion on the roads.

(iii) *State ownership is a means of controlling monopoly*

As we have seen, 'natural' monopolies are to a large extent inevitable. It is argued that controlling such monopolies, especially the public utilities, by state ownership ensures that they will work in the public interest and not merely for high profits.

(iv) *A pricing policy can be adopted which allows a highly capitalised industry to break even on all costs*

As was shown in the previous chapter, where initial fixed costs are very high – e.g. in electricity supply – it is impossible to charge a single price which will generate sufficient revenue to cover total costs. However, by creating a monopoly which can discriminate between customers and charge different prices to each according to what they are willing to pay, total revenue can be increased. On the other hand, since such monopolies are essential public utilities, it is held that they should be under direct state control.

(v) *The efficiency of key industries must be guaranteed*

There are certain industries, e.g. iron and steel, coal and power, upon which most other production depends. Others, e.g. atomic research, are vital for defence. Such industries, it is argued, should not be regarded merely as a source of private profit (with their expansion or contraction depending upon this) but be run by the state in the wider interests of the nation.

(vi) *Productivity will increase through improved attitudes of employees*

It is argued not only that workers will enjoy better working conditions but that the fact that the state is the employer and not a firm striving for shareholders' profits will have a psychological benefit resulting in increased worker productivity.

196

(b) The public corporation as a form of business organisation

When the government embarked on its nationalisation programme in 1945, the disadvantages of the government-department form of organisation discussed above were highlighted. The industries being transferred from the private sector were concerned with economic functions, not the administration of particular policies. As such they served the everyday needs of the whole community, and so their contact with people was much greater than in traditional fields of government. This meant that the House of Commons, as a supervisory body, would have been overworked by parliamentary questions. Moreover, accountability through parliament would have made it difficult to pursue long-term objectives because the minister in charge could change with a reorganisation of government. Finally, civil servants

Fig 11.5 *organisations for providing goods and services*

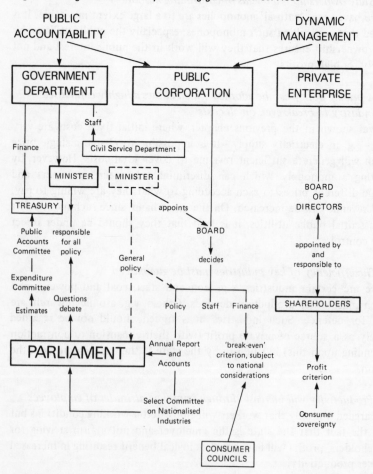

are not chosen to provide the dynamic and imaginative management required for large commercial undertakings.

The answer to these defects was to make the nationalised industries the responsibility of public corporations. The objective was to get the best of both worlds: on the one hand the world of energetic industrial enterprise found in the market economy; on the other the world of accountability to the public, to whom it belongs and whom it serves (fig 11.5).

(c) Organisation of the nationalised industries
The organisation of the nationalised industries, based on the principles outlined above, presents some common features.

(i) The boards are 'bodies corporate'. This means that they have a legal identity and therefore, like a company, have a life of their own, can own property and can sue and be sued in the courts.

(ii) Assets of the industry are vested in the board, and the nationalising act usually gives the board instructions as to its general responsibilities. Thus the National Coal Board is charged with:

(1)   Working and getting coal in Great Britain.

(2)   Securing the efficient development of the industry.

(3)   Making supplies of coal available, in such quality, size, quantity and price as may seem to be best calculated to further the public interest in all respects.

(iii) A minister is given overall control. He exercises, as it were, the shareholders' rights in a company, the 'shareholders' being the community. It is the minister, therefore, who appoints the board's members, though the nationalising act usually specifies their general qualifications. In addition the minister may give the board general directions as to how it is to perform its functions with regard to matters which appear to him to affect national interests, e.g. by authorising capital development, supervising borrowing and appointing auditors.

In this way the boards enjoy freedom in their day-to-day operations but possible subordination in general policy. While they are not subject to parliamentary questioning on details of administration, they are required to submit annual reports to parliament, which are usually debated for a day.

(iv) In financial and staffing matters the boards are free from Treasury control. Originally they were expected to pay their way, taking one year with another, free from state subsidy; but with some, e.g. British Rail, this has proved impossible. They engage their own staff, arranging pay and conditions of service through employees' organisations.

(v) To provide some direct representation for consumers, *consumers' councils* have been established for the coal, electricity, gas and transport industries. They consist of twenty to thirty unpaid members appointed by the minister. Nominations for membership are from bodies he selects as being representative of consumers, e.g. women's organisations, professional associations, trade unions and trade associations. While the coal industry has two national councils, one for industrial and the other for domestic users, the 'consultative councils' of other industries are organised on a regional basis. These councils (1) deal with complaints and suggestions from consumers, and (2) advise both the boards and the minister of the views of consumers. Unfortunately, because of ignorance, remoteness from the offices or general lack of confidence, consumers have so far made little use of these councils.

To sum up, public corporations are made accountable through:

   (i) the responsibility of the minister for appointing board members and ensuring that the board's policies harmonise with the government's overall economic strategy;

  (ii) parliament, which examines how the minister exercises his

Fig 11.6 *the organisation of a nationalised industry*

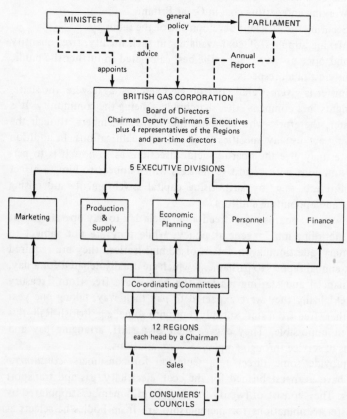

responsibilities, probes (through its Select Committee on the Nationalised Industries), and debates the boards' annual reports;
(iii) consumers' councils.

The detailed organisation of boards has varied; we can illustrate from the coal and electricity industries.

The Coal Industry Nationalisation Act 1946 set up the National Coal Board, and this determines the rest of the organisation of the coal industry. In practice there has been re-organisation from time to time. At present all but the three collieries in Kent are grouped in seventeen areas, each controlled by a director responsible to the NCB. The day-to-day working of the collieries is under the direction of colliery managers.

It seems, however, that originally the problem of size was underestimated, for later nationalising acts have tended towards decentralisation. Thus the Electricity Council, established in 1948, is really only a central representative body for the industry as a whole, and is composed mainly of the chairmen of the twelve area boards, with an independent chairman or vice-chairman appointed by the minister. The area boards were themselves set up by the nationalising act, and the assets of the industry were vested in them. They were also given the *statutory* responsibility for the distribution of electricity. Each board adopted its own pattern of organisation and arrangements for fulfilling its statutory obligations.

Circumstances, however, may change, requiring a new organisation. For instance, the discovery of natural gas meant that distribution had to be organised centrally. Thus in 1973 the original twelve area boards (similar to those for electricity) were replaced by a single British Gas Corporation, which took over the assets of the area gas boards.

(d) Economic problems of nationalisation and efficiencv in the public sector

Apart from the constitutional problems – internal organisation, the minister's exact responsibilities, the extent of and opportunities for parliamentary review – many economic problems still remain to be resolved.

First, problems arise because often nationalised industries are monopolies. On the demand side there is some loss of consumers' sovereignty. For instance, a person can choose initially between gas, electricity, coal and oil for central heating, but thereafter is more or less committed. Should he resent subsequent price rises, the ultimate sanction – taking his custom elsewhere – is hardly available. On the supply side, too, there are grounds for concern. Prices are fixed with the object of covering costs, but what guarantee is there that costs are kept to a minimum by efficient operation? It is often felt that periodic independent efficiency investigations should be made, or some form of private competition allowed, e.g. in postal services.

Second, problems of co-ordination arise in managing these vast industries, and already there has been some movement towards greater decentralisation, e.g. in electricity, postal services and telecommunications. However, these same problems exist in the private sector, and there seems little reason why state industry should be inferior in its ability to solve them.

Third, some economists have criticised investment decisions in many of the nationalised industries, arguing that there has been over-investment in the coal industry and possibly in the railways. Scarce capital could have been better employed elsewhere, e.g. in the construction of motorways. Although some error is bound to occur in a dynamic economy (the discovery of natural gas, for instance, upset the NCB's projections of future demand for coal), there is a feeling that initially the nationalised industries were favoured in the allocation of capital because the government had a vested interest in their success. The present requirement is that any investment project should show a minimum return of 10% on capital.

Fourth, the nationalised industries have not yet really discovered how and when to award wage increases, especially when losses are being made! Threats of strikes in these basic industries, e.g. coal and railways, have led to government intervention, and an aggravation of the wage–cost inflationary spiral.

Finally, although the industries were expected to pay their way, taking one year with another, some have failed to do so. Partly this has resulted from a miscalculation of demand and costs; partly it has been due to the government's use of the nationalised industries to further wider aims, such as price stability (e.g. by restricting increases in the price of gas, coal, electricity, fares, etc.), income redistribution (e.g. by encouraging free travel for senior citizens), social policy (e.g. by retaining loss-making rural railway lines), and full employment and regional balance (e.g. by supporting shipbuilding on Clydeside and the north-east coast).

As a result, the government has had to write off accumulated deficits (e.g. on coal and railways) or subsidise heavily (e.g. shipbuilding). More than that, these wider policy objectives have prevented some nationalised industries from following pricing policies which would have enabled them to break even. The difficulty with many nationalised industries, as we saw above, is that fixed costs are so high that no *single* price can generate sufficient revenue to cover total costs. While the electricity-supply industry has used price discrimination and a two-part tariff to enable it to break even, other industries, notably the railways, have been allowed to operate price discrimination only in a downward direction, fares being reduced where demand is elastic (e.g. on the part of students and senior citizens) but not raised where demand is inelastic (e.g. on the part of commuters and rural passengers). Generally speaking, those who use the services should bear the cost; this is fair and also makes for economy in consumption. Only where there are identifiable external benefits are subsidies to cover deficits justified.

11.4 OTHER QUASI-GOVERNMENTAL BODIES

Although the public-corporation form of organisation was highlighted by the post-1945 nationalisation programme, the practice of setting up of semi-independent government bodies subject to some public control has a much longer history. Even in Tudor times the commissioners of sewers had supervisory duties regarding the disposal of sewage, and in the eighteenth century the turnpike trusts were responsible for providing and maintaining certain roads.

During the twentieth century, however, the number of such semi-independent bodies has increased considerably, e.g. the National Trust, the University Grants Committee, the National Film Finance Corporation, the Milk Marketing Board, the British Council. All are concerned with the allocation of resources, and all are subject to some degree of public control – even though in some cases, e.g. that of the Chruch Commissioners, this only means submitting an annual report to parliament.

Recent expansion of these quasi-autonomous national governmental organisations ('Quangos') has provoked criticism. Such growth has arisen mainly because the state has increasingly intervened in the provision of goods and services. The objective has been to allow these bodies to operate with the minimum of ministerial control so that they can formulate their own policies, cover the particular needs of the regions for which they are responsible and, in certain cases, accept the risks inherent in running a commercial enterprise. Such Quangos cover regional water authorities, regional health authorities, the Equal Opportunities Commission, the Manpower Services Commission, the Commission for Racial Equality, the Health and Safety Executive, the development corporations of new towns and, most controversial of all, the National Enterprise Board.

PART V

FINANCE AND BANKING

FINANCE

12.1 MONEY

(a) What is money?

It is possible to exchange goods by a direct swap. But barter is rare in advanced economies. Where there is a high degree of specialisation, exchanges must take place quickly and smoothly. Hence we have a 'go-between': money.

Anything which is generally acceptable in purchasing goods or settling debts can be said to be money. It need not consist of coins and notes. Oxen, salt, amber, woodpecker scalps and cotton cloth have at times all been used as money. In fact the precise substance, its size and shape, are largely a matter of convenience and custom. But whatever is used, it should be immediately and unquestioningly accepted in exchange for goods and services. Thus the use of the particular good should be backed by custom, and people must feel that it will retain its value by remaining relatively scarce.

Sometimes an attempt is made to confer acceptability by law. In the UK notes have unlimited *legal tender*, in that a creditor *must* accept them in payment of a debt. But a commodity does not have to be legal tender for it to be money. Nor can legislation ensure that it will be acceptable.

In West Germany after the Second World War, cigarettes were preferred to the Reichsbank mark in payment for goods.

(b) The functions of money

Money, it is usually stated, performs four functions:

   (i)   It is a *medium of exchange*, – the oil, as it were, which allows the machinery of modern buying and selling to run smoothly.
   (ii) It is a *measure of value and a unit of account*, making possible the operation of a price system and automatically providing the basis for keeping accounts, calculating profit and loss, costing, etc.

(iii)   It is *a standard of deferred payments*, – the unit in which, provided its value is stable, loans and future contracts are fixed. Without money there would be no common basis for dealing in debts – the work, for example, of such institutions as insurance companies, building societies, banks and discount houses. By providing a standard for repayment, money makes borrowing and lending much easier.

(iv)   It is a *store of wealth*, – the most convenient way of keeping any income which is surplus to immediate requirements. More than that, because money is also the medium of exchange, wealth stored in this form is completely liquid: it can be converted into other goods immediately and without cost. Indeed, it is this 'liquidity' which is the most distinctive characteristic of money, and it results in money's playing an active rather than a merely neutral part in the operation of the economy.

(c) The supply of money

The supply of money consists of:

(i) *Coins and notes*

Since these are regarded as the small change of the monetary system, sufficient coins and notes are always provided for the everyday convenience of the community.

(ii) *Bank deposits*

While purchases of everyday goods – bus-rides, cigarettes, petrol, etc. – are usually paid for in coins and notes, about 80% (in value) of all transactions are effected by cheque. When a person writes a cheque he is instructing his bank to transfer deposits in his account to the person to whom he owes money. Bank deposits therefore act as money.

The two definitions of money in official use are: M_1 which consists of coins and notes and bank deposits held on current accounts, and M_3, which consists of M_1 plus bank deposits held in deposit accounts. M_3 is over twice as large as M_1.

How most such deposits are 'created' by banks is described in the next chapter.

12.2 THE PROVISION OF LIQUID CAPITAL

(a) The need for liquid capital

Where expenditure exceeds the receipts of firms or of the government, the deficit has to be bridged by borrowing. Such funds come from the community, which lends savings. Saving represents refraining from spending on consumer goods, thereby setting free resources for the production of capital goods required by firms or for additional expenditure by the government.

(b) Markets for liquid capital

The market is the institution which brings borrowers and lenders together, making funds available to firms and the government at a price – the rate of interest. But, because finance is required by different types of firm, by the government and by the nationalised industries, for different purposes and for different periods of time, there is a great variety in the types of loan available and in the institutions providing or arranging such loans. Nevertheless, markets can be classified into two broad groups: (i) the *money markets* (dealing in short-term loans) and (ii) the *capital market* (where medium- and long-term capital is raised). The joint-stock banks (the major source of firms' working capital) and the Bank of England (which exercises a general control over the availability of finance) are discussed in chapter 13.

Fig 12.1 *the provision of finance in the United Kingdom*

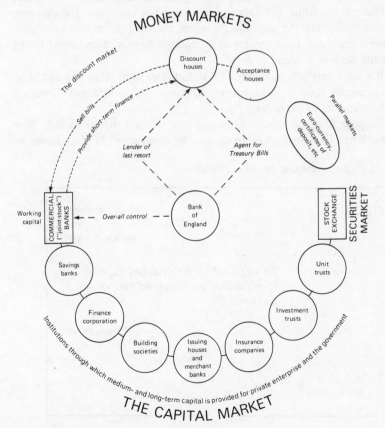

None of the money markets nor the capital market are formal organisations in that buyers and sellers meet regularly in a particular building to conduct business. Instead they are merely a collections of institutions which are connected, in the case of the money markets by dealings in bills of exchange and short-term loans, and in the case of the capital market more loosely – through channelling medium- and long-term finance to those requiring it. Moreover, as we shall see later, within each market there is a high degree of specialisation.

Because it is such a large borrower, the government's requirements tend to dominate these markets, affecting the rates which have to be paid on short- and long-term loans. The complete structure is shown in simplified form in fig. 12.1.

12.3 MONEY MARKETS

(a) The discount market

Bills of exchange are an important source of short-term finance – the commercial bill for firms, the Treasury bill for the government. The discount market comprises the institutions linked by dealings in bills – discount houses, merchant banks acting as acceptance houses, commercial banks and the Bank of England.

It is customary in foreign trade for an importer to be allowed a period of grace, usually three months, to pay for goods. This is arranged through a *commercial bill of exchange.*

Suppose A in London is exporting cars worth £10,000 to B in New York. When he is ready to ship the cars, he draws up a bill of exchange, as

Fig 12.2   *a commercial bill of exchange*

```
£10,000                                    A's address

                                           25 April 1980

            Three months after date, pay to me or
            to my order Ten Thousand Pounds, value
            received.

                                      (Signed) 'A'


To 'B',
    B's address.
```

shown in fig 12.2. This is sent to B, together with copies of the shipping documents to prove that the cars are on the ship. B accepts the bill by writing 'Accepted' and his signature across the face of the bill, and then returns it to A. This acceptance of the bill by B is necessary before the original *bill of lading*, the documentary title to the cars, is handed over.

A can now do one of three things: (i) hold the bill until it matures; (ii) endorse the bill and then get a merchant to whom he is indebted to take it in settlement; or (iii) sell the bill, usually to a discount house.

Fig 12.3 *operations of the discount market*

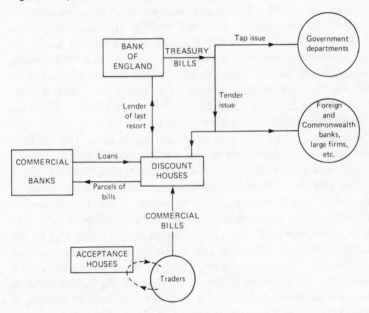

(i) *Discount houses*

Probably A will choose the latter course. So, after endorsing it, he takes it to one of the eleven *London discount houses*. The exact amount paid for the bill will depend on the length of time to maturity, the prevailing short-term rate of interest and the opinion of the discount house as to B's financial standing. If the bill still has three months to run and the prevailing rate of interest on that class of bill is 12%, the discount house will pay about £9,700 for it. This process is known as 'discounting'. Thus, while A quickly regains liquidity by selling the bill, B obtains three months' credit, during which time he will probably sell the cars.

Bills are not usually held for the full three months. Instead after about a month, they are sold in 'parcels' to the commercial banks, who like to have so many maturing each day.

(ii) *Acceptance houses*

If B is a well-known firm of high financial standing, the accepted bill is, from the risk point of view, almost as good as cash. However, as bills are drawn on firms in all parts of the world, little may be known about B. Thus the discount house is either reluctant to discount the bill or will only do so at a high rate of interest. The difficulty can be overcome by getting a firm of international repute to 'accept' responsibility for payment should B default. It is obvious that any firm accepting such a bill must have adequate knowledge of the creditworthiness of the trader upon whom the bill is drawn. Such knowledge is possessed by the merchant banks, such as Lazards, Barings and Rothschilds, who commenced as traders but later specialised in financing trade in particular parts of the world. In their capacity of accepting bills such merchant banks are known as *acceptance houses*. For the service, they charge a small commission of about ¾%, which is paid willingly because the rate of discount on a 'bank bill', i.e. one bearing the name of an acceptance house, is lower than on a 'trade bill' (a bill accepted only by a trader) or on a 'fine trade bill' (where the merchant is of good standing).

In recent years the business of accepting has declined. This has been due to: (i) the diminished use of the commercial bill in international trade; (ii) the decline of London as the world centre for financing foreign trade; and (iii) the increased competition of the commercial banks in accepting bills, largely through the development of the 're-imbursement credit'. With this, B, the importer, induces his own bank in New York to secure an acceptance credit for him in London, which means that he can instruct A to draw the bill on the London branch of his own bank or on a London bank or acceptance house. The New York bank makes itself responsible for the payment of the bill, and so all the London bank or acceptance house has to do is to satisfy itself as to the financial standing of the New York bank. This simpler procedure means that re-imbursement credits can be granted at very low rates of interest.

The decline in the use of the commercial bill coincided with a large increase in government borrowing through Treasury bills. A Treasury bill is really a bill of exchange drawn by the Treasury on itself, usually for a period of three months (ninety-one days), though occasionally two-month bills (sixty-three days) are issued. Since such bills are only short-term loans, they represent the government's cheapest method of borrowing (see p. 328). Treasury bills are issued in denominations of £5,000 upwards, and since the minimum sale is for £50,000 they are primarily for institutional investors.

(iii) *The commercial banks*

The commercial banks fulfil two main functions in the discount market – providing the discount houses with funds and holding bills to maturity.

The discount houses do not themselves have sufficient finance to buy all the bills, commercial and Treasury, offered them. They overcome this difficulty, however, by borrowing money from the commercial banks at a comparatively low rate of interest. Then, by discounting at a slightly higher rate, they make a small profit. The banks are willing to lend at a low rate because the loans are of short duration, often for only a day, and need not be renewed if there is a heavy demand for cash from their ordinary customers. For the discount houses, the trouble involved in the daily renewal of this money at call and the slight risk of its non-renewal is compensated for by the comparatively low rate of interest charged.

The commercial banks can earn a higher rate of interest by themselves holding bills for a part of their currency. However, by convention they do not bid for them directly but buy them from the discount houses when they still have about two months to run.

(iv) *The Bank of England*
The Bank of England enters the discount market as follows.

First, it is the agency by which the government issues Treasury bills. This issue is achieved by two methods, 'tap' and 'tender'. Government departments, the National Savings Bank, the Exchange Equalisation Account, the National Insurance Fund and the Bank of England Issue Department, all of which have funds to invest for a short period, can buy what bills they want at a fixed price, i.e. 'on tap'. This price is not published.

The discount houses and other purchasers (such as Commonwealth and foreign banks) can obtain their issue by 'tender'. Every Friday, the Treasury, acting through the Bank of England, invites tenders for a specified amount of bills, usually between £200 and £300 million.

Second, the Bank of England is the 'lender of last resort'. When the discount houses are pressed for money because the commercial banks will not renew their 'call money', the Bank of England will lend to them at the declared 'minimum lending rate' (see p. 228).

(b) Parallel money markets
As a result of restrictions placed on bank lending, new markets in short-term loans developed to meet the specific requirements of particular borrowers and lenders. Indeed the existence of such markets has encouraged funds to be lent short-term, since they have made it easier for lenders to regain liquidity.

The following are the most important of these comparatively new markets:

(i) *Inter-bank deposits*
This is a market bringing together all banks, including merchant banks, British overseas banks and foreign banks, so that those having funds surplus

to their immediate requirements can lend to those having outlets for short-term loans.

(ii) *Local-authority deposits*
Local authorities borrow on the open market and are willing to make use of very short-term money. Brokers now exist for placing with them short-term funds of banks, industrial and commercial companies, charitable funds, etc. Such brokers also deal in longer-term local-authority bonds.

(iii) *Negotiable certificates of deposit*
Certificates of deposit enable the banks to borrow for periods from three months to five years. They are like bills of exchange drawn on banks by themselves. For the bank they are for a longer period than an ordinary time deposit, thus facilitating medium-term lending. For the lender they offer a higher rate of interest, while the market in them means that they can be sold whenever cash is required.

(iv) *Euro-currency balances*
Euro-currency deposits are simply funds which are deposited with banks outside the country of origin but which continue to be designated in terms of the original currency. The most important Euro-currency is the dollar. As a result of the USA's continuing adverse balance of payments, branches of European banks have built up dollar balances as customers were paid for exports. These balances are offered to brokers in London (where interest rates have been higher than in New York), and are placed mainly with companies or banks (e.g. Japanese) operating on an international scale to finance foreign trade or investment. While the dollar still dominates the market, other European currencies are now dealt in, chiefly the Deutschmark and the Swiss franc.

(v) *Other markets*
Smaller specialist markets have developed in *finance-house deposits* and *inter-company deposits*. Thus finance houses have obtained funds by issuing bills which are accepted by banks and discount houses. Similarly, in periods of tight credit, firms which are short of finance turn to other companies which temporarily have funds to spare.

12.4 THE CAPITAL MARKET

Whereas the money markets developed to supply short-term finance to trade and the government, industry obtains most of its 'working' capital from the commercial banks (see chapter 13). But long-term capital for both the public and private sectors is obtained through the capital market.

Fig 12.4 *the capital market*

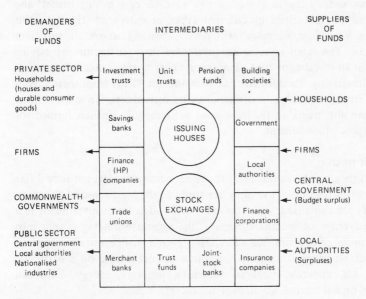

DEMANDERS OF FUNDS / INTERMEDIARIES / SUPPLIERS OF FUNDS

PRIVATE SECTOR
Households
(houses and durable consumer goods)

FIRMS

COMMONWEALTH GOVERNMENTS

PUBLIC SECTOR
Central government
Local authorities
Nationalised industries

Intermediaries: Investment trusts, Unit trusts, Pension funds, Building societies, Savings banks, Government, Finance (HP) companies, Local authorities, Trade unions, Finance corporations, Merchant banks, Trust funds, Joint-stock banks, Insurance companies; ISSUING HOUSES; STOCK EXCHANGES

Suppliers: HOUSEHOLDS, FIRMS, CENTRAL GOVERNMENT (Budget surplus), LOCAL AUTHORITIES (Surpluses)

Notes:
(1) Arrows merely indicate direction, not particular intermediaries.
(2) Intermediaries collect relatively small amounts of capital which are channelled to where they are wanted.
(3) Some intermediaries are mainly concerned with old issues.
(4) Issuing houses assist the movement of funds; stock exchanges provide a market in old securities and thus encourage the provision of new funds.

As can be seen from fig 12.4, this consists of, on the one hand, the suppliers of long-term capital and, on the other, those requiring such capital, the two being connected by a number of intermediaries, usually of a specialist nature. Some of these intermediaries have already been described; here we look briefly at the others.

(a) Insurance companies

Insurance companies receive premiums for insuring against various risks. Some of these premiums, such as those for insuring ships and property, are held only for relatively short periods – having, apart from the profit made, to be paid out against claims. But with life insurance, endowments and annuities, premiums are usually held for a long time before payments are made. Hence insurance companies have large sums of money to invest in long-term securities. These investments are spread over government and other public stocks, the shares and debentures of companies, property and mortgages. Today 'institutional investors', of which insurance companies are the most important, supply the bulk of savings required for new issues.

(b) Investment trusts

Investors usually try to avoid 'putting all their eggs in one basket' and therefore buy securities in different types of enterprise. However, this requires knowledge of investment possibilities and, above all, sufficient resources. The small investor can overcome these difficulties by buying shares in an investment trust. This invests over a wide range of securities, and after paying management expenses the net yields from these investments are distributed as a dividend on its own shares. Thus investment trusts are not 'trusts' in the legal sense but merely companies formed for the purpose of investment.

(c) Unit trusts

Unit trusts are a development of the investment-trust idea, but they differ in two main respects. First, they are trusts in the legal sense of the term. Trustees are appointed, while the trust deed often limits investments to a specified range of securities. Second, the aggregate holding is split into many 'units' of low nominal value. Thus even a small investment covers a range of securities, though it is possible to concentrate on a particular group, e.g. minerals, financial securities, property, energy, European growth, capital accumulation, high income, etc.

Many unit trusts have schemes linked with insurance, to which savers subscribe on a regular basis. While most of the funds are used to purchase existing securities, trusts do make capital available for new investment, particularly when they take up 'rights' issues of companies whose shares are already held.

(d) Savings banks

The National Savings Bank and trustee savings banks provide savings facilities for small depositors, since holdings are limited. Deposits are invested in securities, mostly government and similar stock, prescribed by the trustees.

(e) Trust, pension and trade-union funds

All these accumulate income which is re-invested in government securities, shares, property, etc.

(f) Building Societies

These have a specialised function – the supply of long-term loans on the security of private dwelling-houses purchased for owner-occupation. Their funds are derived chiefly from money invested in them by the general public, but their shares are not dealt in on the stock exchange, being cashable upon notice. Their liquid reserves are usually invested in government stock and local-authority bonds.

(g) Finance companies

These borrow savings from the public and obtain loans from banks in order to finance hire-purchase of both consumer goods and machinery. The rates at which they borrow are comparatively high because of the greater lending risks involved, and for a similar reason the rates at which they lend are high. Many joint-stock banks now engage in hire-purchase finance through their own subsidiary finance companies.

12.5 THE STOCK EXCHANGE

(a) A market in 'old' securities

A stock exchange is really an organised market for exchanging 'securities', i.e. claims to loans or shares. Although there are stock exchanges in most of the larger cities of the United Kingdom, the London exchange is by far the most important and henceforth will be referred to as 'the stock exchange'. A glance at the financial pages of any daily newspaper will reveal the nature of the securities dealt in – British funds (government stock and the stock of the nationalised industries), Commonwealth and foreign-government stock, corporation stock (issued by local authorities such as the Greater London Council and by public-utility undertakings such as the Thames Water Authority) and the stocks and shares of all types of industrial and commercial companies.

By the second half of the seventeenth century a recognisable market was dealing in the shares of trading companies, government-sponsored lottery tickets, seamen's pay-tickets and, above all, in the loans contracted by Charles II and James II (which formed the nucleus of the National Debt officially recognised by William III in 1688). Since then, the National Debt has been the mainstay of the stock exchange's activity.

(b) Members and their work

The stock exchange is privately owned, and the 'proprietors' are the members who between them hold the shares which provided the capital for its buildings. Its affairs are controlled by an elected council of thirty-six members.

Members are either 'brokers' or 'jobbers', but they are not allowed to act in both capacities.

A *stockbroker* acts as the agent for his clients, executing business on their instructions and giving them investment advice. He earns commission on the business he transacts, but he is not allowed to advertise. In effect he acts as the link between the investing public, who wish to buy and sell securities, and the *jobber*, the actual dealer who buys and carries a stock of securities in order to resell them later. The difference between broker and jobber is best shown by an example.

216

Mr A wishes to buy 800 25p ordinary shares in Unilever Ltd. He therefor telephones his broker or bank manager (who will contact whichever broker acts for the bank), giving him the necessary instructions. He will either name the maximum price at which he will buy or instruct the broker to buy at the lowest price possible. On the floor of the Stock Exchange the broker goes to that part which specialises in the leading industrial ordinary shares. He approaches a jobber and enquires the price of 25p Unilever ordinaries, but he does not say whether he wishes to buy or sell. Suppose the jobber replies, 'Four-sixty to four-sixty-six.' This indicates that he is prepared to buy at the lower and to sell at the higher price. The difference between the two prices is known as the 'jobber's turn' and is the normal source of the jobber's profit, the size of spread depending on the jobber's estimate of the risk involved in dealing in that particular security. The broker can accept the price, try to get the jobber to lower his price, or else move on the other jobbers in the hope of doing better. Let us suppose that he considers 466p satisfactory. He then informs the jobber that he wishes to buy 500 shares, the bargain is struck, and both broker and jobber make notes in their dealing books. The broker,

Fig 12.5 *a contract note*

INVOICE NO.   1475   To. Mr A.N. Other
                      Client No. 436485

BARGAIN DATE
AND TAX POINT
  7th November 1979

WE THANK YOU FOR YOUR INSTRUCTIONS AND ADVISE HAVING **BOUGHT** FOR YOUR ACCOUNT SUBJECT TO THE RULES AND REGULATIONS OF THE STOCK EXCHANGE

AMOUNT	STOCK OR SHARES	PRICE	CONSIDERATION		
800	Unilever Limited Ordinary 25p Shares	466p	3728	00	N
	TRANSFER STAMP		75	00	N
	CONTRACT STAMP			60	N
	COMMISSION 1½% on money		55	92	T
	TOTAL VAT @ 15%			8	38
	FOR SETTLEMENT 19 November 1979	£	3867.90		

SPENCER THORNTON & CO.
MEMBERS OF THE STOCK EXCHANGE

CONTRACT NOTE AND TAX INVOICE
FOR SERVICES RENDERED

WE RECOMMEND THAT THIS DOCUMENT
BE RETAINED FOR FUTURE REFERENCE

having arranged the deal, sends to Mr A, or to the bank acting for him, a contract note (fig 12.5).

The transfer stamp represents revenue charged on all transfer deeds (except British government stock). It is charged only on purchases. All bargains have to be settled on the next 'account day', which usually falls fortnightly on a Tuesday, though government and municipal stock are 'for cash', meaning that settlement is immediate.

(c) Economic functions

Critics of the stock exchange tend to ignore its real functions and to concentrate on its speculative aspects. It is true that the facilities offered by the stock exchange do provide openings for speculation. The fortnightly account allows a speculator to buy securities at the beginning and sell at a profit or loss within fourteen days without ever having to put up any money. A speculator who buys securities because he thinks the price will rise is said to be a 'bull'; he hopes to sell them at a profit before the end of the account. On the other hand, a 'bear' sells securities he does not possess because he expects the price to fall before they have to be delivered. Sometimes, if a client's credit stands high with his broker or if he can put up security, he may be permitted to 'carry over' his commitments from one account to the next. Such a transaction is known as 'contango'.

The difficulty concerning speculation is that both optimism and pessimism are contagious and so the market becomes extremely susceptible to both over-confidence and panic. Indeed, expectations are 'self-fulfilling': people who expect the price of securities to rise bid for them, thereby sending up their price, and vice versa. The result is that the prices of stocks and shares may be written up or down not through changes in their earnings prospects but simply through waves of confidence or mistrust.

Even so, we must not forget that some speculation may be advantageous. Expert professional operators such as jobbers tend to steady prices through their function of holding stocks (see below). This also permits securities to be bought and sold at any time, thereby making them more liquid. The great difficulty occurs in distinguishing harmful speculation from genuine investment, for with all investment there is a certain element of risk. In any case the magnitude of the speculative business must not be over-estimated. Most purchases represent genuine investment conducted on behalf of investment trusts, insurance companies, pension funds, building societies and private individuals.

The truth is that, for the following reasons, an organised market in securities is an indispensable part of the mechanism of a capitalist economy.

(i) *It facilitates borrowing by the government and industry*
If people are to be encouraged to lend to industry and the government, they must be satisfied that they will be able to sell an investment easily

should the need arise. Such an assurance is offered to any holder of a quoted security by the stock exchange, for it provides a permanent market. Indirectly, therefore, the stock exchange encourages savers to lend to the government or to invest in industry.

(ii) *Through the jobbers it helps to even out short-run price fluctuations in securities*

Whilst the jobber himself may often speculate, in the short run he acts as a buffer to speculation by outsiders. This is because he does not merely 'match' a buyer with a seller but holds stocks of securities. Since he specialises in dealing in certain securities, he obtains an intimate knowledge of them. Thus, when the public is pessimistic and selling, he may be more optimistic in his outlook and consider that the drop in price is not likely to continue. He therefore takes these securities on to his book. Similarly, when the public is rushing to buy, he will, when he considers the price has reached its zenith, sell from his stocks. The effect in both cases is to even out the fluctuations in price, for in the first case he increases his demand as supply increases, and in the second he increases supply as the demand increases.

(iii) *It advertises security prices*

The publication of current stock-exchange prices enables the public to follow the fortunes of their investments and to channel their savings into profitable enterprises.

(iv) *It protects the public against fraud*

The *official list* of securities is a guarantee that securities listed are reputable. Permission to deal is not given to members unless the stock exchange council is satisfied on this score, and it may be withdrawn if any doubts arise about the conduct of a company's affairs. Moreover, the council insists on a high standard of professional conduct from its members. Should any member default, the investor is indemnified out of the Stock Exchange Compensation Fund.

(v) *It reflects the country's economic prospects*

The movement of the market acts as a barometer which points to the economic prospects of the country – whether as 'set fair', or otherwise.

BANKING

13.1 THE BRITISH BANKING SYSTEM

(a) Types of banks in the UK

(i) *The commercial or joint-stock banks*
These banks, which are dominated by the 'Big Four' (Lloyds, Barclays, the National Westminster and the Midland) operate through a network of branches throughout the country. Their importance in the financial system stems from the fact that most of their business is conducted by way of cheques which are cleared at the London Clearing House. Indeed, the six member banks of the London Clearing House are often referred to as 'clearing banks', and other banks have to do their clearing through one of these. As we shall see, this system of clearing allows them to economise in the use of cash, so allowing them to 'create' credit which serves as money.

(ii) *The central bank*
This is the Bank of England, which, on behalf of the government, exercises ultimate control over the financial system.

(iii) *Merchant banks* (see p. 210).

(iv) *Foreign and commonwealth banks having branches in the UK*

(v) *The National Savings Bank*
This operates mainly through post offices, collecting relatively small savings and selling Premium Bonds, National Saving Certificates and Savings Bonds.

(vi) *Trustee savings banks* (see p. 214).

(vii) *The National Giro*
This exists largely as a cheap and easy means of paying bills.

(viii) *Finance companies* (see p. 215).

Easily the most important of the above are the joint-stock banks. But attention must also be given to the Bank of England, especially with regard to its influence on the operation of the joint-stock banks.

13.2 JOINT-STOCK BANKS

(a) The cheque system
Banks are companies which exist to make profit for their shareholders. They do this by borrowing money from 'depositors' and re-lending it at a higher rate of interest to other people. Borrowers are private persons, companies, public corporations, the money market and the government. The more a bank can lend, the greater will be its profits.

People who hold a current account at a bank can settle their debts by cheque, a very convenient form of payment. But the use of cheques is advantageous to banks. Thus, to advertise their business, induce customers to pay by cheque rather than by cash and encourage people to deposit money with them, banks perform many services outside their main business of borrowing and lending money – keeping accounts, making standing-order payments, providing night-safe facilities, paying bills by credit transfers, purchasing securities, transacting foreign work, storing valuables, acting as executors, etc.

(b) The cheque as a substitute for cash
Cheques lead to a reduction in the use of cash. Suppose that I have paid £100 cash into my banking account. Imagine, too, that my builder banks at the same branch and I owe him £50. I simply write him a cheque for that amount, and he pays this into the bank. To complete the transaction, my account is debited by £50, and his account is credited by that amount. What it is important to observe, however, is that in the settlement of the debt no actual *cash* changes hands. A mere book entry in both accounts has completed the transaction.

Perhaps my builder will, towards the end of the week, withdraw some cash to pay his workers' wages. But it is likely that most of his payments, e.g. for building materials, petrol and lorry servicing, will be by cheque. Similarly, while I may withdraw some cash from the £50 still standing to my account to cover everyday household expenses, the probability is that many of my bills, e.g. my club subscription, half-yearly rates and mortgage repayments, will be settled by cheque or by a credit transfer directly from my account. Furthermore, even where cash is withdrawn, this is often compensated for by cash being paid in.

With the development of the cheque system the proportion of cash required for transactions has decreased. Let us assume a simple model in which the banks operate free from government control but have discovered that in practice only 10% of their total deposits need be retained in cash to cover all demands for cash withdrawals. In short, only £10 of my original deposit of £100 is needed to form an adequate cash reserve.

(c) The creation of credit

It is obvious, therefore, that £90 could be lent by the bank to a third party without my being the wiser. What is not quite so obvious is that the bank can go further than this – and does!

Let us assume that there is only one bank and that all lending is in the form of advances (see p. 224). When a person is granted a loan by his bank manager, all that happens is that the borrower's account is credited with the amount of the loan, or alternatively that he is authorised to overdraw his account up to the stipulated limit. In other words, a deposit is created by the bank in the name of the borrower.

When he spends the loan, the borrower will probably pay by cheque. If this happens, there is no immediate demand for cash. There is no reason, therefore, why the whole of my cash deposit of £100 should not act as the safe cash reserve for deposits of a much larger sum created by the bank's lending activities.

Fig 13.1 *how a bank creates credit*

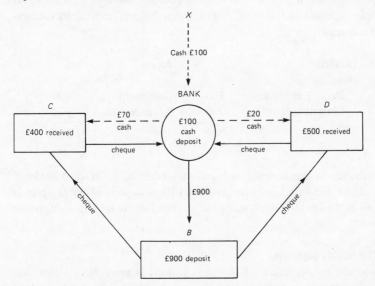

But the bank must not overdo this credit creation. Our model has assumed that, to be safe, cash must always form one-tenth of total deposits. This means that the bank can grant a loan of up to £900. Because it is the only bank, there is no need to fear that cheques drawn on it will be paid into another bank and eventually presented for cash.

The process of credit-creation is illustrated in fig 13.1. X pays £100 in cash into the bank. This allows the bank to make a loan of £900 to B, who now settles his debts of £400 and £500 by sending cheques to C and D. These cheques are paid into the bank. C withdraws cash rather heavily, in the sum of £70; but this is compensated for by D, who only withdraws £20 in cash. This leaves £10 cash – enough to cover the average withdrawal which X is likely to make. While these cash withdrawals are being made, other cash is being paid in, thereby maintaining the 10% ratio.

In practice there are many banks, but for the purpose of credit creation they are virtually one bank because they are able to eliminate a large demand for cash from each other by their clearing arrangements through the London Clearing House. Moreover, banks keep in line as regards their credit creation. Were one bank to adopt, say, a 6% cash ratio, it would find that, because its customers were making such a large volume of payments to people who banked elsewhere, it would be continually called upon to settle a debit with other banks in cash at the end of the day's clearing, so that its cash reserve would fall below the safe level.

(d) The effect of lending on the bank's balance-sheet
Suppose that the receipt of the £100 in cash and the loan to B are so far the sole activities of the bank. Ignoring shareholders' capital, its balance-sheet will read:

Liabilities	£	Assets	£
Deposits:			
Deposit account	100	Cash in till	100
Current account	900	Advances	900
	1,000		1,000

The advance to B is an asset; it is an outstanding debt. On the other hand his current account has been credited with a deposit of £900 – just as though he had paid it in. It can be seen, therefore, that *every loan creates a deposit.*

(e) The bank's objectives
In practice the structure of the bank's assets is more varied than this. Creating deposits in order to lend at a profit entails risks. First, the loan

may not be repaid. Second, and more important, there may be a run on the bank for cash: the original depositor may wish to withdraw his £100, or B, C and D may require between them an abnormally large amount of cash. Any suggestion that the bank could not meet these demands would undermine confidence.

Hence, although a permanent cash reserve is essential, a bank must have other lines of defence so that in an emergency it can raise cash easily and quickly. Instead of lending entirely by advances, which a borrower usually requires for at least six months, some loans must be restricted to a shorter period, even to just a day. But, the shorter the period of the loan, the lower will be the rate of interest the bank earns. On the other hand, it wants profit for shareholders to be as high as possible. Thus it is limited in its lending policy both quantitatively and qualitatively. Not only must credit be restricted to a multiple of the liquid reserves but it must also afford adequate *security, liquidity, and profitability*.

As regards *security*, the bank endeavours not to lend if there is any risk of inability to repay. Collateral, e.g. an insurance policy, the deeds of a house or share certificates, is regarded more as a weapon to strengthen its demand for repayment than as a safeguard against default.

Liquidity and *profitability* pull in opposite directions – the shorter the period of the loan, the greater the bank's liquidity but the less it will earn by way of interest. The difficulty is resolved by a compromise: (i) loans are divided among different types of borrower and for different periods of time; and (ii) the different types of loan are kept fairly close to carefully chosen proportions. In short, the bank maintains a 'portfolio' of assets.

(f) The distribution of a bank's assets

We can see how in practice a bank reconciles conflicting aims if we study its sterling assets. These, apart from its cash, buildings and goodwill, are its debts outstanding – the loans it has made. The position is shown in figs 13.2 and 13.3.

(i) *Money at call and on short notice* are very short-term loans to discount houses which enable the latter to discount bills of exchange and hold them for a month or so before passing them on to the banks.

(ii) *Bills*, which are Treasury bills, local-authority bills and trade bills, are obtained chiefly from the discount houses (though some may be discounted directly for customers) and are held for the remainder of their currency, usually two months.

(iii) *Other market loans* are loans to banks and local authorities, and trade bills above the 2% limit, all of which are not 'eligible reserve assets' (see p. 226).

(iv) *Investments* are medium and long-term government securities bought on the open market.

224

Fig 13.2 *the nature and distribution of a bank's main assets*

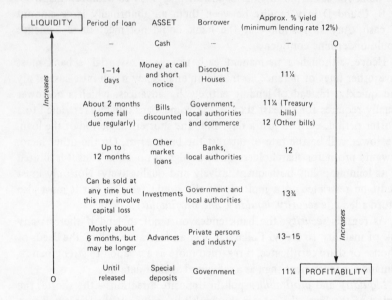

LIQUIDITY	Period of loan	ASSET	Borrower	Approx. % yield (minimum lending rate 12%)
	–	Cash	–	– 0
	1–14 days	Money at call and short notice	Discount Houses	11¼
	About 2 months (some fall due regularly)	Bills discounted	Government, local authorities and commerce	11¼ (Treasury bills) 12 (Other bills)
	Up to 12 months	Other market loans	Banks, local authorities	12
	Can be sold at any time but this may involve capital loss	Investments	Government and local authorities	13¾
	Mostly about 6 months, but may be longer	Advances	Private persons and industry	13–15
0	Until released	Special deposits	Government	11¼ PROFITABILITY

Increases (on liquidity axis, upward) — *Increases* (on profitability axis, downward)

(v) *Advances*, to nationalised industries, companies and personal borrowers, are the most profitable (1–3% above base rate) but also the least liquid of all the bank's assets. The main object of bank advances is to provide the working capital for industry and commerce. The type of loan preferred is 'self-liquidating' within a period of about six months, as with a farmer who borrows at the beginning of the year in order to buy fertilisers and pay wages, repaying the bank when he sells the harvest. Firms, however, are often allowed to 'roll over' their overdrafts.

Generally banks refrain from providing long-term capital for firms, leaving this to the capital market (see p. 212–15).

(vi) For a discussion of *Special Deposits* see p. 227.

It must be emphasised that, apart from cash and bank buildings, these assets are covered only by credit created by the bank. For example, Treasury bills and government securities are paid for by cheques which will increase the accounts of the sellers. If they are new issues, there is an addition to the government account at the Bank of England; if they are old issues, the bank is virtually taking over from somebody else a loan already made to the government. In writing these cheques the bank increases its liabilities, for book-entry deposits have to be created to cover them. This 'pyramid of credit', created to buy earning assets and to make loans upon a minimum 12½%-liquid-assets basis, is shown in fig 13.3.

Fig 13.3   *the pyramid of bank credit*

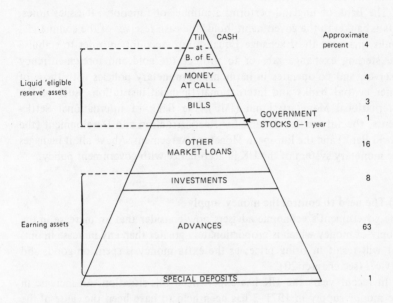

(g) Modification of the cash-ratio approach

Our explanation of credit creation has followed traditional lines: credit bears a fixed relationship to cash reserves. Today, however, the monetary authorities (i.e. the Bank of England acting as agent for the Treasury) now regard cash simply as the small change of the monetary system, to be varied according to the needs of trade. In any case banks are more concerned with their general liquidity position than with the one item of cash. This ori ;inally stemmed from the introduction of the Treasury bill, which through government support became almost as good as cash. Improved markets for loans, e.g. the money markets described in chapter 12, also increase liquidity to the extent that such loans can be regarded as 'near money'.

It follows, therefore, that if the authorities wish to control the money supply, they must operate on other assets which the banks hold in order to change total deposits.

13.3 THE BANK OF ENGLAND

(a) Functions of the Bank of England

The Bank of England, established in 1694, remained a joint-stock company until it was nationalised in 1946. However, nationalisation merely formalised its position as a 'central bank' - the institution which, on behalf of the government, exercises the ultimate control over the policies of banks and other financial institutions.

The Bank of England performs a number of functions. It issues notes, acts as banker to the government, holds the cash reserves of the commercial banks, manages the Exchange Equalisation Account in order to stabilise the sterling exchange rate or to protect the gold and foreign-currency reserves, and co-operates in harmonising monetary policies with those of other central banks and international financial institutions, such as the International Monetary Fund (IMF), the Bank of International Settlements, the International Bank for Reconstruction and Development (the World Bank) and the European Monetary Agreement. Above all, it manages the monetary system of the UK in accordance with government policy.

(b) The need to control the money supply

The government's economic advisers now consider that an increase in the supply of money which is proportionately greater than any increase in output will result in rising prices as the extra money is spent on goods and services (see chapter 20).

In recent years the UK has experienced this situation. An increase in the money supply in 1971-2 has been held to have been the cause of the 27% inflation rate of 1973-4. Again, in 1975-6, spending by the central government, the local authorities and the nationalised industries exceeded their revenues, and the need to cover much of this deficit (the Public-Sector Borrowing Requirement) by an increase in the supply of money led to inflationary pressure and the run on sterling (see again chapter 20). Indeed, one condition of the IMF loan to support sterling was that the money supply should be brought under control. Such a policy entails raising the rate of interest and restricting the ability of the banks to create credit. Responsibility for this rests with the Bank of England.

(c) The weapons which the Bank of England can employ

(i) *The minimum-reserve-assets ratio*

The policy by which credit is controlled is founded on the ability of the Bank of England to dictate to the banks and other lending institutions the minimum liquidity ratio which they shall maintain.

Each bank is required to observe a minimum-reserve ratio (set at 12½% since 1971) of 'eligible reserve assets' to 'eligible liabilities'. This ratio is more or less fixed, and is therefore not a weapon for short-term monetary adjustments.

Eligible reserve assets comprise: balances with the Bank of England, other than special deposits; Treasury bills; company-tax-reserve certificates;

money at call; local-authority bills eligible for re-discount at the Bank of England (up to a maximum of 2% of eligible liabilities); and British government securities with one year or less to maturity. Broadly speaking banks would regard these as their liquid assets.

Eligible liabilities refer broadly to net bank deposits (excluding foreign-currency deposits and deposits having an original maturity of over two years).

It is important to note that this ratio applies to *all* banks; not merely to the clearing banks.

(ii) *Open-market operations*

With a liquidity ratio of 12½%, a given change in eligible reserve assets held by the banks will change total deposits by eight times the amount. The Bank of England can therefore adjust the money supply by varying the eligible reserve assets held by the banks.

This it achieves by buying or selling government securities in the open market. Suppose, for instance, it sells long-term securities. The increase in the supply offered lowers their price (i.e. raises the rate of interest) until the total offering has been bought by the banks or by their customers. But cash will be necessary to pay for them, and so the banks' cash balances at the Bank of England fall. In other words the liquid reserve assets held by the banks are reduced and, if previously banks had made loans to the maximum possible extent, they will be forced to squeeze their advances.

Alternatively the Bank of England may put the pressure on the short end of the market by varying the weekly offer of Treasury bills. Inasmuch as these bills are bought initially outside the banks, the cash balances of the bank's customers can be made to fall, and hence the cash of the banks will likewise fall.

(iii) *Funding*

A deliberate policy of converting government short-term debt into long-term debt is known as 'funding'. It is achieved by open-market operations, as described above, over an extended period. What happens is that the Treasury bill offer is reduced, the government raising the finance it requires by selling medium- and long-dated securities instead.

(iv) *Special deposits*

More fundamental changes in the supply of credit can be effected through calls for special deposits. Banks are required to deposit with the Bank of England a certain percentage of their total eligible liabilities. These special deposits do not count as eligible reserve assets and inasmuch as they are raised by selling such liquid assets, there is a 'multiplier' effect on the size of the bank's assets.

(v) *Supplementary deposits*

When the money supply, chiefly bank credit, is rising too quickly, the Bank of England may apply the 'corset', requiring supplementary deposits from the banks. These are automatically payable if a bank's interest-bearing deposits (thus excluding current-account deposits) rise faster than a specified rate. This target rate of growth is fixed periodically by the Bank of England. The proportion of the excess to be deposited with the Bank of England rises progressively according to the extent of the excess growth, and may be as high as 50%.

Supplementary deposits, unlike Special Deposits, earn no interest. This means that, when the target rate of growth is exceeded, it ceases to be profitable for a bank to compete for deposit money by paying high rates of interest. Thus the pace of monetary expansion is restrained without forcing short-term interest and bank lending rates to unacceptable heights.

(vi) *Minimum lending rate*

The minimum lending rate (formerly Bank Rate) is the rate at which the Bank of England will help the discount houses as a lender of last resort. The rate is announced on a Thursday, and any change in it signals the direction in which the authorities require interest rates to move.

(vii) *Requests*

A policy of allocating credit by the market is not entirely satisfactory, especially when an attempt is being made to hold down the rate of interest. Thus from time to time the monetary authorities issue instructions to the banks, requiring them to discriminate against certain borrowers, e.g. property developers, but to favour others, e.g. exporters.

(viii) *Directives*

The Bank of England, if authorised by the Treasury, can issue directives to any banker to ensure that its requests and recommendations are implemented. So far this power has not had to be used, the banks having observed the requests of the Bank of England.

(d) Conclusion

Monetary policy is unlikely to rely on a single weapon, since the use of one reinforces the others. While today the emphasis is on controlling the total money supply (see p. 325), the different weapons also enable the Bank of England to influence the structure of interest rates in order to induce shifts in the portfolios of both the public and the banks in the desired direction.

PART VI
THE LEVEL OF
ECONOMIC ACTIVITY

THE FULL EMPLOYMENT
OF RESOURCES

14.1 THE NATURE OF THE PROBLEM

(a) The limit to production
Although at any one time resources are limited, they have two important
characteristics: (i) they are capable of alternative uses, and (ii) they can be
increased over time. The first enables us to make the most of what we
have; the second allows us to improve our lot. We can illustrate the situation as follows.

Suppose that, during a year, a country can, with all its resources fully
employed, produce the following alternative combinations of agricultural
produce and manufactured goods (in unspecified units):

Agricultural produce	+	Manufactured goods
100		0
80		25
60		40
40		45
20		48
0		50

By plotting these alternative combinations we obtain a 'production-
possibility curve' (fig 14.1). This shows the various combinations of
agricultural produce and manufactured goods open to country X with its
limited resources and given technology. Note that the curve is concave to
the origin. This is because factors of production are not equally suited to
producing agricultural produce and manufactured goods. It can be seen
from the table that as more resources are transferred to producing manufactured goods, an ever-smaller quantity of manufactured goods is received
for each 20 units of agricultural produce given up. In short, both manufactured goods and agricultural produce are produced under conditions of
diminishing returns.

Fig 14.1 *a production-possibility curve*

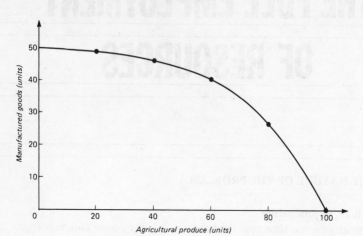

The production-possibility curve shows that, in order to obtain as high a standard of living as possible, country X must be concerned with:

(i) *The allocation of resources*

Because resources can be used in alternative ways, it is necessary to choose between manufactured goods and agricultural produce. The particular combination chosen should be the one which yields maximum satisfaction.

(ii) *The full employment of resources*

While it is impossible to produce a combination of agricultural produce and manufactured goods which lies to the right of the curve, any assortment on the origin side means that the country is not maximising its output because some resources are idle. A combination of goods on the production-possibility curve can be obtained only if there is full employment.

(iii) *The growth of resources*

Over time, the production-possibility curve must be pushed further from the origin so that a larger assortment of both agricultural produce and manufactured goods can be obtained.

(b) Micro- and macro-economics

So far we have concentrated mainly on the first problem – the allocation of a given quantity of resources between different uses. By dividing the economy into a number of comparatively small parts, we have been able to study how each part functions – the demand of consumers in a particular market, the behaviour of the firm, the price of the commodity, and so on. Such study is known as 'micro-economics'. Thus, if we ask ourselves what forces determine the price of potatoes, the rent of an acre of land in London, the dividend on a particular equity or the wage of a Nottingham bus-driver, we are dealing with micro-economic questions.

We now turn to the second and third problems, full employment and growth. These are concerned with the economy as a whole. They give rise to a series of general questions. How do fluctuations in the overall level of employment occur? How can overall demand in the economy change? How do firms in general respond to such a change in demand? What brings about changes in the general level of prices? Such questions are the concern of macro-economics.

Referring back to fig 1.3, micro-economics is concerned with the centre of the diagram – an examination of a particular market and of the connection between one market and another, e.g. those for pencils and pens. But it does not analyse the relationship of any one market to the system as a whole. This is covered by macro-economics, which examines in aggregate the two outer flows, of goods and services and of factors of production.

(c) The method of macro-economics

Because micro- and macro-economics differ in the types of subject they study, their methods of analysis also differ. A simple analogy will explain why.

We can investigate the working of a motor-car by examining its different parts in isolation from one another. Thus we look at the wheels, then the gearbox, the engine, the carburettor, the electric fuel-pump, and so on. In this way we can find out how each part of the car works in detail.

Now, while such an examination is very important and useful, it has its limitations. This is because we just spotlight one component and see how it operates, *ignoring the rest of the car*. It will not enable us to predict what will happen if, for instance, we replace a one-litre engine by a two-litre engine. We cannot assume that, 'other things being equal', the larger engine will make the car run faster. There will be certain 'feedbacks' on the other parts of the car which will affect its running efficiency as a whole. Thus the larger engine may be too powerful for the gearbox; the carburettor may be unable to supply sufficient fuel; the suspension may not be capable of withstanding higher speeds; and so on. It is not enough to examine how one part of the car works in isolation; we have also to consider how the various components are interrelated, and the relative importance of each.

The same applies when we study how an economic system works. The micro approach will only take us a certain distance, for it merely examines how small parts of the economy operate in isolation. Changes which are simultaneously taking place in other parts of the economy and in the level of activity in general are ignored by inserting the phrase 'other things being equal'. So are the repercussions – the feedbacks – which may result from the single change being analysed.

Now this is legitimate enough if we are analysing a comparatively insignificant part of the economy, for example a small industry. Thus if we wish to discover the effects of an increase in the demand for pencils, we are unlikely to make serious errors by assuming 'other things equal', for such a change is unlikely to cause repercussions on the economy as a whole.

But what if we are examining the effects of a considerable increase in the demand for cars? The car industry is a significant part of the whole economy, and so we cannot merely analyse the effects in isolation, stopping at the point where the price of cars rises or the wages of car workers increase. To indicate the full economic results, we shall have to consider (i) possible 'feedbacks' on the demand for cars, and (ii) repercussions on the economy as a whole – which in turn can produce further feedbacks. For one thing, we shall have to know the level of employment in the economy. If this is low, the increased demand for cars may lead to a considerable expansion of activity throughout the economy, leading to a further increase in the demand for cars. On the other hand, if the economy is already running at full employment, the increased demand may merely cause higher prices.

(d) Simplifying by aggregating

Although, when dealing with changes in the economy as a whole, we cannot assume 'other things being equal', we still need to simplify if we are to build up a satisfactory model. This we do by 'aggregating' variables into a few broad groups.

The main aggregates we examine in macro-economics are national income, national output and national expenditure. But we can also deal with sub-aggregates and analyse the factors that determine these. Thus, in analysing national expenditure, we examine consumption spending, investment spending, government spending, export receipts, spending on imports, etc. Similarly, when looking at national income, we consider wages, rent, and profits (see chapter 15). Aggregating in this way enables us to handle all the different variables so that we can bear in mind the effects which a change in any one of them will have on the other groups and upon the level of activity as a whole (see chapter 16).

(e) The economic system

What we have said so far must not be taken to imply that particular markets and the economy as a whole are mutually exclusive. To return to our analogy of the car, all the parts of a car are 'ticking over' when the car is running. Each bit of the carburettor and gearbox, and the way each is functioning, affect the overall running of the car. And how the car is driven will influence the performance of the individual parts – the engine, the suspension, the wheels, and so on. So it is with the economy. The millions of independent decisions made by individual firms and consumers affect the overall functioning of the economy. For example, each decision of an individual firm regarding alterations to its factory, plant or stocks affects the amount of investment spending which the economy as a whole is undertaking. And the firm's decisions will also be influenced by the price of its product – which in its turn depends upon the demands of individual purchasers.

Both micro- and macro-economics are necessary, therefore, to an understanding of how the economy functions. However, before considering the influences on the level of activity, we look at the determinants of the material standard of living of a country (that is, the current position of the production-possibility curve) and the factors upon which growth depends (that is, the movement of the curve outwards from the origin).

14.2 FACTORS DETERMINING A COUNTRY'S MATERIAL STANDARD OF LIVING

Since people can enjoy only what they produce with their limited resources, the production-possibility curve shows the limit to their material standard of living. Because income is not evenly distributed, however, what we are talking about is an average standard of living, usually measured by the national income per head of the population (see chapter 15).

The factors which limit the standard of living can be classified as internal and external, the latter resulting from economic relationships with the rest of the world.

The most important *internal* factors are:

(a) Original natural resources
Obviously, 'natural resources' cover such things as mineral deposits, sources of fuel and power, climate and the fertility of the soil and fisheries around the coast, but also included are geographical advantages, such as navigable rivers or lakes, which help communications.

While national output increases as new techniques or transport developments allow natural resources to be exploited, the exhaustion of mineral resources works in the opposite direction. Moreover, where a country's economy is predominantly agricultural, variations in weather may cause its output to fluctuate from year to year.

(b) The nature of the people, particularly of the labour force

Other things being equal, the standard of living will be higher the greater the proportion of workers to the total population and the longer their working hours.

But the quality of the labour force is also important. This will depend upon the basic characteristics of the people – their health, energy, adaptability, inventiveness, judgment and ability to organise themselves and to co-operate in production – together with the skills they have acquired through education and training.

(c) Capital equipment

The effectiveness of natural resources and of labour depends almost entirely upon capital equipment. Thus machinery is necessary to extract oil and minerals, a turbine generator to harness a waterfall, and hotels to exploit Spanish sun and beaches. Similarly, the output of workers varies almost in direct proportion to the capital equipment and power at their disposal. Indeed, the most important single cause of material progress is investment, the addition to capital.

(d) The organisation of resources

To achieve the maximum output from scarce factors of production, they must be organised efficiently. Have we the correct proportion of machinery to each worker? Is the production of the particular good being carried on in the best possible locality? Could the factors be better deployed within the factory? Such questions have to be answered by those organising production.

(e) Knowledge of techniques

Technical knowledge is acquired through capital expenditure on research and invention. Further capital expenditure is necessary to develop discoveries, e.g. to utilise our present knowledge of nuclear energy. Nevertheless the rapid increase of the standard of living of the UK over the last hundred years has largely been due to the development and application of new inventions such as the steam engine, the internal-combustion engine, electrical power and electronics.

(f) Political organisation

A stable government promotes confidence and thereby encourages saving and investment in long-term capital projects.

To the above we have to add what can be termed *external* factors:

(g) Foreign loans and investments

A net income from foreign investments means that a country obtains goods or services from other countries without having to give goods and services in return, and vice versa. Generally speaking, welfare from this source is only likely to fluctuate over a long period.

(h) The terms of trade
In the short run fluctuations in the terms of trade are likely to be far more important in changing material welfare, especially if the country has, like the UK, a high level of imports and exports.

By the *terms of trade* we mean the quantity of another country's products which a nation gets in exchange for a given quantity of its own products. Thus, if the terms of trade move in a nation's favour, it means that it gets a larger quantity of imports for a given quantity of its own exports. This happens because the prices of the goods that are imported have fallen relative to the prices of those exported. Thus the 1973 increase in the price of oil reduced the standard of living of the importing countries and raised that of the oil producers.

(i) Gifts from abroad
Gifts made to countries for purposes of economic development and defence improve the standard of living of the receiving countries.

14.3 GROWTH

(a) The meaning of 'growth'
When there are unemployed resources, the economy's *actual* output is below its *potential* output; in terms of fig 14.2 the economy is producing inside the production-possibility curve, at point A. Here output can be increased by the essentially short-term policy of increasing aggregate demand in order to absorb unemployed resources (see chapter 18).

Fig 14.2 *economic growth*

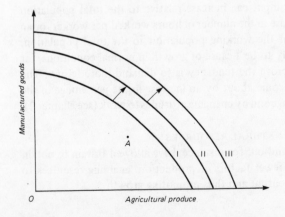

But, by itself, full employment of an economy's resources does not necessarily mean that the economy will grow. Growth is essentially a long-run phenomenon – the *potential* full-employment output of the economy is *increasing* over time. In terms of fig 14.2, whereas full employment simply means that the economy is producing on a point on the production-possibility curve I, growth means that, over time, the curve is pushed outwards to II and III.

Increases in the productive capacity in the economy over time are usually measured by calculating the rate of change of real gross national product per head of the population (see chapter 15). However, when people talk about 'growth' they are thinking chiefly of the difference it makes to the standard of living rather than to output itself. Allowances have to be made, therefore, for defects of GNP as an indication of the standard of living (see chapter 15).

(b) How is growth achieved?
There are three basic causes of growth:

(i) *A rise in the productivity of existing factors*
In the short run, productivity may be raised by improvements in organisation, which secure, for example, more division of labour and economies of large-scale production, or a more intensive use of capital equipment (e.g. the adoption of shift-working). Physical improvements for the labour force, e.g. better food and working conditions, may also increase productivity.

In the longer run, more significant increases can come with education and the acquisition of capital skills. These really represent, however, an increase in the capital invested in labour.

(ii) *An increase in the available stock of factors of production*

(1) A RISE IN THE LABOUR INPUT
The size of the labour input can increase relative to the total population through either an increase in the number of hours worked per worker, or an increase in the ratio of the working population to the total population. The first is hardly likely to be a cause of growth in normal conditions, for as living standards improve the tendency is to demand more leisure. The second, however, may come about by an increase in the percentage of the population of working age and by changing attitudes to work (see chapter 2).

(2) DEVELOPMENT OF NATURAL RESOURCES
North Sea natural gas and oil, for instance, have allowed Britain to obtain her fuel supplies from fewer factors of production, enabling resources to be transferred to other output and thus promoting growth.

Fig 14.3 *factors leading to growth*

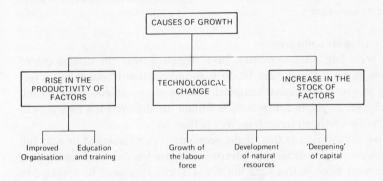

(3) ADDITIONAL CAPITAL EQUIPMENT

Here we must distinguish between 'widening' and 'deepening' capital. Widening capital – adding similar capital equipment – is necessary if the labour force increases, in order to maintain the existing capital – labour ratio and thus output per head. Suppose 10 men, digging a long ditch, have 5 spades between them. If the labour forces is increased to 20 men the capital-labour ratio falls from 1:2 to 1:4 unless 'widening' takes place – that is, unless another 5 spades are provided to maintain the existing ratio. 'Widening' does not increase productivity; it simply prevents diminishing returns to labour setting in.

'Deepening' capital occurs when the capital-labour ratio is increased. If, for example, when there were 10 spades to 20 men, the men were given a further 10 spades, the capital-labour ratio would be raised to 1:1.

(iii) *Technological change*

All we have done in our example so far has been to increase the stock of a given kind of capital equipment, spades. Over time, however, productivity can be raised much more significantly by technological improvements. Thus the 20 men and their spades may be replaced by a single trench-digger and its driver. Because this does the job more quickly and efficiently the remaining 19 men are released for other kinds of work.

In practice, all three causes are usually operating at the same time to increase productivity. Thus, as the labour force or natural resources are expanded, new capital is required, and this allows for the introduction of new techniques.

The speed with which new capital and improvements are introduced also depends upon the price of capital equipment relative to the wages of the labour for which it can be substituted. Over time, wages have tended to rise relative to the cost of capital equipment. This has been marked since World War II; the effect has been to increase the rate of technological change in such industries as agriculture, cargo handling, transport, ship-building and mining.

(c) Constraints upon growth

The preceding discussion may have suggested that the attainment of growth is easy; all we have to do is to increase our labour input, invest more in education, capital equipment and research and encourage techni-cal change. In practice, however, as Britain has discovered, a high growth rate is often difficult to achieve. Why is this?

The main reason is that, if the economy is functioning at or near full employment, growth through investment means less current consumption. If we want more factors – machines, roads, etc. – we must be prepared to have fewer houses, cars, washing-machines and so on. Now, if people *voluntarily* decide to save a higher proportion of their incomes, more resources will automatically be set free for investment. But if people prefer a higher current standard of living, growth through investment can occur only if they are 'forced' to save, e.g. by higher taxation or rising prices. Other constraints upon growth are the desire for leisure, an ageing popula-tion, and the level of research, which determines technological progress.

But, for the UK, the balance of payments has been particularly import-ant, for she is dependent upon imports of raw materials for her industrial production. When the growth rate rises, therefore, her demand for imports rises sharply, whereas exports increase only when production has taken place. This time-lag tends to cause a short-run deficit. When, in the past, Britain's currency reserves have been low, such a deficit has given rise to speculation against sterling, and the outflow of short-term capital from the UK has had to be checked by raising the minimum lending rate and taking other deflationary measures (see chapter 20). As a result, the 'go' of growth has been checked by the 'stop' of the balance-of-payments restraint.

Finally, it should be noted that growth entails costs additional to the reduced current consumption necessary to accumulate capital. Growth usually means change, and the more rapid the growth, the greater the change. Thus in the UK, even though the growth-rate has been relatively low in recent years, coal-mines, cotton factories, shipyards and railway lines have been closed, while the electrical, plastics, aerospace and elect-ronics industries have been developed. Such changes in the structure of the economy are bound to lead to some unemployment (see chapter 18). A higher rate of growth, therefore, means that people have to accept the possibility of changing jobs quite radically, three or four times in their working lives. This will entail retraining and probably moving around the country; and, as techniques change more rapidly, e.g. with the introduc-tion of micro-chips, these processes will happen to a far greater extent than at present.

MEASURING THE LEVEL OF ACTIVITY: NATIONAL-INCOME CALCULATIONS

15.1 THE PRINCIPLE OF NATIONAL-INCOME CALCULATIONS

Fluctuations in the level of activity are monitored by quantitative information on the national income. Although the collection of statistics proceeds continuously, the principal figures are published annually in *National Income and Expenditure* (the *Blue Book*).

The principle of calculating national income is as follows. Income is a flow of goods and services over time: if our income rises, we can enjoy more goods and services. But for goods to be enjoyed they must first be produced. A nation's income over a period, then, is basically the same as its output over a period. Thus, as a first approach, we can say that national income is the total money value of all goods and services produced by a country during the year. The question is how we can measure this money value.

We can tackle the problem by studying the different ways in which we can arrive at the value of a table.

Fig 15.1 shows that the value of the table can be obtained by taking the

Fig 15.1 *the value of the total product equals the sum of values added by each firm*

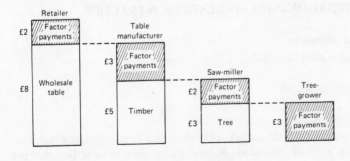

value of the final product (£10) or by totalling the value added by each firm in the different stages of production. Thus the output of the tree-grower is what he receives for the tree (£3) which, we will assume, cost £2 in wages to produce, leaving £1 profit. The output of the sawmiller is what he receives for the timber (£5) less what he paid for the tree. Again, this output (£2) is made up of wages and profit. And so on. The total of these added values equals the value of the final table. Thus we could obtain the value of the table by adding the *net outputs* of the tree-grower (forestry), the sawmiller and the table-maker (manufacturing) and the retailer (distribution).

Alternatively, instead of putting these individual outputs in industry categories, we could have added them according to the type of factor payment – wages, salaries, rent or profit. This gives us the *income* method of measuring output.

Thus, if we assume (i) no government taxation or spending and (ii) no economic connections with the outside world, we can obtain the national income either by totalling the value of final output during the year (i.e. the total of the value added to the goods and services by each firm) or by totalling the various factor payments during the year – wages, rent and profit.

There is, however, a third method of calculating the national income. The value of the table in fig 15.1 is what was spent on it. If the table had sold for only £9, that would have been the value of the final output, with the final factor payment – profit to the retailer – reduced to £1. Thus we can obtain the national income by totalling *expenditure* on final products over the year.

It must be emphasised that the money values of output, income and expenditure are *identical by definition*. They simply *measure* the national income in different ways. This was shown by the fact that factor payments were automatically reduced by £1 when the table sold for £9 instead of £10.

Before we proceed to examine in more detail the actual process of measuring these three identities, it is convenient if we first consider some of the inherent difficulties.

15.2 NATIONAL-INCOME CALCULATIONS IN PRACTICE

(a) General difficulties
Complications arise through:

(i) *Arbitrary definitions*

(1) PRODUCTION
In calculating the national income, only those goods and services which are paid for are normally included. Because calculations have to be made in

money terms, the inclusion of other goods and services would involve imputing a value to them. But where would you draw the line? If you give a value to jobs which a person does for himself – growing vegetables in the garden or cleaning the car – then why not include shaving himself, driving to work, and so on? On the other hand, excluding such jobs distorts national-income figures, for, as an economy becomes more dependent on exchanges, the income figure increases although there has been no addition to real output! (see p. 250).

An imputed money value is included for certain payments in kind which are recognised as a regular part of a person's income earnings, e.g. goods produced and consumed by a farmer.

(2) THE VALUE OF THE SERVICES RENDERED BY CONSUMER DURABLE GOODS

A TV set, dishwasher, car, etc., render services for many years. But where would we stop if we imputed a value to such services? A toothbrush, pots and pans, for example, all render services over their lives. All consumer durable goods are therefore included at their price when bought, subsequent services being ignored.

The one exception is owner-occupied houses. These are given a notional rent to keep them in line with property owned for letting, whose rents are included, either directly or as profits of property companies. This also prevents national income falling as more people become owner-occupiers!

(3) GOVERNMENT SERVICES

Education and health services, although provided by the state, are no different from similar services for which some persons pay. Consequently they are included in national income at cost. But what of certain other government services? A policeman, for instance, when helping children to cross the road is providing a consumer service. But at night his chief task may be guarding banks and factories, and in doing so he is really furthering the productive process. To avoid double-counting, this part ought to be excluded from output calculations. In practice, however, it would be impossible to differentiate between the two activities, and so all the policeman's services – indeed all government services (including defence) – are included at cost in calculating national output (see p. 249).

(ii) *Inadequate information*

The sources from which data are obtained were not specifically designed for national-income calculations. For instance, the Census of Production and the Census of Distribution are only taken at approximately five-year intervals. As a result many figures are estimates based on samples.

Information, too, may be incomplete. Thus not only do income-tax returns fail to cover the small-income groups, but they err on the side of understatement.

But it is 'depreciation' which presents the major problem, for what firms show in their profit-and-loss accounts is affected by tax regulations. Since there is no accurate assessment of real depreciation, it is now usual to refer to gross national product (GNP) rather than to national income (see p. 248).

(iii) *The danger of double-counting*

Care must be taken to exclude transfer incomes when adding up national income (see p. 245), the contribution to production of intermediary firms when calculating national output (see p. 246) and indirect taxes when measuring national expenditure (see p. 245).

A fourth way in which a form of double-counting can occur is through 'stock appreciation'. Inflation increases the value of stocks, but although this adds to firms' profits it represents no increase in real income. Such gains must therefore be deducted from the income and output figures.

(iv) *Relationship with other countries*

(1) TRADE

British people spend on foreign goods, while foreigners buy British goods. In calculating national *expenditure*, therefore, we have to deduct the value of goods and services imported (since they have not been produced by Britain) and add the value of goods and services exported (where income has been earned in Britain).

(2) INTERNATIONAL INDEBTEDNESS

If a father increases his son's pocket-money, it does not increase the family income. Instead it merely achieves a re-distribution, the father having less and the son more. But if the boy's aunt makes him a regular allowance, the family income is increased. Similarly, with the nation: while transfer incomes, e.g. retirement pensions and student grants, do not increase national income, payments by foreigners do. These payments arise chiefly as interest and dividends from loans and investments made abroad. In the same way, foreigners receive payments for investments in Britain. Net income from abroad (receipts less payments) must therefore be added to both domestic expenditure and output.

(b) Government calculations of the national income

Figures for GNP are calculated for income, expenditure and output. Because information is incomplete, results are not identical. In practice the expenditure figure is taken as the datum, income and output differences being treated as a residual error.

(i) *National income*

National income is the total money value of all incomes received by persons and enterprises in the country during the year. Such incomes may be in the form of wages, salaries, rent, or profit.

In practice income figures are obtained mostly from income-tax returns, but estimates are necessary for small incomes. Two major adjustments have to be made:

(1) TRANSFER INCOMES

Sometimes an income is received although there has been no corresponding contribution to the output of goods and services, e.g. unemployment-insurance benefit and interest on the National Debt. Such incomes are really only a re-distribution of income within the nation – chiefly from taxpayers to the recipients. Transfer incomes must therefore be deducted from the total of all incomes.

(2) INCOME FROM GOVERNMENT ACTIVITIES

Personal incomes and the profits of companies are obtained from tax returns. But the government also receives income from its property and may make a profit from such sources as the public corporations. Similarly local authorities may show a surplus on their trading activities – water supply, housing, transport, etc. Such income earned by public authorities must be added in.

(ii) *National expenditure*

National expenditure is the total amount spent on consumer goods and services and on net additions to capital goods and stocks in the course of the year.

Figures for calculating national expenditure are obtained from a variety of sources. The Census of Distribution records the value of shop sales, while the Census of Production gives the value of capital goods produced and additions to stocks. But these censuses are not taken every year, and gaps are filled by estimates from data provided by the National Food Survey and the Family Expenditure Survey.

Market prices are swollen by indirect taxes, e.g. VAT, and reduced by subsidies, e.g. on welfare milk and council housing. What we are trying to measure is the value of the national expenditure which corresponds to the cost of the factors of production (including profits) used in producing the national product. This is known as 'national expenditure at factor cost' and is obtained by deducting indirect taxes from and adding subsidies to national expenditure at market prices.

Adjustments necessary for exports and imports have already been referred to (see p. 244).

(iii) *National output*
National output is the total of consumer goods and services and investment goods (including additions to stocks) produced by the country during the year. It can be measured by totalling either the value of the *final* goods and services produced or the *value added* to the goods and services by each firm, including the government.

(c) Gross national product and national income
In the course of production, machinery wears out and stocks are used up. This represents depreciation of capital. If we make no allowance for this but simply add in the value of new investment goods produced, we have *gross national product*. But, to be accurate, the calculation of total output should include only net investment – that is, the value of new investment goods and stocks less depreciation on existing capital and stocks used up. This gives the net national product, which is the true national income for the year (fig 15.3).

(d) Personal disposable income
For some purposes, e.g. as an indication of people's current living standards, a measurement of personal disposable income, that is, what people actually have to spend, is more significant. The necessary adjustments to gross national product to obtain personal disposable income are shown in fig 15.4.

Table 15.1   *Calculations of the national income of the UK, 1978*

INCOME

	£m
Income from employment	98,156
Income from self-employment	13,245
Profits of private companies and public enterprises	22,651
Rent	11,125
Total domestic income	145,177
less Stock appreciation	−4,249
Gross Domestic Product (income-based)	140,928
Residual error	1,071
Net property income from abroad	836
GROSS NATIONAL PRODUCT	142,835
less capital consumption	−18,310
NATIONAL INCOME	124,525

EXPENDITURE

	£m
Consumers' expenditure	96,086
General government final consumption	32,693
Gross capital formation (investment) at home, including increase in stocks	30,746
Total domestic expenditure at market prices	159,525
plus Exports of goods and services	47,636
less Imports of goods and services	−45,522
Gross domestic product at market prices	161,639
less taxes on expenditure	−23,238
plus subsidies	3,598
Gross domestic product (expenditure based)	141,999
Net property income from abroad	836
GROSS NATIONAL PRODUCT	142,835
less capital consumption	−18,310
NATIONAL INCOME	124,525

OUTPUT

	£m
Agriculture, forestry and fishing	3,715
Mining and quarrying	4,467
Manufacturing	40,690
Construction	8,610
Gas, electricity and water	4,772
Transport	7,677
Communication	4,011
Distributive trades	14,687
Insurance, banking, and finance and business services	5,170
Public administration and defence	10,197
Public health and educational services	9,674
Other services	18,680
Ownership of dwellings	8,578
Total	140,928
Residual error	1,071
Gross domestic product	141,999
Net property income from abroad	836
GROSS NATIONAL PRODUCT	142,835
less capital consumption	−18,310
NATIONAL INCOME	124,525

Source: National Income and Expenditure (Blue Book) 1979

Fig 15.2 *summary of gross-national-product calculations*

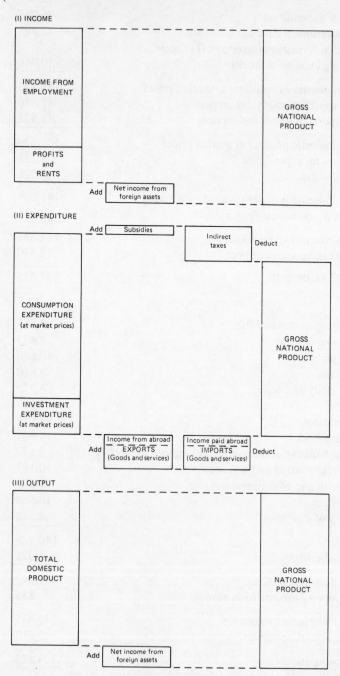

Fig 15.3 *gross national product and national income*

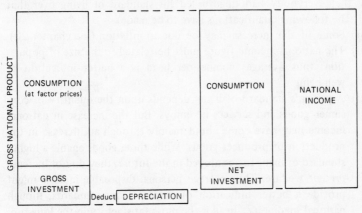

Fig 15.4 *the relationship between gross national product and personal disposable income*

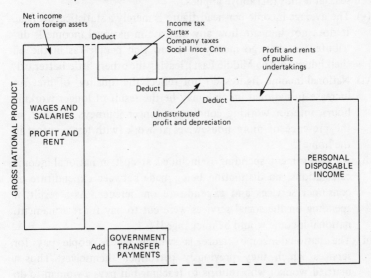

15.3 USES OF NATIONAL-INCOME CALCULATIONS

(a) To indicate the overall standard of living

Welfare is not identical with wealth (see p. 25), but wealth bears the closest single relationship to it. Income, the flow of wealth, is therefore the nearest indication of welfare.

Nevertheless, the national-income figure cannot be accepted solely at its face value. Thus, although the national income of the UK was £32,000 million in 1967 and £124,525 million in 1978, it does not automatically follow that everybody had quadrupled his standard of living over that period. The following qualifications have to be made:

(i) Some of the increase may be due to inflation (see chapter 20).

(ii) The national-income figure must be related to the size of population; thus average income per head is a better indication of well-being.

(iii) A person's standard of living depends upon the quantity of consumer goods and services he enjoys. But the increase in national income may have come about mainly through an increase in the production of producer goods. While these goods enable a higher standard of living to be enjoyed in the future, they do not increase *present* welfare. Thus average personal disposable income might provide a better indication of current living-standards, though national income per head is the more satisfactory in the long run.

(iv) The increase in national income may have come about through a surplus of exports over imports. This represents investment overseas, and thus (iii) above applies.

(v) The average-income-per-head figure is merely a statistical average. It does not indicate how any increase in national income is distributed; it may go mostly to a few rich people (as in the oil sheikhdoms of the Middle East), leaving the others little better off.

(vi) National-income figures do not reflect the 'quality' of life. An increase in national income may be the result of longer working hours, inferior working conditions, longer journeys to work, or the presence of more housewives at work (with less comfort in the home).

(vii) All government spending is included at cost in national-income calculations, no distinction being made between expenditure on consumer services and expenditure on defence. As a result, if spending on the social services were cut to pay for re-armament, national income would be unchanged!

(viii) The national-income figure is swollen when people pay for services which they previously performed themselves. Thus a married woman who returns to teaching but pays a woman to do her housework adds to the national income twice – although the only net addition is her teaching services.

(ix) Because national-income figures are based on private costs and benefits, external costs or benefits do not enter into the calculations. Thus the erection of electricity pylons would be included at cost, no allowance being made for the social cost of spoiling the landscape.

(b) To compare the standards of living of different countries

Comparisons of the national incomes of different countries are often necessary for practical purposes. How much help should be given by the rich countries to the very poor? Which are the very poor countries? What contribution should be made by a country to an international body, such as the United Nations, the EEC and NATO? What is the war potential of a country as indicated by its GNP per head?

But, when used to compare countries' standards of living, national income figures must be subjected to qualifications additional to those mentioned in (a) above.

(i) Because figures are expressed in different currencies they have to be converted into a common denominator. Using the exchange rate for this purpose is not entirely satisfactory, for the rate is determined by factors other than the internal purchasing powers of currencies, e.g. capital movements.

(ii) Different people have different needs. The Englishman has to spend more on heating than the Indian. Obviously, the Englishman is no better off in this respect – though the national-income figures, by valuing goods at cost, would indicate that he is.

(iii) The proportion of national income spent by different countries on defence varies. Countries which spend less can enjoy consumer goods instead, but average national income does not indicate the difference.

(iv) Countries vary as regards the length of the average working week, the proportion of women who work, the number of jobs which people do for themselves, the degree to which goods are exchanged against money and the accuracy of tax returns. Some allowance must be made for each of these factors.

(c) To calculate the rate at which a nation's income is growing

Is the national income growing? Is it growing as fast as it should? Are the incomes of other countries growing faster? Is there sufficient investment to maintain future living-standards? The answers to these and similar questions can be found by comparing national-income figures, though for the reasons given above some caution must be observed.

(d) To establish relationships which arise between various parts of the economy

If, for example, national-income figures revealed a relationship between the level of investment and growth, or between educational expenditure and growth, or between profits and the level of investment, such information would be useful in planning the economy.

The figures might also indicate trends, e.g. changes in the output of different industries, which are helpful to firms in planning production, though more use is likely to be made of specific government statistics.

(e) To assist the government in managing the economy

Some central-government planning is now regarded as essential for achieving full employment, a stable currency and a satisfactory rate of growth. But this requires having figures for the various components of the national income, such as consumption spending, investment, exports and imports. How they can be used will be explained later.

THE DETERMINATION OF
THE LEVEL OF ACTIVITY

16.1 THE LINK BETWEEN SPENDING AND PRODUCTION

(a) The circular flow of income

We will begin by repeating in simplified form the identity which exists between income and expenditure. Take a simple example. A teacher buys a table from a carpenter. With the money he receives, the carpenter pays the timber merchant for the wood, who in turn pays the man who cut the wood. But where did the teacher obtain the original money to buy the table? Simply from the carpenter, the timber merchant and the tree-feller, who each use part of their receipts to pay fees to the teacher for instructing their children. So with the other goods the teacher buys. Thus there is a circular flow of income – one person's spending becomes another person's income. Spending is therefore necessary for earnings.

The same applies to the economy as a whole; at any one time spending equals income. Suppose, for instance, that all production in the economy is in the hands of a giant firm which owns all the land and raw materials and employs all the labour. The firm's income consists of the receipts from the sale of its product. Since it owns all the raw materials and land, these receipts must equal what it pays out in wages and what it has left in profits. This was the principle upon which we measured national income.

Since spending on goods determines the receipts and thus the profits of firms, it is of vital importance in deciding the level of their output and thus of the aggregate level of activity. To explain more fully, we use fig 16.1, which shows the money flows which correspond to the movement of factors and goods in the outer ring of fig 1.3 – payments by firms for factors and expenditure of households on goods. The first represents income of households; the second represents receipts of firms.

If spending on goods and services is maintained, factor payments can be maintained; in other words the profitability of production is unchanged and thus firms have no cause to vary output. If, however, for some reason

Fig 16.1   *the circular flow of income*

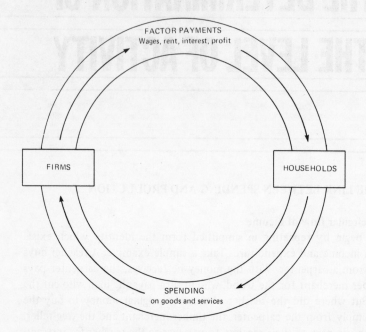

or another, spending should fall, some of the goods produced by firms will not be sold, and stocks will accumulate. On the other hand, if spending on goods and services increases, stocks will be run down. Production has become more profitable and, as a result, output is expanded.

Three important points emerge from our discussion so far:

(i)   There is no impetus towards a contraction or expansion of production if spending on goods and services equals spending (including normal profits) by firms on factors of production.

(ii)   The level of production, and therefore of employment, is closely related to the level of spending.

(iii)   There is nothing to guarantee that spending will be sufficient to ensure a level of production where all factors are fully employed.

Definitions and assumptions

Before we show how changes in spending occur, we must make simplifying assumptions.

We define net profit as gross profit less retentions for depreciation. We assume:

(i) *All retentions for depreciation are actually spent on replacement investment*

Thus, when in future we speak of 'investment' it refers solely to net additions to fixed capital and stocks, i.e. net investment.

(ii) *All net profit is distributed to the owners of the risk capital*
This means that there is no 'saving' by firms.

(iii) *There is no government taxation or spending*

(iv) *There are no economic connections with the outside world; it is a 'closed' economy*
From the above assumptions it follows that: (1) the sum of the factor payments is equal to national income (equals national output) as defined in chapter 15; and (2) income equals disposable income.

(v) *There are no changes in the price level*
Thus any changes in the money value of national income reflect changes in real output.

(vi) *The level of employment is directly proportionate to the level of output*
In practice this may not be strictly true: existing machinery, for example, may be able to produce extra output without additional labour. But the simplification does allow the level of employment to be linked directly with the level of national income.

16.2 REASONS FOR CHANGES IN AGGREGATE DEMAND

(a) Aggregate demand
Our task, therefore, is to discover why changes occur in the national income (hereafter symbolised by Y). Now, as we have just shown, Y depends upon the level of spending, which we shall refer to as aggregate demand (abbreviated to AD). Thus we can find out why Y changes by discovering why AD changes.

(b) Changes in AD
Let us return to our example of the teacher. Suppose he earns £6,000 in a given year. Most of it will be spent on consumer goods and services – but not all. Some will probably be put aside for a 'rainy day'. That part of income which is not spent we can say is 'saved'. What happens to it? The money could be hidden under the mattress; in that case it is obviously lost to the circular flow of income. But the teacher is more likely to put it in a bank, where it is safer and earns interest. Nevertheless, at this point it is still lost to the circular flow. Saving represents a 'leak' from the flow of income.

So far, however, we have looked only at spending on consumer goods. But spending may also be on capital goods. Firms borrow money from their banks (and other institutions) for such purchases. Thus the sum deposited by the teacher stands a good chance of being returned to the circular flow of income by being 'invested', i.e. spent on capital goods or additions to stocks. Investment, therefore, can be regarded as an 'injection'. And, if exactly the amount of money saved by households is spent by firms on investment, the level of AD is maintained (fig 16.2), and Y is unchanged.

But suppose that the amount saved does not coincide with what firms wish to invest. This can come about either by a change in the amount invested or by a change in the amount spent by consumers.

Let us first assume that consumers' spending remains constant. If now firms reduce the amount they borrow for investment, AD is smaller. On the other hand, if firms increase their investment, AD will be larger.

Alternatively the amount of income spent on consumer goods may alter. Investment, we will now assume, remains unchanged. Here, if more is spent out of a given income, AD will increase; if less, AD decreases.

What it is important to recognise is that in an economy where people

Fig 16.2 *the level of income maintained through investment*

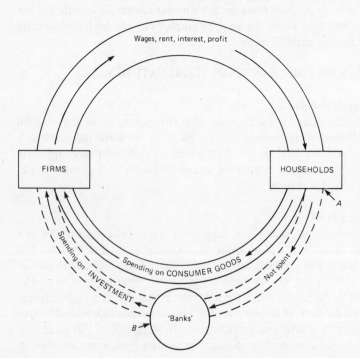

are free to dispose of their income as they please, and where firms are largely left to make their own investment decisions, a difference can easily exist between the amount of income which people plan to 'save' (i.e. which they do not wish to spend) and the amount which firms wish to invest. This is because, in their spending, households and firms act for different reasons and mostly independently of each other. Two questions have therefore to be asked: (i) What determines spending on consumer goods and therefore saving (at position A)? (ii) What determines investment spending (at position B)?

In our analysis, consumption, that is spending on consumer goods and services, will be given the symbol C; saving, i.e. income not spent on consumption, S; investment, i.e. spending on net additions to capital goods and stocks, I.

16.3 CONSUMPTION SPENDING

(a) Consumption and saving by households: 'personal saving'

Income is received as wages or salaries, rent, interest and profits. With it households buy the consumer goods they need. That part of income which is not spent has been defined as 'saving'. Hence $Y=C+S$, $C=Y-S$, and $S=Y-C$.

C and S, therefore, are merely two sides of the same coin. Thus, whenever we consider C or S, we must examine the factors which influence both spending the thrift.

Spending decisions are more important in the short run, for a person's first concern is to maintain his standard of living. They are influenced by:

(i) *Size of income*

A small income leaves no margin for saving. Only when a man has satisfied what he considers are his basic needs will he save a part of his income. Indeed, if current income falls below this level, he may spend some of his past savings or borrow in order to maintain the standard of life he is accustomed to.

But we can go further. As income increases, the proportion spent tends to decrease; or, as it is often put, there is a *diminishing marginal propensity to consume*.

The above conclusions are illustrated diagrammatically in fig 16.3, where the curve C shows how consumption changes with income.

Below an income of OD there is 'dis-saving'. At OD all income is consumed. At higher incomes the proportion spent falls and saving occurs. This diminishing marginal propensity to consume is shown by the decreasing slope of the consumption curve: for any given increase in income, the extra amount spent grows successively smaller.

258

Fig 16.3 *the relationship between consumption and income*

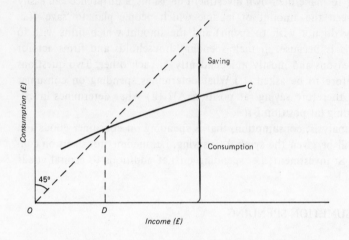

(ii) *The timelag in adjusting spending habits*

It takes time for a person to adjust his standard of living as his income increases. In the short period, therefore, saving increases.

The above two factors explain the *shape* of the consumption curve – how spending changes as income changes. But we still have to account for the position of the curve – what determines the proportion of any given income which is spent. This amount can vary (that is, the position of the C curve may change) as a result of:

(iii) *Changes in disposable income*

We have assumed that firms have distributed all net profits and that there are no government taxation or transfers. In practice both profit distribution and government taxation will affect the size of income available for spending. Increasing direct taxation, for instance, would, by reducing disposable income, lower the C curve.

(iv) *Government policy*

By its fiscal policy the government can influence the proportion of income consumed. Thus the replacement of indirect taxes by a more progressive income tax or a higher corporation tax would tend to take more from savers and less from spenders and so have the effect of increasing consumption.

(v) *The distribution of wealth in the community*

Because the proportion of income saved usually increases with income, greater equality of incomes is likely to reduce the aggregate amount saved out of a given national income. Re-distributive taxation therefore tends to increase total consumption.

(vi) *The invention of new consumer goods*
In recent years family cars, TV sets, hi-fi equipment, central heating and dishwashers have all induced spending, especially when backed by intensive advertising.

(vii) *Hire-purchase and other credit facilities*
A decrease in the initial deposit or an extension of the period of repayment encourages spending. Easier bank credit does the same.

(viii) *Anticipated changes in the value of money*
If people consider that the prices of goods are likely to rise, they bring forward their spending rather than save for the future.

(ix) *The age-distribution of the population*
Since most saving is done by people over thirty-five years of age, an ageing population will tend to reduce the propensity to consume of the community as a whole.

In the long period, people have some concern for their future standard of living, and *thrift* exercises a greater influence on the disposal of income.

The main *factors determining thrift* are:

(i) *Size of income*
As already shown, saving increases as income increases and at an increasing rate.

(ii) *Psychological attitudes*
Some communities are by nature more thrifty than others, providing against sickness, unemployment and old age, and for the education of dependants. On the other hand, ostentation – the desire to 'keep up with the Joneses' – may provide a motive for a high rate of spending.

(iii) *Social environment*
Apart from influencing the general attitude to saving, environment can be a major factor in other ways. Such institutions as savings banks, building societies, insurance companies and unit trusts encourage regular thrift, so that much saving out of income is contractual.

Political conditions, too, influence saving habits. Countries continually threatened by war or revolution do not provide the stable background necessary to encourage thrift.

(iv) *Government policy*
The government can influence people's attitude to saving in a variety of ways. In the UK it tries to stimulate personal saving through the rate of interest offered, income-tax concessions (e.g. on National Savings Bank

interest) and special devices (e.g. Savings Certificates, Premium Bonds and index-linked SAYE). On the other hand, a comprehensive state social-insurance and pension scheme may reduce personal saving.

At one time it was thought that people could only be induced to post-pone consumption, i.e. to save, by offering interest as compensation. This view, however, is now largely rejected, chiefly because much saving is contractual, e.g. insurance and mortgage payments. The dominant factor is the *ability* to save, i.e. the level of income.

Under our simplifying assumptions that all net profits are distributed and that there is no government taxation or spending, all saving is done by households. But saving can be achieved through retentions by businesses and the government (fig 16.4). In order to consider these, we will tempor-arily relax the two assumptions above.

Fig 16.4 *saving in the UK, 1978*

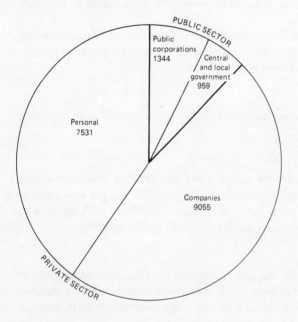

(b) Business saving

Saving by businesses (which in volume remains fairly stable) is achieved by not distributing to shareholders all the profits made in a year. Some profits are usually retained, either to be 'ploughed back' for the expansion of the business, or to be held as liquid reserves in order to meet tax liabilities or maintain dividends when profits fluctuate. The chief factors affecting this type of saving are:

(i) *Profits*

Transfers to reserves are dependent upon and stimulated by the level of current profits. In practice, therefore, business saving is determined principally by the level of AD.

(ii) *Subjective factors*

Profits are likely to be retained when directors are expansion-minded or financially prudent.

(iii) *Government policy*

An increased tax on *distributed* profits or a 'dividend freeze' would be likely to increase company saving.

(c) Government saving

Central-*government* saving is achieved chiefly through a 'budget surplus', revenue exceeding current government expenditure. The surplus may be necessary: (i) to provide for the government's own investment and loans; and (ii) to ensure that, with personal and business saving, total saving will be sufficient to prevent an inflationary AD from developing (see chapter 20).

Apart from a budget surplus, saving can occur in other forms, e.g. when national-insurance and pension contributions exceed current payments.

Recently central-government expenditure has been so high that the difference has had to be covered by borrowing. A Public Sector Borrowing Requirement (see p. 339) means that there is dis-saving.

Public corporations are similar in many ways to ordinary businesses. But, as their operations are more directly under government control and their capital requirements are largely covered by the Treasury, their saving and investment are included under the public sector.

Local authorities, too, may have a budget surplus, but in practice they account for only 6% of total saving.

Thus in the public sector saving is determined chiefly by government policy, economic and political.

(d) Conclusion

In the private sector, spending (and therefore saving) depend upon (i) the level of Y, i.e. the size of AD, and (ii) other factors influencing the amount spent out of income. In comparison with changes in AD these other factors are fairly stable. Hence the main factor affecting short-term changes in consumption spending is the size of AD!

We have therefore to look elsewhere for the reason why AD changes. It is to be found in the comparative instability of the other form of spending – investment.

16.4 INVESTMENT SPENDING

(a) What do we mean by 'investment'?

Investment, for purposes of national-income calculations, is spending over a given period on the production of capital goods (houses, factories, machinery, etc.) or on net additions to stocks (raw materials, consumer goods in shops, etc.).

It is important to distinguish between this definition and what is often referred to as 'investment' – putting money in a bank or buying securities. In national-income analysis, investment takes place only when there is an actual net addition to capital goods or stocks.

Investment takes place in both the private and public sectors.

(b) Investment in the private sector

A firm will only spend on investment if it thinks that it will eventually prove profitable. There are, therefore, two main considerations to bear in mind: (i) the expected yield from the investment; and (ii) its cost.

The *yield* on the investment will depend largely on the demand for the consumer good the firm produces (see p. 162). In *estimating* such demand, the firm is most likely to commence from a position regarding which it does have some definite knowledge, i.e. the present demand for those goods. If that demand is buoyant and has remained so for a fairly long period, the firm will probably view the future optimistically. On the other hand, if present demand is low and has shown itself resistant to attempts to increase it, the future, to say the least, will appear somewhat gloomy. But since the current demand for goods, i.e. the level of consumption, depends chiefly on the level of income, we can say that, the higher AD is, the greater investment is likely to be.

Technical developments, like the internal-combustion engine, atomic energy, automation and North Sea gas and oil, give an added impetus to investment.

Furthermore, the effect of government policy has to be considered. Changes in policy add to uncertainty. Is corporation tax likely to be increased? Will inflation compel the government to carry out restrictive policies? In contrast the government may stimulate private investment by subsidies or generous tax allowances, and revive optimism by increasing its own investment.

This brings us to the *cost* of investment. This is represented by the cost of borrowing money to finance it – the rate of interest (chiefly that on debentures). A low rate tends to stimulate investment. If the rate rises, marginal projects cease to be profitable, and so the level of investment falls (see p. 163).

However, whether the rate of interest has a major influence on investment is doubtful. For one thing, investment decisions, especially for large firms, are the result of long-term planning. Any alteration of plans just because of a change in the rate of interest might throw the whole programme out of phase. For another, firms allow a considerable safety margin when deciding on investment, probably expecting to recover its cost within five years. This margin is thus sufficient to absorb a relatively small rise in the rate of interest. Even the holding of stocks may not be affected by the rate of interest. Convenience is more likely to decide the minimum held. In any case the rate of interest may be only a small part of the cost of holding stocks – warehousing, etc., being relatively far more important. Above all, compared with firms' expectations, the rate of interest is of secondary importance. Thus, especially when it comes to reviving investment, a fall in the rate of interest tends to have little effect.

(c) Investment in the public sector
Capital expenditure is incurred by the central government, nationalised industries and local authorities.

Fig 16.5   *investment in the UK 1978 (£ million) (net fixed capital formation at home and value of physical increase in stocks and work in progress)*

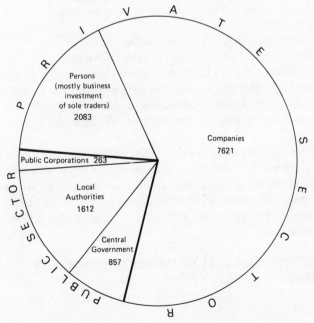

Source: National Income and Expenditure (Blue Book) 1979

Much of central-government investment is fairly stable, depending chiefly on policy commitments. To a large extent, too, the same is true of the capital expenditure of the nationalised industries, for in deciding whether or not to expand their capacity they will be guided by their social obligations as well as by their financial positions. Thus in periods of un-employment they might increase their investment.

Local-authority investment tends, however, to react to changes in the rate of interest. This is especially true of spending on new dwellings. If, after applying government grants, the cost of borrowing is not covered by the rents charged, increased rates have to be levied.

Because this may be disastrous politically, local-authority house-building may be reduced to mere slum clearance.

The real importance of public investment is that it is subject to direct government control. Thus, should private investment be deficient, the government can increase its spending on its own capital projects.

(d) Summary

Employment depends upon the level of AD – the total amount of money spent on the goods produced. AD fluctuates according to the relationship between intended saving and investment.

   (i)   AD expands if:
       (1) investment increases but saving remains unchanged;
       (2) saving decreases but investment remains unchanged.
   (ii)   AD contracts if:
       (1) investment decreases but saving remains unchanged;
       (2) saving increases but investment remains unchanged.

In practice investment is more liable to frequent change than is saving. Whereas firms' expectations are highly sensitive to new conditions, people's spending habits are fairly stable. Fluctuations in the level of AD, and therefore of income, are thus mainly the result of changes in the level of investment.

There is another important way in which saving differs from investment in the process of income creation. Whereas an increase in investment will, other things being equal, automatically produce an increase in saving through an expansion of income, an addition to saving need not lead to an increase in investment. Instead income merely contracts until what is saved from it equals investment.

16.5 THE EFFECT ON THE LEVEL OF INCOME OF CHANGES IN INVESTMENT

(a) The 'multiplier'

Given no change in saving, an increase in investment spending will raise the level of income by more than the increase in investment. Firms producing capital goods will take on additional workers. A part of these workers' earnings will be spent, providing additional income for shopkeepers and others, who in turn will spend a part of their extra income. There is thus a 'multiplier' effect. How the process works in real life can be illustrated from Nevil Shute's *Ruined City*. The shipyard in the town obtained an order for three tankers. 'A shop, long closed, reopened to sell meat pies. . . A man who gleaned a sack of holly in the country lanes disposed of it within an hour. . .A hot roast chestnut barrow came upon the streets, and did good trade.'

The multiplier is defined as the

$$\frac{\text{increase in income}}{\text{increase in investment}}$$

Its size depends upon the fraction of additional income which is spent, that is, the marginal propensity to consume (see p. 257). Suppose investment increases by £100 million a year, and that households spend half of any additional income. Producers of capital goods can now pay an extra £100 million on wages, rent, interest and profit. Households receiving this extra income spend £50 million with shopkeepers who, in their turn, spend £25 million. The sum of these additional incomes will eventually total £200 million. The multiplier equals 2.

To generalise, the multiplier equals

$$\frac{1}{1 - \text{the marginal propensity to consume}}$$

If, in the above example, the marginal propensity to consume had been $\frac{3}{4}$ instead of $\frac{1}{2}$, income would have increased by £400 million, giving a multiplier of 4. Since the marginal propensity to consume + the marginal propensity to save = 1, we can write the multiplier as equalling $1/s$, where s equals the marginal propensity to save.

(b) Diagrammatic representation

Fig 16.6 presents the essentials of the determination of the level of income. It is assumed that investment is autonomous, that is, its level is independent of the level of income (as shown by the horizontal line I). Saving varies with income. Initially saving is negative – households maintain spending at a low level of income by drawing on accumulated savings or by borrowing. When income increases and dis-saving becomes unnecessary, only $\frac{2}{3}$ of additional income is spent, $\frac{1}{3}$ being saved as shown by the line S having a constant slope of $\frac{1}{3}$.

The equilibrium level of income is Y, where S=I. At any income less than this, AD will expand because I is greater than S; and vice versa.

Fig 16.6 *the effect on income of an increase in the level of investment*

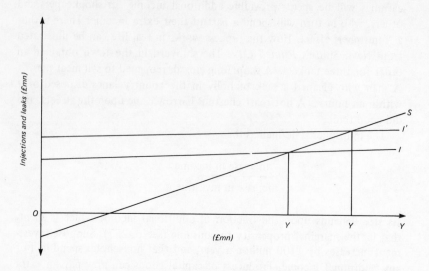

If now investment increases to I', there will be a new equilibrium level of income, Y'. Diagrammatically, the multiplier equals YY'/II', i.e. 3. Similarly, income would decrease if the level of investment fell below I.

16.6 LEAKS AND INJECTIONS IN GENERAL

In the above discussion, saving has been the only leak from the flow of aggregate demand. Similarly investment has represented the sole injection. However, the relaxation of the assumptions that there is no government and a closed economy introduces the consideration of other leaks and injections.

Direct taxation takes income from households, leaving them with less available spending power. Indirect taxes siphon off a part of consumer spending to the government, thereby reducing firms' receipts. Thus taxation is a leak from the circular flow of income. On the other hand, it can be put back by government spending – an injection.

Finally we have to consider the effect of imports and exports. When British households spend on foreign goods and services, there is a leak of AD from the circular flow, since this spending is received by foreign firms. On the other hand, spending by foreigners on British goods and services is received by British firms, and therefore represents an injection (fig 16.7).

These other leaks – taxation and imports – and injections – government spending and exports – affect AD and Y in the same way as do, respectively, S and I.

Fig 16.7 *total leaks and injections*

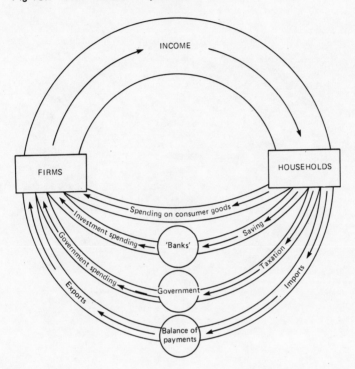

268

PART VII
INTERNATIONAL
TRADE

INTERNATIONAL

TRADE

17.1 WHY INTERNATIONAL TRADE?

(a) How international trade arises

International trade arises simply because countries differ in their demand for goods and in their ability to produce them.

On the demand side, a country may be able to produce a particular good but not in the quantity it requires. The USA, for instance, is a net importer of oil. On the other hand, Kuwait does not require all the oil she can produce. Without international trade most of her deposits would remain untapped.

On the supply side, resources are not evenly distributed throughout the world. One country may have an abundance of land; another may have a skilled labour force. Capital, oil, mineral deposits, cheap unskilled labour and a tropical climate are other factors possessed by different countries in varying amounts.

Nor can these factors be transferred easily from one country to another. Climate, land and mineral deposits are obviously specific. Labour is far more immobile internationally than within its own national boundaries. Capital, too, moves less easily; exchange controls, political risks and simple ignorance of possibilities may prevent investors from moving funds abroad.

Because factors are difficult to shift, the alternative – moving the goods made by those factors – is adopted. What happens, therefore, is that countries specialise in producing those goods in which they have the greatest comparative advantage, exchanging them for the goods of other countries.

(b) The advantages of international trade

(i) *It enables countries to obtain the benefits of specialisation*

Specialisation by countries improves their standard of living.

(1) It is obvious that without international trade many countries would have to go without certain products. Britain, for instance, has no gold or aluminium, and Sweden no oil.

(2) More important, many goods can be enjoyed which if produced at home would be available only to the very wealthy, for instance bananas, spices, oranges and peaches in Britain. But this benefit can be applied generally to all imports. The 'law of comparative costs' shows that, provided countries differ in the relative costs of producing certain goods, they can probably gain by specialisation and trade.

Suppose that there are two countries, A and B, each producing just two commodities, wheat and cars. Each has the same amount of capital and the same number of labourers, but A has a good climate and fertile soil compared with B. On the other hand, B's workers are far more skilful. All factors are fully employed.

When both countries divide their factors equally between the production of wheat and cars, they can produce as follows:

Country	Wheat (units)	Cars (units)
A	500	100
B	100	500
Total production	600	600

But if A specialises in producing wheat and B concentrates on cars, total production would be 1,000 wheat and 1,000 cars. There is thus a net gain of 400 wheat and 400 cars to be shared between them.

Here the gains are obvious, because A is better at producing wheat and B at producing cars. But suppose A also has skilled labour and capital, and is better at producing both wheat and cars, as follows:

Country	Wheat (units)	Cars (units)
A	500	300
B	400	100
Total production (no specialisation)	900	400

Are there still gains to be achieved by specialisation? Provided the rate at which cars can be exchanged for wheat lies within the range $3-1\frac{1}{4}$, the answer is yes. The reason for this is that A's superiority in producing cars is far more pronounced than her superiority in producing wheat for with the same factors she can produce three cars for every one of B's, but only one-and-a-quarter units of wheat for one of B's. Relative, rather than absolute, advantages are what are really important. The result is that if A specialises in producing cars, leaving B to produce wheat, total production will be 600 cars and 800 wheat.

Suppose now that world conditions of demand and supply are such that 2 wheat exchange for 1 car; i.e. the price of cars is exactly twice that of wheat. A now exchanges 200 cars for 400 wheat, giving her a total of 400 wheat and 400 cars, and B 400 wheat and 200 cars.

It can be seen, therefore, that through specialisation B is 100 cars better off. But has specialisation improved A's position? She now has 400 cars but only 400 wheat, a gain of 100 cars but a loss of 100 wheat. But by her own production she would have had to go without $166\frac{2}{3}$ wheat in order to obtain the extra 100 cars. Thus we can conclude that she too is better off.

The above explanation must be refined to allow for:

(1) DEMAND
The law of comparative costs merely shows how two countries can specialise to advantage when their opportunity costs differ. But until we know the demand for goods we cannot say definitely whether specialisation will take place or, if it does, to what extent it takes place. Thus, although a country may be favourably placed to produce certain goods, a large home demand and thus a relatively high price may mean that it is a net importer of that good.

(2) TRANSPORT COSTS
These reduce possible gains and therefore make for less specialisation. Indeed, it is conceivable that transport costs could so offset A's superiority in making cars that B found it better to produce her own requirements.

(3) CHANGES IN THE CONDITIONS OF SUPPLY
Few production advantages are permanent. Climate and, to a large extent, mineral deposits persist, but new techniques can make factors more productive. Thus India now exports cotton goods to Britain!

(4) INTERFERENCE BY NATIONS WITH THE FREE MOVEMENT OF GOODS
By customs duties, quotas, exchange controls, physical controls, etc.

(ii) *By expanding the market, international trade enables the benefits of large-scale production to be obtained*
Many products, e.g. computers, aircraft and cars, are produced under conditions of decreasing cost. Here the home market is too small to exploit fully the advantages of large-scale production. This applies particularly to small countries such as Switzerland. In such cases international trade lowers costs per unit of output.

(iii) *International trade increases competition and thereby promotes efficiency in production*

As we have seen, any restriction of the market makes it easier for one seller to gain control. In contrast, international trade increases competition. A government must always consider the risk of a monopoly developing when it gives protection to the home industry by tariffs, etc.

(iv) *International trade promotes beneficial political links between countries*

Examples of this are the EEC and the Commonwealth, where trade is still an important link.

17.2 THE PATTERN OF THE UK'S OVERSEAS TRADE

(a) Trade with other countries

From our study of the reasons for international trade we can deduce the likely pattern of the UK's trade. Since, in the first place, trade arises because resources are unequally distributed, we have to ask: (i) What are the factors of production of which the UK can be said to have relatively plentiful supply? (ii) What are the factors of production in which she is deficient?

In answer to (i), we can point to her coal reserves and skilled working population, and the stock of machinery and factories which has been built up in the past through the thrift of her people. In addition she has a high proportion of very skilled and highly educated administrators, engineers and technicians, and commercial and financial experts. All such persons can render services to other countries, particularly the less developed. Thus administrators go abroad to start businesses and engineers plan and construct buildings and bridges, while commercial and financial experts and institutions perform services for countries other than the UK.

As regards (ii), however, the UK lacks land (chiefly for agriculture, because of the size of her population); plentiful supplies of very cheap, unskilled labour; certain minerals (such as nickel, zinc, aluminium and copper); certain chemicals (such as sulphur and nitrates); and the climate which is necessary, in terms of both warmth and rainfall, for the production of many foodstuffs (such as cane sugar, vegetable oils and tropical fruit), beverages (such as tea, coffee and cocoa) and raw materials (such as cotton, rubber and tobacco).

Thus, analysing the problem simply from the aspect of the distribution of resources, we can say something in a general way, first about the nature of the goods in which the UK deals with the rest of the world, and second about the countries with which she deals.

(b) The commodities of the UK's international trade

The relative supply of the UK's resources suggests that she will mostly export manufactured goods and also render services to other countries. In return she will import raw materials and foodstuffs, together with minerals and chemicals not found in sufficient quantities within her own borders.

Table 17.1   *The UK's imports and exports 1978 (by value)*

	Imports		Exports	
	£m	%	£m	%
Food, beverages and tobacco	6,142	15.0	2,912	7.8
Basic materials	3,326	8.1	968	2.6
Mineral fuels and lubricants	4,831	11.8	2,375	6.4
Manufactured goods	26,106	63.7	30,024	80.4
Miscellaneous (postal packages; live animals not for food)	564	1.4	1,084	2.9
		100		100

Source: Annual Abstract of Statistics

Fig 17.1   *percentage distribution of the UK's imports and exports, 1979*

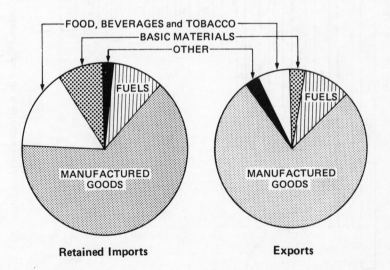

Retained Imports   Exports

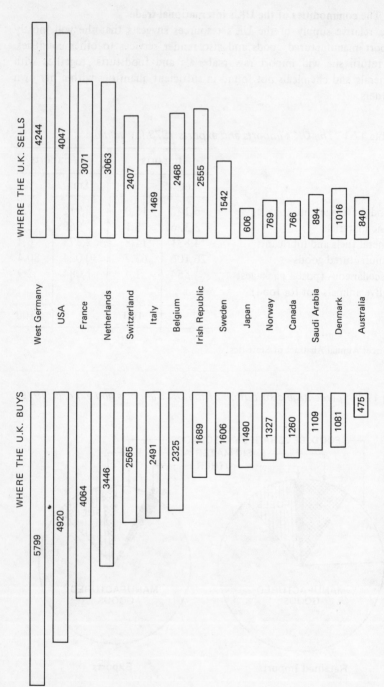

Fig 17.2 *the principal exporters to and importers from the UK, 1979 (£ m)*

The nature of the services rendered by the UK is considered later, but the broad divisions of goods exported and imported support this surmise (table 17.1): 40% of the value of her total imports consists of food, drink, tobacco, basic materials and mineral fuels, while 81% of the value of her total exports is in manufactured goods.

(c) The countries with which the UK trades
Again an analysis of the UK's resources compared with those of other countries suggests that she will import goods from countries having relatively much agricultural land, enjoying a tropical or semi-tropical climate or possessing the minerals and chemicals which she herself lacks. Where these countries need the UK's manufactured goods, as in the case of Australia, imports from them can be paid for directly by the export of such goods as wool. But where the country, like the USA, does not require manufactured goods, imports have to be paid for indirectly. This is achieved through triangular or multilateral trade. Thus Malaysia and South Africa export tin and gold respectively to the USA, but the latter sends comparatively little to them directly in exchange. Instead she exports such goods as wheat, cotton, tobacco and machinery to the UK, which in return settles the USA's bill from Malaysia and South Africa by sending them manufactured goods.

(d) The UK's trade with the Commonwealth
Table 17.2 shows that, in value, about one-ninth of the UK's trade is with the Commonwealth. Why is this?

The main reason has already been given – it arises because Commonwealth countries have factors of production which are complementary to those of the UK. However, this does not provide a complete picture, for as we suggested earlier there are special reasons why the UK's trade with the Commonwealth should be important.

Table 17.2 *Percentage distribution of the United Kingdom's foreign trade, 1938-78 between Commonwealth countries and the rest of the world*

	Imports %		Exports %	
	1938	1978	1938	1978
Commonwealth countries	38.9	9.0	44.6	13.2
Foreign countries	61.1	91.0	55.4	86.8
TOTAL	100	100	100	100

Source: Annual Abstract of Statistics

First, there exist certain ties which can be summed up in the phrase 'a feeling of brotherhood'. The development of the Commonwealth was pioneered by British emigrants who took with them a common language, common trading methods and a common loyalty to the crown. Today many people there still possess home ties with the UK. Because of such connections it is only natural that these countries should turn to the UK both as a market for their own goods and for their supplies of the goods they need.

Second, the return to British capital invested in the Commonwealth is earned mainly by exporting goods to the UK.

However, when Britain joined the EEC in 1973, preferential tariffs for Commonwealth goods virtually ended, and the importance of Commonwealth trade has decreased.

(e) The UK's trade with the European Economic Community (EEC)
Table 17.3 shows that, in value, over one-third of the UK's trade is with the EEC countries.

Table 17.3 *Percentage distribution of the UK's trade between the EEC and the rest of the world*

	Imports %		Exports %	
	1964	1978	1964	1978
EEC	23.0	40.5	27.6	37.7
Rest of the world	77.0	59.5	72.4	62.3
TOTAL	100	100	100	100

Two points should be noted. First, much of this increase in trade took place even before the UK joined the Common Market, and it is likely to increase with the common external tariff (see below). Second, the trade is mostly in manufactured goods, particularly chemicals, machinery and cars.

The reason is that specialisation is no longer confined to either manufacturing or agriculture. Now, even within manufacturing, different countries concentrate on producing particular goods. Thus Japan's Toyota car appeals to certain people in the UK, while British Minis are wanted in Japan. Such specialisation can give rise to considerable trade between countries which have reached the same stage of industrial development.

17.3 FREE TRADE AND PROTECTION

(a) Controlling international trade
Our earlier analysis suggests that trade should be as free as possible, for only then can maximum specialisation according to the law of comparative

advantage take place. In practice, however, all countries follow policies which, to varying degrees, prevent goods from moving freely in response to differences in relative prices. Methods vary.

(i) *Customs duties*
Customs duties, e.g. the common external tariffs of the Common Market, are both revenue-raising and protective. They become protective when the imported good bears a higher rate of tax than the similar home-produced good.

(ii) *Subsidies*
While countries which subscribe to the General Agreement on Tariffs and Trade (GATT) cannot follow a policy of 'dumping' exports by giving direct subsidies, the volume and pattern of international trade may be influenced indirectly by other means, e.g. government assistance to the shipbuilding industry. Less obviously, welfare benefits, e.g. family allowances and income supplements which keep down labour costs, may give one country a price advantage over another.

(iii) *Quotas*
If demand is inelastic, the increase in price resulting from a customs duty will have little effect on the quantity imported. Thus, to restrict imports of a good to a definite quantity, quotas must be imposed. For instance, foreign films can be exhibited only in a fixed proportion to British films.

Compared with duties, quotas have two main disadvantages. (1) As a result of the artificial shortage of supply, the price may be increased by the foreign supplier or by the importer. Hence, unless the government also introduces price control, it is they who gain the advantage and not the public. (2) Quotas are usually based on a firm's past imports, which makes the economy rigid by penalising the efficient firm wishing to expand.

(iv) *Exchange control*
A tighter check on the amount spent on imported goods can be achieved if quotas are fixed in terms of foreign currency. This necessitates some form of exchange control. Until October 1979, all earnings of foreign currency and claims to foreign currency had to be handed over to the Bank of England, which alone could authorise withdrawals to cover imports, foreign travel and capital movements.

(v) *Physical controls*
A complete ban – an embargo – may be placed on the import or export of certain goods. Thus narcotics cannot be imported, while the export of some strategic goods to Iron Curtain countries is forbidden. Similarly, strict regulations covering the import of live animals (e.g. cattle, dogs and parrots) make trade in them difficult.

(b) Reasons for government control of international trade

In general trade is controlled because governments think nationally rather than internationally. Although people as a whole lose when trade is restricted, those of a particular country may gain.

Many reasons are put forward to justify controls. Occasionally they have some logical justification; more usually they stem from sectional interests seeking to gain advantages. We can, therefore, examine the arguments under three main headings: (i) those based on strategic, political, social and moral grounds; (ii) those having some economic basis; and (iii) those depending on shallow economic thinking.

(i) *Non-economic arguments*

(1) TO ENCOURAGE THE PRODUCTION OF A GOOD OF STRATEGIC IMPORTANCE

Where a nation is dependent on another for a good of strategic importance, there is a danger of its supply being cut off in the event of war. Thus one argument for subsidising aircraft production in the UK is that it will ensure the survival of technical know-how, plant and skilled labour.

(2) TO FOSTER CLOSER POLITICAL TIES

As a member of the EEC, Britain must impose a common external tariff as part of a movement towards political as well as economic unity.

(3) TO PROSECUTE POLITICAL OBJECTIVES

Trade can be a weapon of foreign policy, e.g. in the sanctions against Rhodesia.

(4) TO PROMOTE SOCIAL POLICIES

Although in the past Britain has subsidised her agriculture mainly for strategic reasons, today the purposes are basically social – to avoid depression in rural districts.

(ii) *Economic arguments having some justification*

(1) TO IMPROVE THE TERMS OF TRADE

The incidence of a selective tax is shared between producer and consumer according to the relative elasticities of supply and demand (see p. 337). A government can therefore levy a tax on an imported good to improve the terms of trade if demand for the good is more elastic than the supply, for the increase in price is borne mainly by the producer, while the government has the proceeds of the tax. In practice this requires that: (a) the producing country has no alternative markets to which supplies can be easily diverted;

(b) her factors of production have few alternative uses; and (c) the demand for the exports of the country imposing the tariff is unaffected by the loss of income suffered by countries who now find their sales abroad reduced.

(2) TO PROTECT AN 'INFANT INDUSTRY'

It may be possible to establish an industry if during its infancy it is given protection from foreign competitors already producing on a large scale. It is argued that the guaranteed home market will enable the 'infant' to get over its teething troubles and eventually be strong enough to compete successfully. Britain's car industry, for instance, initially benefited from such protection.

In practice, industries tend to rely on this protection, so that tariffs are never withdrawn; for example, American duties on manufactured goods imposed in the eighteenth century still persist today. Moreover, industries are often encouraged which without protection would have no chance of survival. This leads to maldistribution of a country's resources.

(3) TO ENABLE AN INDUSTRY TO DECLINE GRADUALLY

Fundamental changes in demand for a good may severely hit an industry. Such, for instance, was the fate of the British cotton industry in the 1970s. Restrictions on imports can cushion the shock, giving the industry more time to contract.

(4) TO PREVENT DUMPING

Goods may be sold abroad at a lower price than in the home market. This may be possible because: (a) producers are given export subsidies; (b) price discrimination by a monopoly is possible; or (c) it enables the producer to obtain the advantages of decreasing costs. People in the importing country benefit directly from the lower prices. If, however, the exporter is trying to establish a monopoly which can be exploited once home producers have been driven out, there is a case for protecting the home market.

(iii) *Economic arguments having little validity*

(1) TO RETALIATE AGAINST THE TARIFFS OF ANOTHER COUNTRY

The threat of a retaliatory tariff may be used to influence another country to modify a restrictive policy. While this may be successful, it can induce counter-retaliation, with everybody losing.

(2) TO MAINTAIN HOME EMPLOYMENT IN A PERIOD OF DEPRESSION

Countries may place restrictions on imports to promote employment in the manufacture of home-produced goods. The difficulty is that other countries retaliate, thereby leading to an all-round contraction in world trade. GATT was set up to prevent this from happening (see below).

(3) TO PROTECT HOME INDUSTRIES FROM 'UNFAIR' FOREIGN COMPETITION

The demand that British workers must be protected from competition by cheap, 'sweated' foreign labour usually comes from the industry facing competition. The argument, however, has little economic justification. First, it runs counter to the principle that a country should specialise where it has the greatest advantage. That advantage may be cheap labour. Second, low wages do not necessarily denote low labour costs. Wages may be low because labour is inefficient through low productivity. What is really significant is the wage cost per unit of output. Thus the USA can export manufactured goods to the UK even though her labour is the most highly paid in the world. The threatened industry can compete by improving productivity to reduce wage-cost per unit. Third, a tax on the goods of a poor country merely makes the country poorer and its labour cheaper. The way to raise wages (and the price of the good produced) is to increase demand in foreign markets. Indeed, if imports from poor countries are restricted, other help has to be given. Thus, by importing cheap manufactured goods from Hong Kong, Britain reduces the amount of aid which is necessary. Fourth, protection, by reducing the income of the poorer countries, means that they have less to spend on Britain's exports. Last, the policy may lead to retaliation or aggressive competition elsewhere, thereby making it more difficult for the protecting country to sell abroad. One reason why Japan captured many of Britain's foreign markets for cotton goods was that her sales to Britain were restricted by protective barriers.

While restriction of trade tends to lower living standards, there may be benefits – economic, political and social. Thus protection to an industry may be given because home workers cannot adjust quickly to other occupations or industries. Usually, however, such economic gains are doubtful. Others cannot be measured, and it has to be left to politicians to decide where the balance of advantage lies. It must, however, always be remembered that protection creates vested interests opposed to subsequent removal.

(c) The General Agreement on Tariffs and Trade (GATT)

The General Agreement on Tariffs and Trade, established in 1947, has three major objectives: (i) to reduce existing trade barriers; (ii) to eliminate discrimination in international trade; and (iii) to prevent the establishment of further trade barriers by getting nations to agree to consult one another rather than take unilateral action. It operates as follows.

Member nations meet periodically to 'agree' on a round of tariff reductions. Here the 'most-favoured-nation' principle applies – any tariff concession granted by one country to another must automatically apply to all other participating countries. Thus, if the EEC agrees to reduce her tariff on American automatic vending machines by 5% in exchange for a 5% reduction in the American tariff on EEC man-made fibres, then both concessions must be extended to every other member of GATT.

Today over one hundred nations subscribe to GATT. Through the organisation, a progressive reduction in tariffs has been achieved, and the principle has been established that problems of international trade should be settled by co-operative discussion rather than by independent unilateral action. But difficulties have arisen. (i) The principle of reciprocity means that low-tariff countries have to begin from inferior bargaining positions, and the concessions they can make are thus limited. Such countries may, therefore, prefer a low-tariff regional arrangement, such as the EEC. (ii) In certain circumstances the 'most-favoured-nation' principle may deter a country from making a tariff reduction to another country for the simple reason that it has to be applied to all. (iii) The articles of the agreement have had to be waived to allow for special circumstances – balance-of-payments difficulties, American protection of her agriculture, the UK's imports from the Commonwealth, the establishment of 'infant' industries in the underdeveloped countries and the discriminatory character of the EEC.

17.4 THE BALANCE OF PAYMENTS

(a) Paying for imports

Occasionally international trade takes the form of a barter arrangement, one country agreeing to take so much of another country's produce in exchange for so much of its own. Normally, however, exchanges are arranged by private traders who, according to relative prices, decide whether it is profitable to export and import goods.

But each country has its own currency. This fact is important for two reasons: (i) sufficient foreign currency has to be obtained to pay for imports; and (ii) a rate has to be established at which one currency will exchange for another.

We can approach the question of how imports are paid for by considering the purchases made by a housewife, Mrs Jones. Each week she buys a variety of goods. However, there are at least seven sources from which she could obtain the money to pay for them.

The most usual is the week's earnings. From her husband's allowance, say, Mrs Jones pays the shopkeeper as she collects her goods. It must be noted, however, that what Mrs Jones is really doing is exchanging the goods which Mr Jones has specialised in producing for the other goods needed. Thus, if Mr Jones is a tailor, the money from the suits he sells buys Mrs Jones the goods she needs. Furthermore, money is often earned not by making goods but by performing services. Thus Mrs Jones herself may earn wages by working for the shopkeeper. Also, interest on savings may provide some current income. Provided that all the weekly expenses are met out of this combined weekly income, we should say that the Jones family was 'paying its way'.

It might happen, however, that Mrs Jones's expenditure was not covered by the current weekly income. This might occur, for instance, because she bought a costly good, such as a washing-machine. In such circumstances, she would have to raise the money from other sources. First, she could draw on her savings. Second, she could sell some goods from her household stock, such as the piano or the TV set, for which she had a less urgent need. Third, she might be able to borrow the money from a friend or, what amounts to the same thing, ask the shopkeeper to forgo being paid for the time being. Finally, if she were extremely fortunate, she might be able to obtain a gift of money, say from a doting father. Such methods of payment would be fairly satisfactory provided that her savings were gradually replenished, or the assets sold were replaced by others of equal value, or the loan was repaid during the lifetime of the good. Otherwise Mrs Jones would not be paying her way. If over-spending continued, her savings would eventually run out, her home would be sold up and more loans or credit from the shopkeeper would be unobtainable.

Broadly speaking, a nation trading with other nations is in exactly the same position as Mrs Jones. The same alternatives are open to it in paying

Fig 17.3 *how exports pay for imports*

for imports. The main source is receipts from current exports. Fig 17.3 shows how exports earn foreign currency. Importing and exporting are arranged by firms, and payments are arranged through banks, who exchange the currency of one country for the currency of another *provided that they have the necessary reserves of that currency*. Such reserves are earned by customers who export to foreign countries.

Let us assume that £1 sterling exchanges for $2 and that there are no currency restrictions. Suppose a British merchant, X, wishes to import cotton from A in the USA to the value of £10,000. The American exporter requires payment in dollars, for all his payments, e.g. his workers' wages, have to be made in dollars. Hence the importer goes to his bank, pays in £10,000 and arranges a 'documentary credit'. The bank cables its branch in New York, authorising it to make the equivalent dollar payment to A on production of the necessary documents, e.g. the bill of lading (see p. 209). (Most banks have branches in foreign capitals; if not, they engage local banks to act for them.) But how is it that the branch has dollars available to honour the draft?

We can see the answer if we imagine that another British firm, Y, has sold £10,000 worth of sports cars to an importer, B, in the USA. This firm wants payment in pounds sterling. Hence the American importer of the cars pays $20,000 into his bank in the USA, and the same procedure follows. It is obvious that the two transactions – buying cotton from the USA and selling sports cars to the USA – balance each other. The British bank's branch has had to pay out dollars, the American sterling. The British bank has received sterling, the American bank dollars. If the two get together, their requirements match. (In practice it is more likely that they would meet their needs through the foreign-exchange market.) The dollars to pay for the cotton are obtained by selling the sports cars, and *vice versa*. In short, exports pay for imports.

(b) 'Exports' in the wider sense

In this connection the term 'exports' needs qualification. In the same way that Mrs Jones received payment for her services to the shopkeeper, so a nation may receive payment not only for goods but also for services rendered to other countries. Goods exported are termed 'visible exports' because they can be seen and recorded as they cross frontiers. On the other hand, services cannot be seen and recorded; they are therefore called 'invisible' exports. Nevertheless, since services involve payments by persons from abroad, they are exports.

The main sources of invisible earnings and payments are:

(i) *government expenditure abroad*, e.g. on overseas garrisons and diplomatic services;

(ii) *shipping services*, e.g. for an American travelling in the QE2 or shipping exports in a British merchantman;

(iii) *civil aviation*;

(iv) *travel*, e.g. sterling required by an American tourist for spending on a visit to London;

(v) *other services*, e.g. royalties earned on books and records, and income from the transactions of overseas oil companies which ship direct from wells and refineries abroad to other countries;

(vi) *interest, profits and dividends from overseas investments*;

(vii) *private transfers*, e.g. remittances to relatives abroad.

Payments for any of the above transactions involve changing into another country's currency. Thus they represent imports to the paying country and exports to the receiving country.

(c) The balance-of-payments accounts

The account presented by a country of its monetary transactions with the rest of the world are known as the 'balance of payments' (table 17.4).

(i) *Current account*

On the one hand the current account shows the foreign currency which has been *spent* on *imported goods* and *invisibles* in the course of the year, and on the other the foreign currency which has been *earned* by *exporting goods* and *invisibles*.

That part of the current account showing payments for *goods* exported and imported is known as the *visible balance* (formerly the *balance of trade*). Where the value of goods exported exceeds the value of goods imported, we say that there is a favourable visible balance. If the opposite occurs, the visible balance is unfavourable. Too much, however, must not be read into the terms 'favourable' and 'unfavourable'. In the first place we have to know the reasons for the unfavourable balance. It may be brought about, for instance, by an increased demand for raw materials - which will later be exported in the form of manufactured goods. Second, a favourable or unfavourable visible balance can be reversed when invisibles are taken into account.

When we add payments and income on the invisible items to the visible balance we have the *current balance*.

There is no special reason why earnings from goods and invisibles exported between 1 January and 31 December in any one year should equal expenditure on the goods and invisibles imported during that period. How often, for instance, does what you earn during the week tally exactly with what you spend?

The current account is therefore likely to show a difference between earnings and expenditure. When the *value* of goods and invisibles exported

Table 17.4 *The balance of payments of the UK, 1978 (£m)*

CURRENT ACCOUNT
  Visible trade
    Exports (f.o.b.)   + 35,432
    Imports (f.o.b.)   − 36,607
    Visible balance   − 1,175
  Invisibles (net)
    Government   −   697
    Shipping   −   171
    Civil aviation   +   348
    Travel   +   955
    Financial and other services   + 2,854
    Interest, profits and dividends +   836
    Private transfers   − 1,918
    Invisible balance   + 2,207

    CURRENT BALANCE   + 1,032

TOTAL CURRENCY FLOW
  Current balance   + 1,032
  Investment and other capital flows (net)   − 2,931
  Balancing item   +   773

  Total currency flow   − 1,126

OFFICIAL FINANCING—drawings on (+),
  repayments or additions to (−)
    Foreign currency borrowing   − 1,203
    Official reserves of gold and foreign currency   + 2,329

                                                         + 1,126

Source: Annual Abstract of Statistics

exceeds the *value* of goods and invisibles imported, we say that there is a surplus current balance; when the reverse occurs, we say that there is a deficit. But, again, too much should not be made of the terms 'surplus' and 'deficit'. The current account is only part of the statement covering a nation's overseas financial transactions. Capital flows must also be scrutinised.

(ii) *Investment and other capital flows*

If current transactions were a country's only dealings with the world, the balance-of-payments accounts would be quite simple. A surplus of £100 million, for example, would add that amount to the reserves or allow the country to invest that amount overseas or to pay off short-term borrowings from abroad. A deficit would reduce the reserves or have to be financed by disinvestment or short-term borrowing abroad.

But capital flows also affect a country's ability to build up reserves or to pay off debts. Thus investment by private persons resident in the UK in factories or plant overseas (whether directly or by the purchase of shares), or a loan by the British government to an underdeveloped country, leads to an outflow of capital and the spending of foreign currency. Similarly, investment in the UK by persons overseas, or borrowing abroad by the British government, local authorities, nationalised industries or companies, leads to an inflow of foreign capital and the receipt of foreign currency. Whereas the current account covers *income* earning and spending in the course of the year, the term 'investment and other capital flows' covers the movement of *capital* in and out of the country. This capital may be short- or long-term.

Adding capital flows to the current balance gives the *total currency flow*.

(iii) *Total currency flow*

The total currency flow shows how much foreign currency is earned or is required to cover (1) the current balance, (2) investment and other capital flows, and (3) the 'balancing item', the difference between the total value of transactions recorded and the actual amount of foreign currency gained or lost as shown in the Bank of England's accounts.

(iv) *Official financing*

Even a net currency *outflow* must have been covered by foreign currency. For instance, imports will have been paid for even though receipts may not have been currently earned. *Official financing* shows how this has been achieved. Similarly, if there is a net currency *inflow*, the official financing account shows how the balance has been disposed of. It is in this sense that we can say that the balance of payments always balances.

Suppose that there is a net currency outflow. This can be covered by the monetary authorities by: (1) official borrowing from the IMF or from the monetary authorities of other countries; and (2) drawing on the UK's reserves of gold and foreign currency.

As we shall see, a net currency outflow cannot go on indefinitely. Measures to correct it, especially when the main cause is a persistent deficit on the current balance, will have to be taken.

Fig 17.4 *the balance of payments, 1979 (£m)*

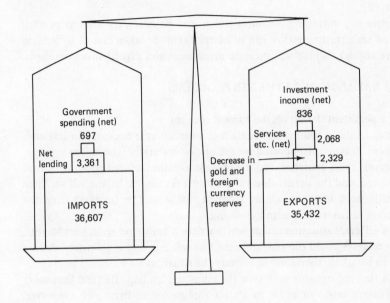

Government spending (net) 697

Net lending 3,361

IMPORTS 36,607

Investment income (net) 836

Services etc. (net) 2,068

2,329

Decrease in gold and foreign currency reserves

EXPORTS 35,432

Fig 17.5 *the balance of payments in outline*

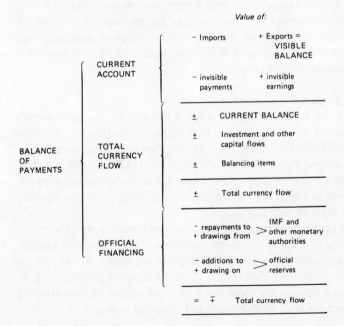

Value of:

CURRENT ACCOUNT

− Imports + Exports = VISIBLE BALANCE

− invisible payments + invisible earnings

BALANCE OF PAYMENTS

TOTAL CURRENCY FLOW

± CURRENT BALANCE

± Investment and other capital flows

± Balancing items

± Total currency flow

OFFICIAL FINANCING

− repayments to + drawings from → IMF and other monetary authorities

− additions to + drawing on → official reserves

= ∓ Total currency flow

Similarly a net currency inflow enables the authorities to (1) repay official borrowing, and (2) add to the UK's reserves of gold and foreign currency.

Here any corrective measures which may be necessary are less painful, for an embarrassing inflow can to a large extent be taken care of by lending more abroad – which will increase investment and capital flows outwards.

17.5 BALANCE-OF-PAYMENTS PROBLEMS

(a) A persistent deficit on the current account

It may be that a country has a deficit in a certain year because, for instance, it spent heavily on imported stocks of raw materials. The following year, however, those materials may be made into manufactured goods which are exported, and the deficit thus turned into a favourable balance. If so, there is little need to worry about a deficit, for it can be financed from the reserves or from short-term borrowing.

A different situation occurs where a deficit continues from year to year. The reserves could run out, and creditors will not lend indefinitely. Action has to be taken, therefore, to remedy the situation.

A first-aid measure is to raise the minimum lending rate (and thus other short-term rates) in order to attract foreign loans. Eventually, however, exports must be increased in value, and imports decreased.

Two basic policies can be followed: (i) reducing expenditure on imports; and (ii) switching expenditure, with foreigners spending more on British exports, and consumers at home spending less on imports in favour of home-produced goods. Both policies can be followed simultaneously (though with a different emphasis on each), but to clarify the issues it is better to consider them separately.

(i) *Reducing expenditure on imports*

Expenditure on imports may be reduced forcibly by the government's imposing import duties, quotas and exchange controls. However, not only is such a policy likely to arouse hostility and even to lead to retaliation by foreign countries, but it offends the spirit of GATT and of the IMF. However, as we saw in chapter 14, imports increase as income expands. Thus one way in which the value of imports can be brought into line with that of exports is by reducing income.

Fig 17.6 explains the situation. We assume an economy with no government spending or taxation, injections consisting of autonomous investment and exports, and leaks of saving and imports related to income. At the current level of income, Y, there is a current balance-of-payments deficit, DF. Assuming exports are maintained, this deficit can be eliminated by bringing down the level of investment to I', reducing income to Y'.

Fig 17.6 *achieving balance-of-payments equilibrium by deflation*

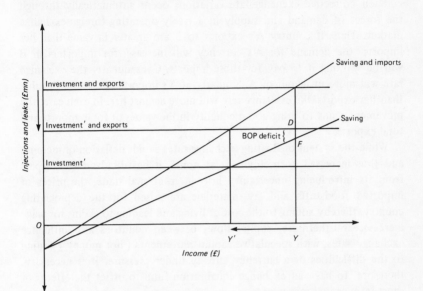

Such a deflationary policy would also tend to put a brake on any rise in home prices. More important, it allows adjustment to take place without altering currency-exchange rates (see below). This has the advantage that it encourages international trade by removing uncertainty as to how much exporters will actually receive for their goods when they are paid for, a consideration important to the UK in view of her dependence on international trade.

But there is a serious disadvantage: a deflationary policy only succeeds at the expense of creating unemployment.

(ii) *Increasing exports and decreasing imports by expenditure switching*
Whilst some switching can be enforced by government control on import expenditure, the most effective method is to alter the relative prices of imports and home-produced goods. Prices of internationally traded goods are composed of (1) the home price and (2) the exchange rate. Thus British exports can be made more competitive in world markets by lowering the rate at which the pound sterling exchanges for foreign currencies. Because fewer units of foreign currency have now to be given up to obtain a pound sterling, foreigners can buy British exports more cheaply. If their elasticity of demand is greater than 1, more revenue will be earned from exports (provided, of course, that supply by British firms can respond to the extra demand). Similarly, imports to Britain now cost more, encourag-

ing people to switch to the relatively cheaper home-produced goods.

Such corrective exchange-rate variations occur automatically through the forces of demand and supply in a freely operating foreign-exchange market. Thus, if country A's exports to B are greater in value than her imports, the demand for A's currency will increase, for importers in B will be wanting it to pay for those imports. Consequently the exchange rate will move in favour of A. Similarly, if A's imports are greater in value than her exports, the exchange rate will move against her. In each case, the movement tends to bring about equality in the values of total imports and total exports.

While the system of floating exchange rates avoids deflation of incomes and thus increased unemployment at home, it has disadvantages. Apart from its introducing uncertainty into international trade, the prices of imported foodstuffs and raw materials are raised for the depreciating country, thereby adding to the cost of living and leading to claims for wage increases. Furthermore, capital flows between countries also influence exchange rates, with speculative capital movements ('hot money') adding to the difficulties of a currency already under pressure. It is necessary, therefore, to have an exchange equalisation fund to offset the effects of short-term capital movements.

(b) The present position of the UK

After 1944 the UK, in common with other Western countries, followed a policy of 'managed flexibility' under the Bretton Woods Agreement. This was an international code of monetary behaviour which operated through the IMF, member countries agreeing on declared rates of exchange to be altered only in accordance with accepted rules.

But maintaining fixed exchange rates in the face of inflation prevented the UK from taking measures to expand its economy. Hence in 1972 the 'pegged' pound was abandoned in favour of fluctuating exchange rates.

Nevertheless, the IMF still monitors international monetary affairs and acts as a 'lender of last resort' in order to tide member countries over temporary balance-of-payments difficulties. In return, however, it may require the recipient country to follow policies judged appropriate to correcting the imbalance.

The Bretton Woods Agreement also established the International Bank for Reconstruction and Development to provide long-term finance for such projects as roads, irrigation and power stations, especially in under-developed countries. Funds are obtained by (i) a 'quota' subscribed by member nations roughly in proportion to their national incomes, and (ii) borrowing on the international market by the issue of bonds backed by the quotas of members. In addition, in order to encourage private lending the bank will, in return for a small premium of $\frac{1}{2}$-1%, guarantee repayment of a loan. Countries which have economically sound projects but cannot obtain loans from private sources at reasonably low rates of interest may borrow from the bank for a period of five to twenty-five years at about 4%.

17.6 THE EUROPEAN ECONOMIC COMMUNITY

(a) Background to the EEC
The two world wars convinced statesmen in western European countries that some form of political unity was desirable, and in 1949 the Council of Europe was created – the basis, it was hoped, of a European parliament. But organisations with definite functions – the Organisation for European Economic Co-operation (founded in 1948), the North Atlantic Treaty Organisation (1949) and the Western European Union (1954) proved more fruitful than did the Council of Europe with its broad aims.

Although these organisations involved co-operation, they were merely voluntary associations, not federal bodies 'exercising supra-national powers in the interests of members as a whole. Although federation was the ultimate aim of European statesmen, they realised that it could only pro-ceed piecemeal and on a functional basis. The first supra-national organisa-tion, the European Coal and Steel Community (ECSC), was formed in 1951 to control the whole of the iron, steel and coal resources of the six member countries – France, West Germany, Italy, Holland, Belgium and Luxembourg. The old divisions created by inward-looking national interests were thus broken down.

The success of the ECSC led to the setting up in 1957 of the Atomic Energy Community (EURATOM), a similar organisation, for the peaceful use of atomic energy, and the European Economic Community (EEC), an organisation to develop a 'common market' between the six member countries. All three communities have now been brought within the EEC.

When first offered membership of these organisations, Britain refused to join. Not only would joining the EEC have weakened Commonwealth ties, but she was also unwilling to forgo the right to follow independent policies in economics and defence. Instead, with six other nations, she joined the looser European Free Trade Area (EFTA).

Contrary to Britain's expectations, the EEC grew in strength, for difficulties were resolved as they arose. Moreover, Britain's trade with EEC countries increased at a faster rate than that with EFTA, since her goods were more complementary to their economies. Accordingly, after pro-tracted negotiations, the UK joined the EEC in 1973.

(b) The institutions of the EEC

The essential point to grasp is that the 1957 Treaty of Rome set up a 'community' whose government and institutions were developed from those of the old ECSC. Britain's position in the institutions is similar to that of France, West Germany and Italy, with the other members, Belgium, the Netherlands, Luxembourg and the Irish Republic, enjoying slightly less representation.

There are four main institutions:

(i) *The commission*

This is the most important organ of the EEC. Its thirteen members (two from the UK) serve for four years. Once chosen, however, the members of the commission act as an independent body in the interests of the Community as a whole, and not as representatives of the governments that have nominated them.

The commission is responsible for formulating policy proposals, promoting the Community interest, trying to reconcile national viewpoints and implementing Community decisions.

(ii) *The council of ministers*

Each member country sends a cabinet minister (usually the foreign secretary) to the council of ministers. This is the supreme decision-making body. Its task is to harmonise the commission's draft Community policies with the wishes of member governments. Proposals and compromise plans are exchanged between the council and the commission. If the council becomes deadlocked, the commission reconsiders the proposal in order to accommodate the views of the opposing countries. Originally it was intended that the council decisions should be on a weighted majority basis, but proposals affecting vital national interests now have to be unanimous.

(iii) *The Court of Justice*

This consists of ten judges appointed by agreement of member governments for six-year terms. Its task is to interpret the Rome Treaty and adjudicate on complaints, whether from member states, private enterprises or the institutions themselves. Its rulings are binding on member countries, Community institutions and individuals.

(iv) *The assembly, or European parliament*

This is a body of 410 elected members (81 from the UK). Members sit according to party affiliation, not nationality. The assembly debates Community policies and also examines the Community's budget. It can dismiss the commission by a two-thirds majority.

(v) *Special institutions*

Apart from the four main institutions above, there are also special institutions to deal with particular policies, e.g. the economic and social committee, the European Investment Bank, the European Social Fund, the European Monetary Co-operation Fund, etc.

(c) Economic objectives of the EEC

The over-riding aim of the EEC is to integrate the policies of its member countries. Its economic policy is based on two main principles: (i) a customs union and (ii) a common market.

(i) *A customs union*

We have to distinguish between a free-trade area and a customs union. The former simply removes tariff barriers between member countries but allows individual members to impose their own rates of duty against outsiders. A customs union goes further. While it too has internal free trade, it also imposes common external tariffs.

The EEC has a customs union, since this is essential for an integrated common market. Otherwise goods would enter the market through low-duty countries and be re-sold in those imposing higher rates.

(ii) *A common market*

In essence the common market of the EEC envisages goods and factors of production as moving freely within the community through the operation of the price system; only in this way can the full benefits of the larger market be realised.

However, this takes time to accomplish. Member countries had already developed their own individual taxes, welfare benefits, monopoly policies, methods of removing balance-of-payments imbalances, full-employment policies and so on. Such differences could disrupt the working of the price system because they would give some members advantages over others. For example, suppose that on joining the EEC Britain had retained purchase tax on refrigerators but had removed it on binoculars. This would weight the possibilities of trade against Italy (which has a comparative advantage in producing refrigerators) and in favour of West Germany (which has a comparative advantage in producing high-grade binoculars).

Alternatively the comparative advantage of some countries may lie in the expertise of the professional services they can provide. Usually this means that such services have to be taken to where the customer is (e.g. know-how regarding property development). There must therefore be mobility of labour within the market, e.g. for property developers.

Emphasis, therefore, has been placed on 'harmonisation' policies. Thus, when Britain joined, arrangements were made for her to adapt certain economic policies towards those of the original members.

(d) Aims of Common Market policy
The Common Market is seeking to achieve:

(i) *Common external tariffs (CET)*
All members will impose tariffs on imports from non-member countries at the same rates.

(ii) *Free trade between member countries*
This involves the removal of all duties, quotas and other barriers to free trade between members.

(iii) *A common agricultural policy (CAP)*
Because the demand for agricultural products tends to be inelastic, changes in the conditions of supply can have far-reaching effects on the incomes of farmers. CAP seeks to support farmers' incomes by maintaining prices on the home market through import levies on imported foods. Three prices are fixed for each product:

(1)   a *target price*, which, it is estimated, will give farmers an adequate return in a normal year;

(2)   a *threshold price*, which is used as the basis for assessing levies on imports; and

(3)   the *intervention price*, at which surplus supplies resulting from a good harvest, or from over-production through too high a threshold price, are bought up by various agencies to be disposed of outside the Market, e.g. butter sold to the USSR.

Obviously CAP confers greater benefits on countries in which agriculture is important (e.g. France) compared with countries which are more dependent on manufacturing (e.g. the UK).

(iv) *Harmonisation of tax systems*
As has already been shown, some standardisation of taxation is necessary in order to remove any 'hidden' barriers to trade. This applies particularly to indirect taxes. In the EEC value added tax (VAT) is to be the basic form of indirect tax, and it is proposed that eventually it will be imposed by all member countries at the same rates.

No proposals exist for harmonising income taxes, but most countries have adopted the 'imputation' system of corporation tax.

(v) *Free movements of persons and capital*
If a common market is to be effective, people and capital must be able to move as freely within the Community as within their own countries.

(vi) *Complete monetary integration*

As we have seen, countries can adjust the prices of imports and exports by varying the exchange rate. If this were allowed within the EEC, it could enable a member to obtain a competitive advantage over others by depreciating its currency. It is agreed, therefore, that eventually all currencies will have fixed exchange rates within narrow limits.

However, world economic depression since 1973 has made countries with relatively weak currencies (e.g. the UK) reluctant to commit themselves to a fixed exchange rate, since maintaining this could entail deflation (see above). Even so, in 1979 all EEC countries except the UK joined the European Monetary System, agreeing to keep their exchange-rate movements within a narrow band.

(vii) *A common regional policy*

Just as one nation cannot allow depressed areas to persist, so the EEC is expected to help regions of high unemployment. Northern Ireland and southern Italy are two such regions. Apart from the establishment of a regional development fund, however, little has so far been done to integrate policies designed to encourage industries to go to problem areas.

(viii) *A common transport policy*

By regulating such items as freight rates, licences, taxation and working conditions, the EEC can seek to ensure that transport undertakings compete on an equal footing. Any hidden advantages enjoyed by one country would distort the free movement of goods within the Community.

(ix) *Common rules on competition*

To prevent the distortion of competition in trade, uniform regulations have been introduced to cover price-fixing, sharing of markets and patent rights.

(x) *A Community budget*

A Community budget is necessary to meet the costs of administration and policies requiring expenditure, e.g. CAP and regional assistance. There are two main sources – import duties and a 1% VAT.

(e) Advantages of belonging to the EEC

Several advantages can accrue to countries by forming a common market.

First, it increases the possibility of specialisation. The EEC provides a market of 260 million people, larger than that of the USA. This allows economies of scale to be achieved, especially as regards sophisticated products requiring high initial research expenditure, e.g. computers, nuclear reactors, supersonic aircraft and modern weapons. Member countries now combine to cover research costs, e.g. for Concorde and the European Airbus.

Second, keener competition in the larger market can result in greater efficiency. Within the EEC there are no trade barriers which in effect protect inefficient firms. Free trade means that goods and services can compete freely in all parts of the market and that factors of production can move to their most efficient uses, not merely within but also between countries.

Third, a faster rate of growth may be achieved. In the EEC's first fifteen years the GNPs of the six original members grew twice as fast as that of the UK, giving them (Italy apart) a higher GNP per head than Britain's. To a large extent this faster rate of growth was the result of increased economies of scale and competition enjoyed by the EEC countries. But it is also possible that the EEC generates growth by the mood it engenders.

Fourth, there could be significant political benefits. As already explained, the ultimate objective of the original advocates of European co-operation was some form of political union. A western Europe which could speak with one voice would carry weight when dealing with other major powers, particularly the USA and the USSR. Moreover, the integration of defence forces and strategy would give its members far greater security.

(f) Problems facing the UK as a member of the EEC
While Britain's membership of the EEC can secure important benefits and allow her to influence its future development, it does pose special problems.

(i) *The CET could lead to the diversion of trade toward less efficient EEC suppliers*
The duties imposed by the customs union may allow firms within the Common Market to compete in price with more efficient firms outside.

Suppose, for instance, that the same machine can be produced by both the USA and West Germany, but – because the American firm is more efficient – its machine is 10% cheaper. In these circumstances Britain would, other things being equal, import from the USA. As a member of the EEC, however, Britain would have to discriminate against the American machine by the appropriate CET, say 20%. This would make the German machine cheaper, and so trade would be diverted to the less efficient producer.

The main problem this poses for Britain concerns foodstuffs, for these have traditionally entered Britain duty-free. As a result, for instance, dairy produce (particularly butter) from New Zealand was able to compete with that of European producers. The imposition of a tariff against New Zealand thwarts this.

(ii) *The CAP has particular disadvantages for the United Kingdom*
There are three main criticisms of the CAP:

(1) The import duties levied on foodstuffs in order to maintain prices for farmers within the Community hit Britain particularly hard. Since she is dependent on imports for half of her food supplies, it is essential to obtain them from the most efficient producer.

The CAP, on the other hand, requires Britain to switch her imports of foodstuffs to dearer producers within the EEC. In doing so she is subsidising, as it were, inefficient methods of farming, e.g. in West Germany.

(2) Over-production (as in the case of butter) occurs because high prices, not demand, encourage supply by EEC countries.

(3) The distortion of the normal pattern of international trade in foodstuffs widens the gap between the rich and poor countries because the latter are often food producers.

(iii) *The UK's trade with the Commonwealth*

While Britain's former EFTA partners and the less developed nations of the Commonwealth enjoy a special association with the EEC, exporters of manufactured goods, among whom are Australia, Canada and Hong Kong, have lost their preferential treatment. In the past, trade has been a strong link between the Commonwealth countries, though it must be recognised that the importance of Britain's trade with the Commonwealth has been diminishing over the past twenty years.

(iv) *Certain producers, such as tomato and fruit growers and fishermen, are particularly hit by EEC rules*

(v) *Britain's contribution to the Community's budget is growing, imposing an additional strain on her balance of payments*

(vi) *Harmonisation of taxation and the adoption of a common monetary system involve some loss of economic sovereignty*

As regards taxation, two examples can be given. First, protection of agriculture by import duties rather than by deficiency payments means that consumers, not taxpayers, pay to maintain Community farmers' incomes. In effect, therefore, the change from subsidies to protective duties is regressive. Second, VAT at present also tends to be regressive since it does not impose a higher rate on luxuries.

But it is through the adoption of the common monetary policy that Britain really stands to lose freedom of action over major economic policy, as this would mean that the price of exports could only be reduced by deflation.

Against this, however, some economists might argue that this will present no problem for Britain provided she can hold her inflation in check – and here the adoption of the EMS requirements would impose the necessary discipline.

(g) Conclusion

Britain's membership of the EEC provides the opportunity for an all-round improvement in her standard of living. But the benefits will only be secured if she braces herself to compete in the larger market. Two major problems must be faced: (i) increasing the rate of capital investment in industry, and (ii) controlling the rate of inflation at home. Each is essential if Britain is to be cost-competitive both within the EEC and in world markets.

PART VIII
MANAGING THE
ECONOMY

FULL EMPLOYMENT

18.1 THE NATURE OF GOVERNMENT ECONOMIC POLICY

(a) Objectives of government management of the economy

In chapter 1 we drew together the various reasons for government interference in the market economy, classifying them under three broad objectives: (i) allocation of resources, (ii) stabilisation and (iii) re-distribution of wealth and income. Again, however, it must be emphasised that rarely are these three broad objectives mutually exclusive. For instance, monetary measures to stabilise the economy will affect the allocation of resources and the distribution of wealth and income. Thus not only does a rise in the rate of interest hit in particular those firms needing large amounts of capital, but it reduces the value of wealth held by persons and institutions who have invested mainly in long-term government stock (see p. 340).

The first objective has already been discussed when dealing with the market economy and the public sector. In the former, the government seeks to improve the allocation of resources by interfering in the market mechanism, e.g. by carrying stockpiles to be used to stabilise the prices of certain agricultural products, and by controlling monopolies. In the latter, allocation of resources is partly based on pricing criteria and partly on political judgments, e.g. on whether to close uneconomic coal-mines and shipyards.

In the remainder of this book we examine stabilisation policy and, within the broader context of public finance, the re-distribution of wealth and income.

(b) Government stabilisation policy

Government stabilisation policy is concerned with:

   (i)   Full employment.
   (ii) Balanced regional development.

(iii)   A stable level of prices.

(iv)   Growth of national income.

(v)   A healthy overseas trading position.

In considering these it is not sufficient to concentrate simply on an examination of individual decisions in particular markets. We have to look at groups as a whole – consumers, firms, trade unions, etc. – and see how they are connected in the whole economic system.

Once again it must be pointed out that these policies often affect each other, the pursuit of one having, as it were, negative side-effects. For instance, an anti-inflationary policy may lead to the unemployment of resources. But not always: some measures may be complementary in that they promote more than one policy. Thus a road improvement scheme to relieve traffic congestion may give work to the unemployed. Usually, however, one objective has to be 'traded off' against another. Mr Harold Macmillan, a former prime minister, has likened the role of the government to that of a juggler whose task' is to keep many balls in the air at the same time. Some balls are going up because they have been given special attention, while others are on their way down.

In the last resort the emphasis put on different policies is a matter of judgment and therefore rests on political views. Our task is to analyse possible measures and suggest their likely consequences. The politician then has to decide where the balance of advantage lies.

18.2 FULL EMPLOYMENT

(a) What do we mean by 'full employment'?

Although today 8% of the working population are unemployed, this compares favourably with the situation in pre-war Britain, where, in the worst year – 1932 – the national unemployment rate was 22.1%. Unemployment means that labour, machines, land and buildings stand idle; as a result, the standard of living is lower than it need be. But the real curse is the human misery that results. Many people, without work for years, lose hope of ever finding a job; in any case skills deteriorate as the period of unemployment lengthens. Thus unemployment is usually discussed in terms of labour.

We say that unemployment exists where people capable of and willing to work are unable to find suitable paid employment. But, where an economy is constantly adapting to changing conditions, there will always be some persons unemployed as they switch jobs or as seasonal or casual works comes to an end. Some 2–3% unemployment must be allowed for, to cover this.

(b) Causes of unemployment

Unemployment may occur for many different reasons, and these must be distinguished if the appropriate remedies are to be applied.

(i) Normal or transitional unemployment

There will always be some people changing jobs. In certain occupations, e.g. unskilled labour in the construction industry, workers are not employed regularly by any one employer: when a particular contract is completed, labour is made redundant. Occasionally, too, workers are discharged when a factory is being re-organised.

Unemployed workers usually register at the local employment exchange, forming a pool of labour from which employers can fill vacancies. But how large should this reservoir of labour be? If it is too large, workers remain unemployed for long periods. If it is too small, production is dislocated by bottlenecks in filling vacancies (with employers holding on to labour not currently needed), by job-switching just for the sake of change and, above all, by strikes in support of claims for higher wages.

(ii) Seasonal unemployment

Employment in some industries, e.g. building, fruit-picking and holiday catering, is seasonal in character. The difficulty is that the skills required by different seasonal jobs are not 'substitutable'. To what extent, for example, can hotel workers become shop assistants in the January sales? Seasonal employment is not completely avoidable. But it can be reduced if a small, regular labour force will work overtime during the 'season' and admit such people as students and housewives during the busy periods. Moreover, the price system may help. By offering off-season rates, hotels at holiday resorts can attract autumn conferences.

(iii) Frictional unemployment

Frictional unemployment occurs where there are unemployed workers from a particular occupation in one part of the country but a shortage of the same type of worker in other parts. Thus today there is a surplus of unskilled and manual labourers in the north of England, whereas firms in the London area have vacancies unfilled.

Two main reasons can be suggested for this type of unemployment – ignorance of available opportunities and immobility of labour.

(iv) International causes

Because the UK is so dependent on international trade, she is particularly vulnerable to unemployment brought about by a fall in the demand for her exports. Such a fall may occur because:

(1) THE PRICES OF UK GOODS ARE TOO HIGH TO BE COMPETITIVE IN WORLD MARKETS

If home prices rise, for example because of wage increases, the export market is likely to be hit severely. The demand for exports is usually highly elastic, since substitutes are often available from competing countries.

306

Fig 18.1   *the effect on employment of a wage increase in an export industry*

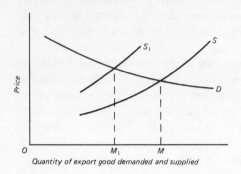

Quantity of export good demanded and supplied

The effect on employment is shown in fig 18.1. The wage increase moves the supply curve from S to S₁. Because demand is elastic there is a considerable fall in the demand for the good, from OM to OM₁. The industry, and therefore employment, contracts.

(2) INCOMES OF MAJOR IMPORTING COUNTRIES MAY BE REDUCED BY A
    RECESSION OR A DETERIORATION IN THE TERMS OF TRADE
    (see p. 34).
If incomes of importing countries fall, their demand for UK goods, especially those having a high income-elasticity of demand, will be likely to decrease. This is what happened following the increase in the price of oil in 1973.

(v) *Structural unemployment*
Structural unemployment, like the frictional type, results largely from the immobility of labour; but in this case it is brought about by long-term changes in the conditions of demand and supply. It is associated, therefore, with major changes in the economy, particularly in the export industries.

On the demand side, there may be a change in any of the factors influencing the conditions of demand. The price of substitutes may fall (Dundee jute products have largely been replaced by plastics), or foreign buyers may switch to competitors' goods (British shipyards have been hit by Japanese competition). On the supply side, new techniques or the exhaustion of mineral deposits may make labour redundant. Automation has reduced ICI's demand for workers at Stockton; exhaustion of the better coal seams has led to the closure of pits in south Wales and mid-Scotland.

Where an industry is highly localised in a particular area, the resulting unemployment may be particularly severe (see p. 311)

(vi) *Cyclical unemployment*

The term 'cyclical unemployment' refers to the alternate booms and slumps in the level of industrial activity which have occurred over the last hundred years. It was the major cause of the high unemployment of the 1930s.

By comparison with those of the 1930s, however, depressions since 1945 have been fairly mild, and are termed 'recessions'. This is because we now know that they are largely associated with an inadequate level of aggregate demand. The rest of this chapter, therefore, shows how our analysis of changes in the level of activity (chapter 16) can be used to reduce cyclical unemployment.

The other types of unemployment are largely the result of frictions – the immobility of labour – which make the price system work imperfectly. Here an approach based on demand and supply in a *particular* labour market can provide an explanation (chapter 19).

18.3 CYCLICAL UNEMPLOYMENT AND GOVERNMENT POLICY

In order to make our explanation simpler, we shall assume a closed economy.

Employment depends upon the level of national income (Y). If the level of AD is too low, the economy will be in equilibrium where Y is below the full-employment level (fig 18.2). Thus the government's task is to estimate that level of AD which will produce full employment without inflation, and then arrange that AD is increased to this level.

The role of the government in controlling the economy can be likened to that of the driver of a car. At no time can the car run on its own, and the man at the wheel has to make continuous steering adjustments. From time to time, too, he is concerned with more definite alterations, varying his pressure on the accelerator, changing gear and even modifying his route to avoid traffic congestion.

But in all these manoeuvres different drivers act differently. Some use the gear-lever rather than the accelerator in reducing speed. Others assess that traffic congestion will not be so bad as to warrant a detour. Nor does the same man do exactly the same things each day. He knows many different routes to work and, being flexible, he chooses that which is most appropriate to the particular traffic conditions.

So it is with the government. Like the driver guessing the traffic congestion along the route, the government has to work from incomplete information in estimating what change in AD is necessary to achieve the desired result and to what extent the measures it adopts will produce that change. It can use two main types of control – monetary and fiscal – but it usually has to combine them in different ways. Not only does one reinforce the other, but a different emphasis has to be placed on each according to the needs of the prevailing conditions. Where a quick change in the direction or tempo of the economy is required, more weight must be given to those measures which begin to work immediately, e.g. reducing taxes in order to increase consumption

(a) Monetary control

Monetary measures are aimed at varying the cost and availability of credit.

The *cost of credit* is the rate of interest which has to be paid. Nevertheless, as we noted earlier, there are doubts about the effectiveness of interest policy in influencing investment. Moreover, apart from being ineffective, interest policy may be undesirable for the following reasons:

(i) It cannot be pursued independently of the general level of world interest rates. If, for instance, the UK retains interest rates which are low in relation to those of the rest of the world, there will be an outflow of sterling balances. On the other hand, high interest rates mean a high cost to the UK of borrowing from abroad, increasing her 'invisible payments' (see p. 286).

(ii) The Public-Sector Borrowing Requirement may be so large that a high interest rate is necessary to attract loans (see chapter 20). It must be remembered, however, that this adds to the burden of servicing the national debt, necessitating higher taxation.

Even so, interest policy cannot be discarded completely as a weapon for regulating the economy. It can be applied quickly and to a fine degree and, if implemented early, can provide advance warning of the authorities' intentions. The psychological effects of changes may be more important than their direct effect on the cost of long-term investment.

The *availability of credit* is concerned with both the *overall level of liquidity* and *selective controls*. The former is now linked to the declared ceilings on increases in the money supply (see p. 184); the latter are exercised mainly through bank advances and hire-purchase.

When it is desired to restrict further expansion, banks are 'requested' to discriminate between different types of borrower; for instance, continuing to grant loans to exporting businesses, but refusing credit to firms concerned with property development.

In order to regulate spending on consumer goods, particularly such durables as cars, furniture, refrigerators and washing-machines, the terms of hire-purchase sales are varied.

In practice monetary policy, by varying the cost and availability of credit, is a weapon against inflation rather than one to promote full employment. Thus reducing the overall level of liquidity, restricting credit and imposing selective controls such as hire-purchase restrictions may be useful in stopping people from spending, but relaxing restrictions may not stimulate them to increase spending.

(b) Fiscal control

Indirectly, fiscal policy can influence private consumption and investment by simply changing the *type* of taxes levied. Thus a switch from indirect taxation would tend to increase consumption, for it would mean greater spending power for poorer people (those having a high propensity to consume). Similarly a movement away from taxes on companies would tend to increase investment through improved profitability.

More directly, AD may be influenced by budgetary policy which adjusts the relationship between government taxation and expenditure. As we have seen, taxation represents an appropriation by the government of a part of private incomes, and will be retained in the circular flow of income only in so far as it is spent by the government. Hence AD will be increased if taxation is less than government spending, and vice versa. If previously the budget was balanced, there would now be a budget deficit, and vice versa. In fig 18.2, current Y is OY, less than the full-employment level OY_{fe}. It is therefore necessary to increase total injections from J to J', e.g. by increased government spending.

Fig 18.2 *achieving a full-employment aggregate demand by budgetary policy*

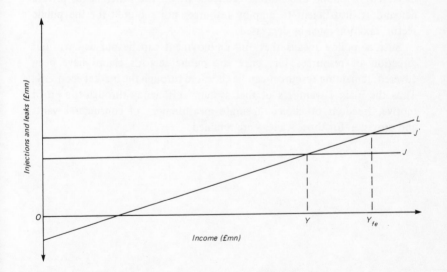

Thus today the budget is regarded, not simply as the means of raising revenue to meet the year's estimated expenditure, but as a weapon to adjust private spending power to the output which available resources can produce given the demands of the public sector. Since the latter are largely determined by policy commitments, the ability to vary public expenditure is limited; it is therefore taxation which takes the strain. Reducing taxation increases disposable income and, provided this increase is not entirely saved, spending will increase (expanding income according to the multiplier).

Such a policy is not without its difficulties. For example, the convention of annual budgets tends to dictate the timing of major adjustments. Moreover, reducing taxes may, because of administrative difficulties, take time to be effective. With PAYE, for instance, new tax tables have to be distributed. Thus fiscal policy may often have to concentrate on putting extra purchasing power quickly into the hands of consumers, e.g. by reducing national-insurance contributions and indirect taxes. Taxation, too, has other objectives than the adjustment of AD – re-distributing income, for instance. Thus policies can conflict. Finally, budgetary policy does not direct demand into those districts and industries where unemployment is highest. Again we see the necessity of having a variety of measures.

Nevertheless, budgetary policy does allow the national product to be allocated between the private and public sectors according to their relative priorities. Certain tasks can be undertaken better by the state – road-building, defence, health care, etc. – and the government must decide on the proportion of the national product which shall be devoted to each of these. Taxes adjust private demand in order to release resources for the public sector. If there is full employment, excessive demand must be increased or public expenditure reduced. If, on the other hand, private demand is insufficient to employ resources not required for the public sector, taxation must be decreased.

Such a policy means that full employment can be pursued without direction of resources for, once the public sector's claims have been covered, remaining resources can be allocated through the market economy. Thus the main advantages of that system – efficiency through the profit motive, freedom of choice, accurate measurement of consumers' wants and provision for those wants – are retained.

BALANCED REGIONAL

DEVELOPMENT

19.1 THE NATURE OF THE PROBLEM

(a) Regional unemployment

Even when there is no overall deficiency of aggregate demand, unemployment may occur through changes in the conditions of demand and supply. Demand may be buoyant for some goods, e.g. electronic equipment, and slack for others, e.g. ships. On the supply side, too, technological change, e.g. automation, can lead to redundancies.

Because of the localisation of industry, the above changes result in some regions enjoying high levels of economic activity whereas others are depressed (table 19.1).

Table 19.1   *Percentage rate of unemployment by region, 14 Feb. 1980*

United Kingdom	6.1
Region:	
South East	3.9
East Anglia	4.7
South West	6.1
West Midlands	5.8
East Midlands	5.1
Yorks. and Humber	6.2
North West	7.7
North	9.2
Wales	8.4
Scotland	9.0
N. Ireland	11.6

Source: Employment Gazette (Department of Employment)

(b) Frictions to the perfect operation of the price system

Theoretically the price system should move workers who become un-employed to other jobs. The fall in the demand for a good, and the conse-quent unemployment, should result in a relative wage fall. On the other hand, where demand is buoyant wages should rise (assuming that AD is adequate throughout the economy as a whole). Such changes in relative wages should move workers from low-wage to high-wage industries, and industries from high-wage to low-wage areas.

In practice, these movements take so long to accomplish that they cannot be left entirely to the free operation of the price system. Labour does not move easily from one industry to another because of occupational immobility, or out of depressed areas because of geographical immobility. Industry may not transfer to depressed areas, because unemployed workers have not the necessary skills or because the saving in wage-costs is insuf-ficient to offset the loss of location advantages. Indeed, national wage agreements, by eliminating pay differentials, undermine the forces which set the price system in motion.

19.2 GOVERNMENT POLICY

(a) General considerations

In deciding upon specific measures to improve labour mobility, the govern-ment must bear in mind that:

(i) Unemployment arising through immobility is far more difficult to cure when cyclical unemployment also exists, for an unemployed man has little incentive to move if there is unemployment even in the relatively prosperous areas.

(ii) Problems arise if only labour and not industry shifts. Where workers move out of an area, their spending power is lost. Here the multiplier operates in reverse to make the area still further depressed. In contrast, 'growth' areas could experience inflationary pressure which may eventually be transmitted throughout the economy.

(iii) Other government interference in the economy may add to the problem of immobility. Thus high rates of income tax whittle away monetary inducements to move and unemployment benefit may reduce the incentive to seek a job elsewhere, while rent control leads to difficul-ties in finding accommodation. Similarly, uniform national wage-rates, insisted upon by many trade unions, eliminate the incentive of lower labour costs to attract firms to areas of high unemployment.

(iv) Usually only a small fraction of the labour force has to move out of a depressed area, since new industries can be attracted to provide work for the remainder. While it is easier for the younger workers to move, this should occur only if absolutely necessary, for their loss can further depress the area.

(v) Many changes of both occupation and area take place in a series of 'ripples'. Thus an agricultural labourer may move to road construction to take the place of the Irish labourer who transfers to the building industry.

(vi) Since government measures take time to become effective, there should be a continuous policy of bringing greater diversity to those areas mainly dependent on one or two industries.

(b) Specific measures to improve occupational mobility

The government's first task must be to improve occupational mobility. Entry into certain occupations should be made less difficult. Here the government can give information on opportunities in other industries and occupations and use its influence to persuade trade unions to relax their apprenticeship rules.

More important, people must be trained in the new skills required by expanding industries. The government's Manpower Services Commission is currently responsible for promoting industrial training. Over fifty government training centres have been set up, and trainees are given financial assistance. Lump-sum redundancy payments were introduced in 1966 to encourage workers to change jobs when their particular skills were no longer required. In the longer period the problem can be tackled by advising school-leavers on career prospects and further training. Today most industries each have an industrial training board responsible for training facilities, paying grants for approved courses and imposing levies on employers to spread the cost.

(c) Measures for dealing with geographical immobility

Obstacles to geographical mobility are more difficult to overcome. Where a whole area is 'depressed' the government can give first aid by placing its contracts there, e.g. for ships, and by awarding it priority for public works, e.g. schools, new roads, and hospitals. In the long period, however, it must take measures which will on the one hand encourage the outward movement of workers and, on the other, induce new firms to move in.

The first group of measures – 'taking workers to the work' – consists of granting financial aid for travelling to new work or towards the cost of moving, providing information on prospects in other parts of the country, and removing artificial barriers such as the shortage of housing accommodation.

The second policy – 'taking work to the workers' – is now regarded as the real long-term solution. It avoids forcing workers to move out of areas to which they are attached, relieves the growing congestion in the Midlands and south-east England, and prevents depopulation in the north, with the loss of 'social capital' which that involves. Above all it recognises that the multiplier works in reverse, so that moving workers out makes the region still further depressed.

On the other hand it can involve firms in higher costs: their desire to establish plant in the south-east is to secure the advantages of localisation, such as a supply of skilled workers or close contact with customers on the Continent.

To move young, expanding firms into the depressed areas the government may use either the carrot or the big stick. So far it has concentrated on the former, though there has been some oblique compulsion through planning requirements. A firm re-locating in one of the Assisted Areas – Special Development Areas (where the need for jobs is most acute), Development Areas and Intermediate Areas, as shown in fig 19.1 – is offered special assistance, the most important forms of which are:

(i) *Regional development grants* for approved expenditure on buildings, works, machinery and plant at the rate of 22% in a Special Development Area and 15% in a Development Area. Since grants are not limited to projects creating employment, they may be used to help with improvements and modernisation.

(ii) *Removal grants* of up to 80% for certain costs incurred in moving to a Special Development area or Development Area.

(iii) *Loans at favourable rates or interest relief* for projects which reduce unemployment.

(iv) *Government factories* for sale or to rent on favourable terms.

(v) *Help for transferring key workers* essential to setting up a new plant.

All the above are in addition to the investment incentives through tax concessions available to manufacturing and service industries throughout the country.

Assistance is also obtained from the EEC's European Regional Development Fund, which was set up in 1975, and loans are available on favourable terms from the European Investment Bank and the European Coal and Steel Community.

The Department of Industry controls the Industrial Estates Corporation, which supervises government-sponsored industrial estates in England. In Scotland and Wales the Industrial Estates Corporations have become the responsibility of the Scottish and Welsh Development Agencies, responsible to the Secretaries of State for Scotland and Wales respectively.

Northern Ireland also enjoys a full range of incentives under separate legislation.

Through its planning powers the government can indirectly use some compulsion. The consent of the local planning authority is necessary for any new building or addition to an existing building. Moreover, if this would create industrial floor-space of more than 50,000 square feet outside the Assisted Areas, an industrial development certificate is also required from the Department of Industry, which relates the request to the level of employment in the region.

In the dispersal of industry the government has, whenever possible, set an example. Thus the Department of Health and Social Security is centred in Newcastle and the National Giro in Bootle, and branches of the Department of Inland Revenue have been moved to Wales.

(d) Regional planning

While development-area policy deals with special districts needing extra help, planning now covers larger areas to ensure a sound infrastructure of public services and a broad-based industrial structure. To this end the

Fig 19.1 *the Assisted Areas as from 1 August 1980*

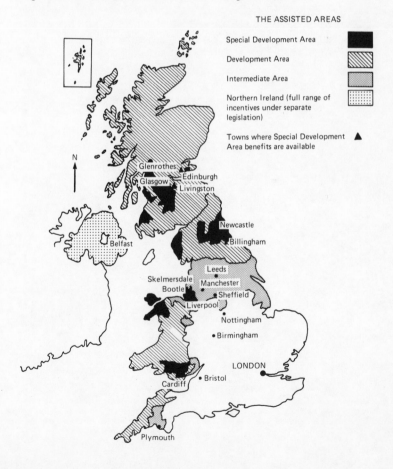

THE ASSISTED AREAS

Special Development Area

Development Area

Intermediate Area

Northern Ireland (full range of incentives under separate legislation)

Towns where Special Development ▲
Area benefits are available

whole country is divided into ten regions (eight for England, one for Scotland and one for Wales), for each of which there is planning on a broad scale as regards the distribution of labour, the diversification of industry and the rate of growth.

Primary responsibility for regional development lies with the Department of Industry. In the seven regions requiring most assistance it has regional industrial boards. These advise generally on applications for selective financial assistance for the development of industry in their regions.

Each region has an economic planning board, consisting of civil servants from the main government departments concerned with regional planning. The board's task is to formulate plans and to co-ordinate the work of the departments concerned. As far as possible the members are brought together in one building.

CURRENCY STABILITY

20.1 THE EFFECTS OF INFLATION

Today the control of inflation is given priority in government policy. To appreciate why, we have to look at the effects of rising prices or – what is the same thing – a fall in the value of money.

(a) Possible benefits

At one time a gently rising price level was not viewed with too much concern. It improved the climate for investment and so helped to maintain AD. Moreover, it tended to reduce the real burden of servicing the national debt: while interest is fixed in money terms, receipts from taxation increase as national money income rises.

The snag, however, is that, once started, the rise in prices is difficult to contain. At first it becomes uncomfortable, producing undesirable results both internal and external. Eventually, the rate of inflation increases. The situation is then serious, for it is much more difficult to reverse the trend. Indeed, it can develop into runaway inflation.

(b) Internal disadvantages

(i) Income is re-distributed arbitrarily. Not only does inflation reduce the standard of living of those dependent on fixed incomes, e.g. pensioners, but it benefits debtors and penalises lenders. Thus the stability upon which all lending and borrowing depends is undermined.

(ii) Interest rates rise, both because people require a higher reward for lending money which is falling in value and also because the government is forced to take disinflationary measures.

(iii) Investment is discouraged by government anti-inflation policy. In practice, controls imposed on prices are more effective than those on costs, particularly wages. The result is an erosion of profits and a disincentive to invest.

(iv) Saving is discouraged because postponing consumption simply means that goods cost more later.

(v) Inefficiency is encouraged because a buoyant seller's market blunts competition as higher prices allow even inefficient firms to survive.

(vi) Inflation generates social unrest because there is competition for higher incomes. Thus, because of rising prices, trade unions ask for annual wage rises. Often demands exceed the rate of inflation, anticipating future rises or seeking a larger share of the 'national cake', i.e. improving their members' real standards of living at the expense of weaker groups.

(vii) the rate of inflation tends to increase, largely because high wage settlements in anticipation of higher future prices help to bring about what they fear.

(c) External effects

Inflation can create serious difficulties for a country dependent on international trade, as Britain has discovered over the past thirty years. Where the level of domestic prices rises relatively to those of foreign competitors, imports increase, since they become more competitive with home goods. Moreover, exports are discouraged by being relatively dearer and because manufacturers find it easier to sell in the buoyant home market. This may lead to balance-of-payments difficulties (see below).

20.2 MEASURING CHANGES IN THE GENERAL LEVEL OF PRICES

(a) Difficulties

The difficulty of measuring changes in the general level of prices is that different kinds of price – wholesale prices, retail prices, security prices, import prices, etc. – change differently. If we tried to measure changes in all prices, therefore, our task would be stupendous. More than that, it would lack practical significance; a measurement which, for instance, included security prices would have little interest to a working man owning no securities. It is usual, therefore, to concentrate on changes in the prices of those goods which are of most general significance – the goods bought by the majority of people.

(b) The method of measuring changes in the price level

Since we are mainly interested in how much the price level has altered between one date and another, it can be measured as a relative change by means of an *index number*. The steps are as follows:

(i) A base year is selected.

(ii) In order to ensure that the same goods are valued over the period under consideration, a 'basket' of goods, based on the current

spending habits of the 'typical' family (in 1979, one where the head has a gross income of less than £160 a week), is chosen.
(iii) The basket is valued at base-year prices, and that value is expressed at 100.
(iv) The same basket is re-valued at current prices.
(v) The cost of the current basket is then expressed as a percentage of the base year. Thus, if the cost of living had risen by 5%, the index for the current year would be 105.

In practice the prices of the selected goods are compared, their percentage changes being 'weighted' according to the relative expenditure on the particular commodity in the base year. Suppose, for instance, that there are only two commodities, bread and meat, upon which income is spent. The index between two years is calculated as follows:

| | | Year 1 | | | Year 2 | | |
	Price	Units bought	Expenditure	Weight	Price	Year II as % of year I	Weighted price relative
Bread	20p	5	100	10	30p	150	1500
Meat	100p	11	1100	110	120p	120	13200
				120			120)14700
							122.5

Index

Year I (base)	100
Year II	122.5

The price in year 2 is expressed as a percentage of the price in year I. This is multiplied by the appropriate weight to give a 'weighted price relative'. These weighted price relatives are then totalled and divided by the total of the weights to give the new index number.

(c) Defects of the index of retail prices

The index of retail prices is based on the method outlined above. But as a means of expressing changes in the value of money it has snags:

(i) The basket and the weighting are merely an arbitrary average. Different income-groups have widely different baskets, and even within the same group the amount spent on each good varies. Thus a change in the index of retail prices does not affect all people equally.

(ii) The basket becomes more unreal the further we move from the base year. For instance, an increase in income changes patterns of expenditure. In an attempt to surmount this defect, the weights are revised each January on the basis of the *Family Expenditure Survey* for the previous year. The index figure for the year is then calculated at current prices (January = 100) and 'linked' to the main base date (15 January 1974) by multiplying the main index figure by the proportionate change in the year.

(iii) Technical difficulties may arise both in choosing the base year and in collecting information. For instance, the base year may prove to be somewhat abnormal because of a particularly high birth rate, while the development of discount stores may upset standardised methods of collecting prices.

Thus an index of retail prices merely *points towards* changes in the cost of living. But if we remember its limitations it provides a useful assessment of changes in the value of money.

20.3 CAUSES OF INFLATION

Experience of inflation over the past twenty-five years suggests that it has no single cause. We can begin, however, by distinguishing initiating influences on both the demand and supply sides.

(a) Demand pull

Our analysis of the determination of the level of activity has suggested that, if there is cyclical unemployment, the situation can be improved by expanding AD. But since output increases as AD expands, prices need not rise initially. However, as full employment is approached, bottlenecks occur in the supply of raw materials and components, and less efficient

Fig 20.1 *an inflationary level of monetary AD*

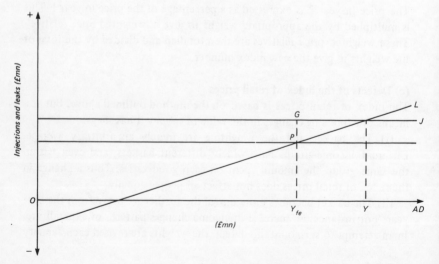

labour has to be employed. As a result output is unlikely to increase at the same rate as AD, so that prices start to rise.

If AD is allowed to expand above the level necessary to produce full employment, extra spending has its impact on a fixed output. Consequently prices are forced up: we are in a true inflationary situation. In terms of fig 20.1, total injections are so high that the equilibrium level of income would be Y. We can say that there is an inflationary gap of GP.

(b) Cost push

The rise in prices can start on the supply side. Thus the prices of imported foodstuffs, raw materials and capital equipment may increase. For example, the fivefold rise in oil prices in 1973-4 triggered off worldwide inflation.

More usually, however, cost-push inflation has followed from demand-pull. Once prices start to rise as the government pursues a full employment policy, trade unions seek compensating wage increases. Indeed, the scale of their demands tends to increase in order to allow for future price rises. Furthermore, the current practice is for such demands to be presented yearly, often irrespective of the rate of inflation and without any justifying increase in productivity.

Generally speaking, employers have not resisted such demands, feeling that product prices can be raised to cover them. This is especially true when they enjoy a monopoly selling power. In practice their expectations are justified, for unless the government imposes financial restraints to make it more difficult for firms to cover higher wages, the increased wages themselves provide the incomes and expenditure to justify higher prices. We have, therefore, what is termed 'cost-push' inflation – prices are being 'pushed up' by an initial increase in costs.

(c) Differences in policy approach

Fig 20.1 suggests that, to cure demand-pull inflation, injections should be cut from J to J', thereby reducing aggregate demand from Y to Y_{fe}. Alternatively, where the basic cause is cost push, the government can urge or impose wage restraint, backing this with restrictions on price rises. In practice, both policies have proved too simplistic.

First, instead of inflation's being merely a condition of excess demand at the full-employment level of output, it is a *process*. An initial price rise generates demands for wage increases which, when granted, push up prices still further, thus leading to new demands for wage rises, and so on. In short, there is an inflationary spiral. Thus the remedy is not a simple piece of surgery to remove excess fat, but rather a fight against a cancerous growth.

The logic of government price-control policy has been to break this spiral: if the rise in prices could be halted, trade unions would have fewer grounds for high wage demands. To back this up the UK has experimented with voluntary wage restraint, statutory wage freezes and the 'social contract' of 1976. In practice, the policy has had only short-term effects, holding wage-rises for about two years. For one thing, it imposes rigidity on the economy, leading to shortages of goods and resources, in particular of skilled labour, in those industries where demand is buoyant. For another, wage-restraint policy has provided for lower-paid workers to benefit by comparison with the higher-paid, e.g. by allowing them flat-rate increases. This has undermined wage differentials, and eventually skilled workers act to have them restored.

Second, at one time it was thought that there was a fairly close inverse relationship between the level of unemployment and the rate of price rises. But in the 1970s the rate of inflation rose even though the level of unemployment increased – a situation often referred to as 'stagflation'. Trade unions in key industries pressed wage-claims although there had been little increase in productivity and irrespective of the fact that some of their members were already unemployed. This suggests that there may be strong sociological factors behind the demand for wage rises, organised labour seeking to re-distribute income in favour of workers generally. Such an objective would also be compatible with the 'structural inflation' view, which stresses that wage rises awarded in the growth industries are in practice conceded in declining industries, e.g. shipbuilding, steel, cars, etc., through the annual process of wage bargaining. Indeed, it is asserted that any norm urged by the government merely reinforces an across-the-board increase since it is interpreted as a minimum for all workers. Furthermore, high wage-claims to re-distribute income irrespective of the level of unemployment become respectable if trade unions can rely on the state to compensate weaker groups who suffer from inflation, e.g. the unemployed, those living on fixed incomes, pensioners, etc. This was part of the logic behind the 'social contract'.

Third, the Keynesian view (derived from the writings of the economist J. M. Keynes) that an increase in the supply of money has only an indirect and muted effect on the level of AD and thus on the price level is now challenged by the 'monetarists', led by Professor Milton Friedman. They assert that increases in the money supply can lead directly to extra spending. In other words, there has been a resuscitation of the quantity theory of money.

(d) The quantity theory of money

The quantity theory of money attributes a rise in the general price level to an increase in the supply of money. Usually it is given precision by being expressed in the form of the Fisher equation: MV=PT, where M is the amount of money available in the economy; V is the velocity of circulation – the average number of times each unit of money changes hands in carrying out transactions; P is the general level of prices; and T is the volume of transactions, the total quantity of goods and services exchanged against money.

If we are concerned with the Fisher equation as a statement of fact, there is nothing to quarrel about, for its two sides are equal by definition. MV, the amount of money multiplied by the number of times each unit changes hands in a given period, is merely the expenditure by buyers of goods and services over the period. Similarly, PT, the average price of goods multiplied by the volume, is simply the receipts of sellers. Since expenditure must be the same as receipts, MV and PT are simply different ways of expressing the same thing.

Nevertheless, the equation is helpful in that it separates the three variables determining the price level. Not only may the volume of goods exchanged against money alter but, more important in the short term, so may money turnover, for the same amount of money may be used many times to finance different transactions. For example, if each £1 of a total sum of £10 is used on average ten times during a certain period, in practice that £10 does the work of £100 where each £1 is used only once.

But, as an explanation of what *causes* changes in the price level, the quantity theory is only valid if T and V can be assumed to be constant. The Keynesian view, as we have seen, is that an increase in AD – and the quantity theory attributes this simply to an increase in M – would increase output if there were less than full employment. In other words, T would increase and P remain unchanged.

On the other hand, modern monetarists hold that, especially in the short term, T is fairly constant, either because of nearly full employment or because of stagflation, where higher expenditure and higher prices do not stimulate growth. But it is their views on V which have aroused the most controversy. Keynes held that V adjusts to changes in M: an increase in M would simply be held in liquid balances, and the effect on spending would only be indirect as a result of the consequent fall in the rate of interest. In contrast, the monetarists assert that V has a degree of stability. As a result, an increase in M can lead directly to additional spending on goods and services, and thus have a direct effect on the price level. While this view still needs substantiating more completely, the experience of the UK and other advanced economies in recent years does seem to indicate a link between an increase in M and an increase in the rate of inflation, prices rising after a time-lag of about two years.

20.4 CONTROLLING INFLATION

(a) A mixture of measures

The foregoing discussion has drawn attention to the fact that there is no *single* cause of inflation. Different factors exert different pressures at different times. Policy, therefore, must consist of a variety of measures, each being applied to a different degree according to the government's reading of the situation. These measures include:

(i) *Exhortation* to moderate wage increases, raise productivity and increase exports.

(ii) *Wage restraint* within a given 'norm', or even a statutory prices-and-incomes policy.

(iii) *Fiscal policy*, mainly higher taxation, to reduce the level of AD.

(iv) *Monetary policy* to reduce spending by making bank credit harder to come by, by imposing hire-purchase controls and by raising the rate of interest.

(v) Rigid *control of the growth* of the overall *supply of money*.

The use of these controls can be illustrated by a brief survey of Britain's economic policy since 1974, the period when inflation developed into a really serious problem.

(b) Britain's economic policy since 1974

Although the Labour government increased food and housing subsidies to keep down the cost of living, during 1974 there was a leap in money wage-rates. In addition, the increase in the money supply over the previous two years began to affect prices. Above all, world inflation resulted from the 1973 rise in the price of oil, and the price of British imports rose. By the end of 1974 inflation in Britain was running at the rate of 27%.

To combat this, the Labour government placed the emphasis on the 'social contract'. On the one hand, trade unions limited their demand for wage increases; on the other, the government agreed to maintain as far as possible the level of employment and the real value of social benefits and to legislate to improve the conditions of employment.

While it helped employment, the high level of AD led to a 1975 current balance-of-payments deficit of nearly £1,700 million. The value of sterling fell, and this was accentuated by the withdrawal of sterling balances. Not only did this raise the price of imports (thereby adding to inflation) but, to prevent the exchange rate falling still further, the Bank of England had to spend heavily from the reserves. By the end of 1976 Britain had to exercise her final borrowing facility with the IMF of £2,350 million.

But this loan was only advanced on condition that Britain introduced acceptable economic measures. The size of the public-sector borrowing requirement was giving cause for concern, for government spending had increased under the 'social contract'. In part it 'had been financed by increasing the money supply, and this was held to be a major cause of inflation. Britain therefore had to agree to cut the PSBR by at least £2,500 million in each of the following two years. The mere announcement of these measures eased pressure on the exchange rate, which continued to improve with the pursuit of anti-inflation measures. By 1978, however, the trade unions were in no mood to limit their wage-demands to the government norm of 5%. In the event, they achieved increases of almost 15%, and the rate of inflation moved once more into double figures.

The return of a Conservative government in 1979 switched the emphasis of anti-inflationary policy from price control, wage restraint and limits to the increase of aggregate demand, to strict control of the money supply. Instead of taking an active role in wage settlements, the government has stood aside, deliberately leaving industries to negotiate their own terms with the trade unions. The government simply warns that high wage increases will, with a strict control of the money supply, result in unemployment; the trade unions are, as it were, being left to learn from hard experience. In the meantime it must be admitted that any 'blood-letting' strikes which result will necessarily hold back improvements in living-standards, something which could be avoided by the exercise of common sense and moderation (see also pp. 156-7).

(c) World inflation
One final point should be noted: the UK's price level cannot be isolated from general world inflation, such as that which followed the large rises in oil prices of 1973, 1974 and 1979. We must, therefore, expect the UK's price level to continue to rise; what we have to ensure is that it does not rise faster than those of foreign competitors in world markets.

GOVERNMENT FINANCE

21.1 GOVERNMENT EXPENDITURE

(a) Limits to government spending

In the 1970s taxation has taken about 40% of the gross national product –
a remarkable increase since 1910, when the figure was only about 10%.
The government is now spending on a much wider range of activities.

Many items of government spending, e.g. pensions, national-debt interest
and grants to local authorities, are unavoidable since by nature they are
basically contractual. It may therefore seem that the government has
merely to estimate its expenditure and imposes taxes to cover it. But this
is not the case.

Since goods and services in the economy as a whole are limited, the
government has to cut its coat according to its cloth, asking such questions
as: What can be afforded for the Arts Council? How much can be given to
local authorities? Can university education be expanded? Can national-
insurance contributions be reduced? The economic problem, involving
decisions at the margin, confronts private persons and the government
alike. The government can only secure more goods and services by allowing the private sector less. In the last resort the division rests on a political
decision.

(b) The distribution of government expenditure

Government spending can be classified under the following headings:
  (i)   *Defence*, which has accounted for about one-sixth of all govern-
        ment spending.
  (ii) *Internal security* – the police, law-enforcement and fire brigades.
  (iii) *Social responsibilities* – education, and protection against the
        hazards of sickness, unemployment and old age.
  (iv) *Economic policy*, covering subsidies to agriculture and industry,
        help for Development Areas, worker training and the provision of
        capital to the nationalised industries.

(v) *Miscellaneous*, including expenditure on diplomatic services, grants to local authorities and – the largest single item – interest on the national debt.

(c) How government expenditure is financed

In the same way that firms have to pay for both variable and fixed factors, the government has to spend not only on single-use goods and services but also on goods which render services over long periods. The first, which involve regular yearly spending, should be paid for out of regular yearly income. But capital spending, on such items as roads, loans to nationalised industries and university building, is more fairly financed by borrowing, for the repayment of the capital then partly falls on future beneficiaries.

Current expenditure is met from two main sources: (i) miscellaneous receipts, chiefly interest on loans, rents, and charges on goods and services (such as medical prescriptions); and (ii) taxation, described in more detail below.

Capital expenditure is mostly covered by government borrowing, which takes the form of:

(i) Short-term loans from the sale of Treasury bills. Originally these were used to bridge the time-gap between expenditure and receipts from taxation, but – because it is cheaper to borrow short than long – they eventually became a major means of government borrowing. Nevertheless the inflationary effects which followed have forced the government to adopt a 'funding' policy (see p. 340).

(ii) Medium- and long-term loans are obtained by selling stock having a minimum currency of five years. Some, such as 3½% War Loan, are undated.

(iii) *'Non-market' borrowing*, through National Savings Certificates, Premium Savings Bonds, etc. and the deposits of the National Savings Bank and Trustee Savings Banks.

21.2 THE MODERN APPROACH TO TAXATION

(a) Taxation and government policy

Until the end of the nineteenth century, the functions of the state were mainly defence and the preservation of law and order, and taxation was levied primarily for revenue purposes.

To meet the vast increase in government spending over the last fifty years, higher rates of taxation have been imposed and new taxes introduced. As we shall see, these additions have provided new means for promoting economic and social policies. Briefly, by its fiscal measures, the government can: (i) influence the allocation of resources, e.g. to allow for social costs and benefits; (ii) exercise an overall control of the economy, mainly to secure full employment or check inflation; (iii)

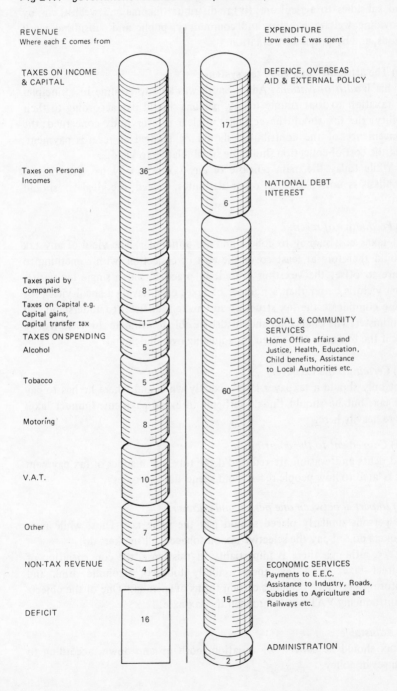

Fig 21.1 *government revenue and expenditure, 1979*

REVENUE
Where each £ comes from

TAXES ON INCOME
& CAPITAL

Taxes on Personal
Incomes — 36

Taxes paid by
Companies — 8

Taxes on Capital e.g.
Capital gains,
Capital transfer tax — 1

TAXES ON SPENDING

Alcohol — 5

Tobacco — 5

Motoring — 8

V.A.T. — 10

Other — 7

NON-TAX REVENUE — 4

DEFICIT — 16

EXPENDITURE
How each £ was spent

DEFENCE, OVERSEAS
AID & EXTERNAL POLICY — 17

NATIONAL DEBT
INTEREST — 6

SOCIAL & COMMUNITY
SERVICES
Home Office affairs and
Justice, Health, Education,
Child benefits, Assistance
to Local Authorities etc. — 60

ECONOMIC SERVICES
Payments to E.E.C.
Assistance to Industry, Roads,
Subsidies to Agriculture and
Railways etc. — 15

ADMINISTRATION — 2

promote economic growth, e.g. through tax allowances for investment and subsidies to agriculture; (iv) re-distribute income and wealth, e.g. by providing welfare benefits and community, public and subsidised merit goods, and by progressive taxation.

(b) The attributes of a good tax system
In his *Wealth of Nations*, Adam Smith was able to confine his principles of taxation to four simple tenets: persons should pay according to their ability; the tax should be certain and clear to everybody concerned; the convenience of the contributor should be studied as regards payment; and the cost of collection should be small relative to yield.

While today the main purpose of any tax is usually to raise money, emphasis is now placed on other attributes. Indeed, the ideal tax should be:

(i) *Productive of revenue*
All taxes cost money to collect and are unpopular. The yield of any tax should therefore at least cover the cost of collection, with something to spare to offset the vexation caused. In practice, too, a single tax with a high yield is better than a number of taxes each having a small yield, for these complicate the tax structure and make it difficult to understand and administer. The Chancellor should also be able to estimate the yield from a tax if the budget is to be used for adjusting overall demand.

(ii) *Certain to the taxpayer*
Not only should a taxpayer know exactly when and where he has to pay his tax, but he should find it difficult to evade payment. Indirect taxes score heavily here.

(iii) *Convenient to the contributor*
Bad debts and evasion are reduced if the time and manner of tax payment are related to how people receive and spend their incomes.

(iv) *Impartial between one person and another*
All persons similarly placed should pay the same tax. Thus, while non-smokers do not pay the selective tax on tobacco, all smokers do.

Yet, although there is impartiality in this sense, the concentration of indirect taxes on a few goods – chiefly tobacco, alcoholic drink and motoring – severely penalises certain forms of spending. One of the objects of introducing VAT was to broaden the tax base.

(v) *Adjustable*
A tax should be capable of variation, both up and down, according to changes in policy.

(vi) *Automatic in stabilising the economy*

As we have seen, varying the relationship between government expenditure and revenue is one of the major devices for keeping the economy on an even keel – with full employment but a stable price level. Through tax changes, the Chancellor of the Exchequer can vary the purchasing power of the community. Usually he has to make a deliberate adjustment in his budget, but it is helpful if taxes operate automatically in the desired direction. Thus, when money income increases, so do income tax and VAT yields, thereby reducing inflationary pressure, and vice versa.

(vii) *Harmless to effort and initiative*

This becomes important as direct taxation increases. High rates of income tax, for instance, may induce the taxpayer to take his income in the form of leisure or reduce his willingness to undergo training or seek promotion. The extent to which this occurs, however, is uncertain. If a person has fixed money commitments, e.g. hire-purchase instalments, mortgage repayments and insurance premiums, he may have to work harder to meet them when his income is reduced. Furthermore, if we assume that a high rate of income tax is a disincentive to effort, we infer that people always look upon work as distasteful, while leisure is seen as a pleasurable alternative. This may be true for many, but in the high-income brackets there are some who find their work enjoyable. Last, most workers have to work a 'normal' week, and can only vary their hours as regards overtime.

The disincentive effect is more likely to occur when there is a sudden jump in the rate of tax between one income level and another. People reduce their effort at the higher marginal level.

High direct taxes can also affect enterprise and efficiency. By eroding the wage differentials between skilled and unskilled labour they reduce incentives. Similarly, entrepreneurs are only prepared to accept risks if the rewards are commensurate.

Furthermore, high taxation of profits and income means that the penalty of inefficiency is not borne entirely by the taxpayer. Because income is smaller, less tax is paid and so a part of the cost falls on the government.

(viii) *Consistent with government policy*

Although the tax structure should not change frequently, individual taxes must be constantly reviewed to see how they could be used to promote government policy. To encourage effort, should income from work be taxed at a lower rate than investment income? Will an indirect tax, by raising the cost of living, increase wage-push inflation?

Indirect taxes can be adapted to specific objectives, e.g. cigarettes bear a high selective tax, while exports are 'zero-rated' for VAT (see below).

(ix) *Minimal in its effect on the optimum allocation of resources*

An indirect tax on a particular good results in resources' not being fully allocated according to the preferences of consumers. This may be acceptable where social costs and benefits have to be allowed for. But normally, to maximise satisfaction, consumers spend so that the marginal utility relative to price is equal for all goods. This relationship is destroyed by a tax on one good, for its price rises, resulting in a re-distribution of consumers' expenditure and thus of the factors of production. In addition, taxing its products may disrupt the industry (see below).

Again, selective indirect taxes entail a greater loss to the consumer than an income tax yielding the same amount. Unlike the latter, selective indirect taxes change the relative prices of goods, so that consumers have to re-arrange their patterns of expenditure. This substitution involves a loss of satisfaction in addition to that suffered through the reduction in income.

Finally, direct taxes can affect the supply of factors, particularly capital, to industry. High taxation may discourage saving; it certainly reduces the power to save. This is not serious for large companies, who can borrow on the open market. But the major sources of capital for small businesses are the owners' personal savings and profits ploughed back. Thus income tax and corporation tax deprive small and risky but often progressive companies of much-needed capital.

Not only that, but high direct taxes may repel foreign capital. Although the deduction of income tax on dividends may be refunded, the company still has to bear corporation tax on profits (at 52% in 1980). The amount available to shareholders is therefore less, and the declared dividend correspondingly smaller. Consequently people may prefer to invest in companies operating in countries where there is a higher return to capital – a higher return which is the result not of superior efficiency but simply of lower taxes.

(x) *Equitable in its distibution of the tax burden*

Taxes can be classified according to the proportion of a person's income which is deducted:

(1) A *regressive* tax takes a higher proportion of the poorer person's income than of the richer. Indirect taxes which levy a fixed sum irrespective of income, e.g. television licences, are regressive.

(2) A *proportional* tax takes a fixed proportion of one's income. In 1980 income tax was proportional for the first £11,250 of taxable income, 30% of every £1 being taken in tax.

(3) A *progressive* tax takes a higher proportion of income as income increases (fig 21.2). Income tax is progressive above £11,250 of taxable income since above that progressively higher

Fig 21.2 *the difference between regressive, proportional and progressive taxes*

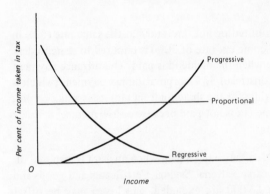

rates apply. Capital transfer tax, which involves graduated rates of tax, is also progressive.

Justification for taxing the rich man more highly than the poor man rests on the assumption that the law of diminishing utility applies to additional income, and that an extra £50 affords less pleasure to the rich man than to the poor man. Thus taking from the rich involves less hardship than taking from the poor. Generally this can be accepted as true, but we can never be sure, simply because there is no absolute measure of personal satisfaction.

21.3 THE STRUCTURE OF TAXATION

Because there are so many effects of taxation no single tax is completely perfect. Consequently there must be a structure of taxation, combining a number of taxes which the government can vary from time to time according to changes in emphasis on different objectives.

The following classification of taxes is based on their methods of payment.

(a) Direct taxes
With these taxes the person makes payment direct to the revenue authorities – the Department of Inland Revenue or the local authority. Usually each individual's tax liability is assessed separately.

(i) *Income tax*
'Taxable income', which is subject to a basic rate (now 30%) with increasing rates above £10,000 is arrived at after allowing deductions depending

on marital status and other personal circumstances. Investment income above £5,000 per annum is subject to a surcharge of 15%.

(ii) *Corporation tax*

All profits, whether distributed or not, are taxed at the same rate (52% in 1980). A part ($\frac{3}{7}$ at an income-tax rate of 30%) is imputed to shareholders and deducted in advance when the dividend is paid. This advance payment is allowed against the mainstream 52% corporation-tax payment (which is always paid in arrears), while for the shareholder it counts as a 'tax credit', and is refundable if income tax is not paid because of low income.

(iii) *Capital gains tax*

A tax is now levied at 30% of any capital gain when an asset is disposed of. Owner-occupied houses, cars, National Savings Certificates and goods and chattels worth less than £2,000 are excluded, and losses may be offset against gains.

Where the gain does not exceed £3,000 in any year, no tax is payable.

(iv) *Capital transfer tax*

Capital transfer tax replaced estate duty in 1974. It applies to lifetime gifts as well as to legacies, though the former generally bear only half the latter's rate of tax. The starting point is £50,000 and rates of duty are progressive, varying according to the size of the transfer – 10% in the £65,000–£70,000 band, increasing to 75% above £2 million. Somewhat lower rates are payable by working farmers on the transfer of their farms.

(v) *Other taxes*

These consist of stamp duties (payable on financial contracts), motor-vehicle duties, Petroleum Revenue Tax and Development Land Tax.

Local rates, levied by district councils, can also be regarded as a direct tax.

Direct taxes yield nearly two-thirds of total revenue. Their great merit is that, being progressive and assessed according to the individual's circumstances, they ensure that the heaviest burdens are placed on the broadest backs. Their progressive character also gives additional weight to their role as built-in stabilisers.

Their main disadvantage is that when the rate of tax is high there may be disincentive effects. As a result indirect taxes also have to be levied.

(b) Indirect taxes

Indirect taxes on goods and services are so called because the revenue authority (the Department of Customs and Excise) collects them from the seller, who, as far as possible, passes the burden on to the consumer by including the duty in the final selling price of the good (see p. 336). They may be *specific* (i.e. consisting of a fixed sum irrespective of the value of the good) or *ad valorem* (i.e. consisting of a given percentage of the value of the good).

Indirect taxes may be divided into:
(i)   Customs duties levied at EEC rates on goods imported from countries outside the EEC.
(ii) Excise duties on home-produced goods and services, e.g. beer, whisky, petrol, cigarettes and gambling.
(iii) Value-Added tax (VAT): an *ad valorem* tax, levied on most goods and services at each stage of production at a basic rate. Thus, using fig 15.1 as an example, a VAT at 15% paid by the consumer on the table in the shop would be £1.50, making a total purchase price of £11.50. The VAT, however, would have been paid at each stage of production: tree-grower 45p; saw-miller 30p; table manufacturer 45p; retailer 30p. In practice each producer would pay to the Customs and Excise the full 15% tax of the goods as invoiced by him *less* the VAT paid by his suppliers of materials, etc., as shown on their invoices. Thus the retailer would pay the Customs and Excise 30p – £1.50 minus the VAT of £1.20 charged to him.

Some goods, e.g. food, coal, gas, electricity, new buildings, books, newspapers, public-transport fares, medicines on prescription, etc. are zero-rated. This means that the final seller charges no VAT *and* can reclaim any VAT invoiced by intermediary producers. Other goods, e.g. rents and medical services, are 'exempt'. Here no VAT is charged by the final seller, but any VAT paid by an intermediary, e.g. for building repairs, cannot be reclaimed.

The main merit of VAT is that it is broad-based, the yield increasing almost proportionately to consumer spending. Moreover, since VAT covers most forms of spending, it does not distort consumer choice as much as a highly selective tax.

On the other hand it can be argued that a general tax on spending is regressive, for it hits those on lower incomes, who spend proportionately more of their incomes, harder. This fact is tempered somewhat, however, by zero-rating goods regarded as necessities.

Indirect taxes give a certain and often an immediate yield and can be adjusted to specific objectives of government policy. On the other hand, by being regressive they undo some of the re-distributive effects of direct taxes.

(c) The distribution of the burden of an indirect tax between consumers and producers

When a good is subject to a selective tax this does not mean that its price will rise by the full amount of the tax. Consider the following demand and supply schedules for commodity X.

Price of X (pence)	Demand ('000 lb.)	Supply ('000 lb.)
12	60	150
11	70	130
10	80	110
9	90	90
8	100	70

The equilibrium price is 9p. Now suppose a tax of 3p is charged on the producer for each unit of X he puts on the market. This means that whereas before the tax he supplied 70,000 units at a price of 8p, he will now only supply this quantity at 11p (because 3p would go in tax). Similarly, 90,000 units will only be supplied at a price of 12p instead of 9p. Thus the effect of the 3p tax can be shown by the shift in the supply curve from S to S_1 (fig 21.3). This gives a new equilibrium price of 11p, the buyer paying 2p more and the producer receiving 1p less, the quantity traded falling from 90,000 units to 70,000 units.

Fig 21.3 *the diagrammatic representation of a tax on the supply side*

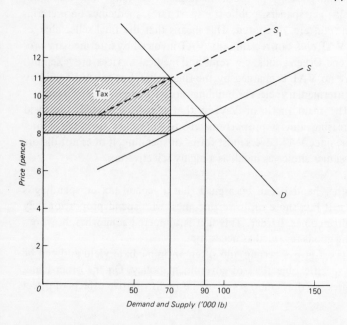

The result is the same if the 3p tax is levied on purchasers. Before the tax, 100,000 units were demanded at a price of 8p. If purchasers now have to pay a 3p tax, this is equivalent to a price of 11p including tax, and so they will demand only 70,000 units. Similarly, for a price of 9p they will demand only 60,000 units instead of 90,000. Thus the effect of the 3p tax imposed on buyers can be shown by the move in the demand curve from D to D₁ (fig 21.4). This gives a new equilibrium price of 11p (8p at which the market is cleared, plus 3p tax), and the quantity traded falls from 90,000 to 70,000.

Fig 21.4 *the diagrammatic representation of a tax on the demand side*

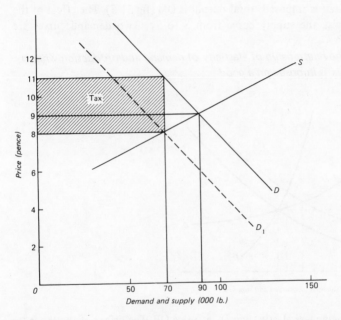

The amount of the tax falling on consumers as compared with that falling on producers is directly proportional to the elasticity of supply as compared with the elasticity of demand. That is:

$$\frac{\text{consumers' share of tax}}{\text{producers' share of tax}} = \frac{\text{elasticity of supply}}{\text{elasticity of demand}}$$

That this proposition is likely to be true can be seen from the following argument. When a tax is imposed, the reaction of the producer is to try to push the burden of the tax on to the consumer, while similarly the consumer tries to push it on to the producer. Who wins? Simply the one whose bargaining position is stronger. This will depend upon the ability to switch to producing substitutes if the price falls as compared with the ability to switch to buying substitutes if the price rises. Now the possibility of substitution largely determines elasticities of supply and demand. Thus the relative burden of the tax paid by producers and consumers depends upon relative elasticities of supply and demand.

(d) The effect of an indirect tax on the size of an industry
The greater the elasticities of demand and supply, the greater will be the effect of a tax in reducing output. We can show this diagrammatically.

(i) *Elasticity of demand*
Before the tax is imposed, total output is OM (fig 21.5). The effect of the tax is to raise the supply curve from S to S_1. Two demand curves are

Fig 21.5 *the relationship of elasticity of demand and production when a tax is imposed on a good*

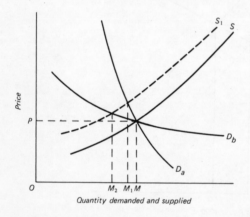

Quantity demanded and supplied

shown, D_a being less elastic than D_b at price OP. The effect of the tax is to reduce output to OM_1 where demand is D_a, and to OM_2 where it is D_b. In the latter case consumers are more able to switch to buying substitutes.

(ii) *Elasticity of supply*
Before the tax is imposed, total output is OM (fig 21.6). The effect of the tax is to lower the demand curve from D to D_1. Two supply curves are shown, S_a being less elastic than S_b at price OP. The effect of the tax is to reduce output to OM_1 where supply is S_a, and to OM_2 where it is S_b. In the latter case producers are more able to produce alternative goods.

This proposition has important practical applications. (i) The government may use a subsidy (which can be illustrated by moving the supply

Fig 21.6 *the relationship of elasticity of supply and production when a tax is imposed on a good*

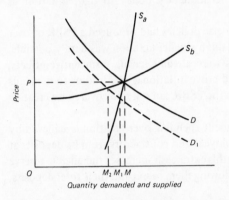

Quantity demanded and supplied

curve to the right) to increase the production, and thus employment, of an industry. The effect will be more pronounced where demand and supply are elastic. (ii) Because the effect of a tax is to reduce production, even a temporary tax may harm an industry. This is particularly so where home demand is elastic and production takes place under decreasing costs, for the smaller demand will raise export prices. Thus a selective tax on cars would not only reduce home demand but also, by doing so, lose economies of scale, thereby putting up prices in both home and foreign markets. Even when the tax is subsequently withdrawn, foreign markets may not be regained.

21.4 THE PUBLIC-SECTOR BORROWING REQUIREMENT (PSBR)

(a) Expanding the level of activity by government spending
As we have seen, the level of aggregate demand may be inadequate to fully employ resources. This is the basis of the Keynesian theory, and the remedy advocated is to increase government spending and reduce taxation to expand aggregate demand. In short, a budget deficit could be used to reduce the level of unemployment.

Keynes recognised that this meant an increase in the national debt – in present-day terms, the public-sector borrowing requirement (see p. 226). But to him, writing in the depression of the 1930s, this presented few real problems, and these were in any case of minor significance by comparison with the benefits of reduced unemployment.

(b) The difficulties raised by a high PSBR
But the 1970s have seen a somewhat different situation. Not only has un-employment risen uncomfortably high, but it has been accompanied by

inflation – a condition often referred to as 'stagflation' (see chapter 20). This has brought the government's budgetary policy to reduce unemployment into direct conflict with its monetary policy to fight inflation, as follows.

By 1976 the government's social policies had produced a PSBR of over £9,000 million a year. Reducing this by higher taxation was hardly possible, since high rates of direct taxes were already having disincentive effects, while higher indirect taxes could prove inflationary by leading to demands for higher wages. In this situation the PSBR can only be covered by creating money or by borrowing.

Initially an excess of government spending over taxation is achieved by the government's paying its employees and contractors from its deposits at the Bank of England. Eventually this extra cash increases the eligible reserve assets of the joint-stock banks, allowing them to expand their total deposits, including advances.

But resorting to the 'printing-press' in this way cannot be a permanent solution. The government has to cover its PSBR by borrowing. Even so, if it does this by the cheapest method – the sale of Treasury bills – it runs into difficulties. The major holders of Treasury bills are the joint-stock banks, and they buy them as the increased offering by the authorities forces up the yield. Such purchases, however, directly add to the banks' eligible reserve assets, allowing them, as above, to increase their deposits. In other words, short-term borrowing involves an inflationary increase in the money supply.

As a result, the government has to rely on long-term borrowing, selling medium- and long-term bonds in the market to the non-bank sector, the institutions and private purchasers. Since such sources of funds rely mainly on current saving, this method is not inflationary. The difficulty, however, is that extra bonds can only be disposed of at a lower price – that is, by a rise in the long-term rate of interest. This has the overall effect of discouraging investment, thereby increasing unemployment and retarding the rate of growth. Nor is this all. Interest payments on this borrowing add to the PSBR. Furthermore, inasmuch as higher interest rates attract funds from abroad, the money supply is increased.

In practice, therefore, fiscal policy cannot proceed independently of monetary policy. Usually the government compromises by increasing borrowing at higher interest rates, setting a ceiling on the increase in the money supply and reducing public-sector spending in order to relieve the pressure from the PSBR.

INDEX

Firm (*cont.*)
    raising capital 81–4, 89,
       217–18, 220, 224
    size of 90–3, 121
    see also Costs of production;
       Factors of production;
       Output
Free market, *see* Private sector
Friedman, Milton 322

G
General Agreement on Tariffs and
    Trade (GATT) 279, 282–3,
    290
Goods and services,
    allocation of 24–5
    value of 45, 205, 241–7
Government department, accounta-
    bility through 185–6, 196
Government grants to local authori-
    ties 191–4, 264, 327
    grants in aid 192
    rate support grant 192–3
Government intervention 24–6, 59,
    79, 177, 183–4, 200, 251,
    303–4, 317
    and cost-benefit analysis
       180–3
    on employment 144, 148–
       52, 304–10, 321, 324,
       338–40
    fiscal policies 309–10, 324,
       328, 340
    on labour 143–4
    monetary policies 226,
       258–62, 303, 308, 324–5,
       340
    nationalisation 194
    objectives of 303
    prices-and-incomes policy
       184, 321–2, 324
    regional policies 312–16
    stabilisation of commodity
       prices 63–4, 200, 303
    trade controls 279–80,
       290–1
Gross Domestic Product 178
Gross National Product (GNP) 238,
    244, 246, 248, 250, 298, 327
Growth, economic 251, 298, 316,
    330, 340
    causes of 238–40

Growth, economic (*cont.*)
    constraints on 240
    definition 237–8

H
Hire-purchase finance 215
Holding company 91
Hypermarkets 101–3

I
Imperial Tobacco Company 89, 91
Imports 244, 249, 251, 266, 272
    controls on 46, 279–82,
       290–1, 296, 335
    from EEC 278, 298–9
    increased demand for 234,
       240, 290, 318
    payment for 34, 283–5,
       286, 288
    quotas 46, 273, 279, 290
    reductions in 291–2
    value of 275–7, 286–7,
       290, 324
Income 332–3
    changes in national income
       255–6, 258, 317
    definition 159, 240, 249
    elasticity of demand 72
    and expenditure 253–4
    government 245
    increase in 40, 53, 72, 102–
       3, 257–9, 264–6, 290–1,
       310, 319, 331
    national 234, 235, 241–51,
       253, 255, 262, 303, 307
    personal disposable 248–9,
       255, 258, 262
    redistribution of 21, 24,
       180–1, 194, 200, 244–5,
       303, 310, 317, 321, 330
    and saving 257–60, 264–6
    transfer 244–5
Independent retail outlets 101,
    102–3
Industrial and Commercial Finance
    Corporation 83
Industry,
    primary 40, 73
    secondary 40, 73
    tertiary 40, 73
Industry, Department of 314–16

55555

Price (*cont.*)
- function of 59–62, 312
- 'future price' 49
- and government policy 24–5, 53, 63–4, 180, 184, 194–5, 200–1, 226, 240, 279, 303–4, 331
- index of retail prices 149, 318–20
- market clearing 46, 56–7, 116–17
- security prices 318
- 'spot price' 49
- *see also* Demand; Supply

Private company 76, 81–3

Private sector 25–6
- demand and 'needs' 178–9
- free market, operation of 45–64
- investment in 262–3
- *see also* Firm; Mixed economy; Public sector

Production, large-scale 21, 23, 32, 87–9, 90, 92, 123, 194–5, 238, 273

Production-possibility curve 231–2, 235, 237–8

Productivity 321–3
- increase in 140, 154, 195, 238–40, 282, 309, 323
- *see also* Growth; Output

Profit 20, 245–7, 251, 260–1
- definition 171–2
- marginal revenue 117–18, 120, 128–31, 152, 154–6, 162–5
- maximising 111, 114, 116–18, 129–32
- monopoly profit 172–4
- net 254–5, 260
- normal 110, 118, 171–3
- role of 172–4
- super-normal 110, 121, 127, 154, 156, 169, 172–3

Public company 76–7, 80, 83–4

Public goods 21, 23, 177, 179–81, 186, 192, 194, 330

Public sector 25, 309–10
- cost-benefit analysis 180–3
- economic efficiency 199–201

Public sector (*cont.*)
- government department 185–6, 196
- local authority 186–94
- nationalised industries 194–201
- and 'needs' 178–9, 310
- 'Quangos' 178, 201
- pricing policy 179–80, 195, 303
- size of 26, 178
- wage-claims in 183–4
- *see also* Local authorities; Mixed economy; Nationalised industries; Private sector

Public-Sector Borrowing Requirement 226, 261, 310, 324–5, 339–40

Public Works Loans Board 191

Q

'Quangos' 178, 201

Quotas, import 46, 273, 279, 290

R

Rates 191–4, 334
- rate rebates 193–4
- rate support grant 192–3

Raw materials,
- as factor of production 118, 274–5, 277, 290
- supply of 34, 48, 320–1
- *see also* Mineral deposits

Recession 307

Regional development 42, 95, 303, 311–16
- EEC policy 297
- government policy 312–16
- planning 315–16
- unemployment 95, 200, 297, 311–12

Regional Development Fund 297, 314

Registrar of Companies 76, 80

Registrar of Restrictive Trading Agreements 133–4

Rent 171–2, 246–7
- of ability 168, 172
- 'commercial' 163–4
- economic 166–70, 172, 174

352

Unemployment (*cont.*)
    and immobility 33, 148, 312
    regional policies 95, 297, 311–12
    and wage increases 72, 109, 154–7, 305–6, 325, 340
Unit trusts 214, 259
United Nations 250

V
Value, exchange 45–6

W
Wage-rates 282, 305
    and demand for labour 123–4, 137–40, 146–8, 152–5, 167, 312
    determination of 144–8, 154–6, 171

Wage-rates (*cont.*)
    and employment 72, 109, 154–7, 305–6, 325, 340
    and government 144, 149–52, 324–5
    and inflation 149, 200, 321–2, 324–5, 340
    minimum wage-agreements 21, 149, 153
    negotiations for 146, 149, 150–7, 183–4, 318
    piece-rates 145–6, 150
    in public sector 183, 200
    and supply of labour 139–40, 143–4, 146–9, 153
    time-rates 145–6, 150
Wages Councils 150–1
Wealth 159–61, 206, 249
    distribution of 21–2, 24, 53, 132, 258, 303, 330
Western European Union 293
Wholesaler 97–9, 101, 103–4